TO…

**THE PRINCE OF DARKNESS**

&

**THE GODFATHERS OF METAL**

On behalf of The Freak and the *both* of us,

THANK YOU

99% of this is true

1%… is just crazy

# WARNING

The following contains Fate & Irony and…

HEAVY "fucking" METAL

**Reader's discretion is advised**

A

**Dreams-Reality-Heart**

Production

In association with

**Devil's Right Hand Inc.**

Professional "Shadow" Services

# PROFESSIONAL SHADOW

### A FAN LETTER & RESUME BY...

# ROB SHADOWS

*Copyright © June 18th 2025*

**By Rob Shadows**

**All rights reserved.**

No part of this book may be reproduced in whole or in part without the expressed consent of the author with the exception of passages quoted for review.

## *DISCLAIMER*

Due to the sensitive and potentially embarrassing nature of the material contained within this volume, all the names of people, places and commercial enterprises have been changed to a fictitious title to protect the guilty from prosecution, and spare the innocent from future harm.

In other words… so we don't get sued, or fucking shot!

# THE LIFETIMES

## (Table of Contents)

MY-BIG-HOUSE..................................................................................viii

1. JUNIOR'S EYES.............................................................................1

2. CHILDREN OF THE GRAVE.......................................................17

3. PARANOID....................................................................................31

4. THE HAND OF DOOM..................................................................57

5. AFTER FOREVER..........................................................................81

6. JOHNNY BLADE..........................................................................104

7. DIRTY WOMEN...........................................................................125

8. SYMPTOM OF THE UNIVERSE..................................................147

9. TOMORROW'S DREAM..............................................................162

10. IRONMAN..................................................................................180

11. ELECTRIC FUNERAL................................................................202

12. LORD OF THIS WORLD............................................................226

13. NEVER SAY DIE........................................................................251

14. HOLE IN THE SKY....................................................................274

15. GOD IS DEAD............................................................................296

16. FAIRIES WEAR BOOTS............................................................322

17. A HARD ROAD..........................................................................345

18. THE WRIT..................................................................................369

19. END OF THE BEGINNING(S)..................................................379

# MY-BIG-HOUSE

All of the events depicted in this book take place in my country of origin, my native nation, my homeland, in…

**MY-BIG-HOUSE.**

In **MY-BIG-HOUSE**, which was founded through time and designed by the ages, the cities within are but giant rooms joined together by highway sized hallways, reaching across the cardinal wings of an ever changing floor plan of four seasons that are host to a land of living skies, majestic boreal forests, the greatest of great lakes, the rockiest of mountains, and the wildest roses upon wide open plains...

In **MY-BIG-HOUSE**, there are no state borders to divide its residents and no provincial boundaries to label tenants within a place, where, everyone is the same regardless of creed, color, race, religion or gender, and where everyone is capable of using The Energy to achieve prosperity and purpose.

In… **MY-BIG-HOUSE** …we are.

## Oct.1 1971

Somewhere between now and then, a fateful union between a restaurant waitress and a long haul trucker gives life to a shining star and a myth in time, whom is ushered into an unlikely family of acute poverty and forced vows that finds an infant boy taking his first steps out of a semi truck upon an ever changing road, until three and a half years later, The Myth would ask Fate and Irony for a little sister…

## Feb. 11, 1975

"Smile…!" *FLASH!*

When a flaming star suddenly burned an immortal image into the mind of an infant shadow, a child with an unnatural name suddenly blinked his way into a curious mortal realm, where his first discoveries was Mom standing there with a strange flash box in her hand, followed by the reflection of his future self known as The Myth, his big brother sitting there giving him a buddy hug. The itchy brown tweed sofa upon which they sat prickled at the skin on his arm, while those little red suspenders with the lapels crisscrossed tightly over his tiny sloped shoulders, pulled the pants up uncomfortably into the crotch of a child who could not speak!

# 1

# *JUNIOR'S EYES*

# THE FORGOTTEN TIMES

## *Home Town, ~ 1983 ~ Labor Slave*

For those about to rock a mad fan's resume, the interview begins after a young Shadow learns to wipe his own ass without falling into the big white bowl of brown submarines, which finds a child of tomorrow taking notice of a material world for the first time, like his toys that lit up with lights and sounds until he threw them against the wall and they no longer functioned, or Fluffy, the white family cat that lit up with lights and sounds after it somehow got trapped in the wood burning stove, only to escape to live on as Smokey, the charred feline with melted ears.

Then, there was that thing called a stereo in the corner of the living room, which lit up with lights and sounds that strangely made little Shadow feel charged up, yet, at the same time, calm on the inside? And lastly, there was that big wooden box on the floor with the black and white screen at its center, which curiously lit up with lights and sounds that revealed a whole other world beyond the four walls of innocence, which made a young and restless kid wonder… "How do they all fit inside there?"

As the sons of a silent mom and a never there father, the television became a teacher and a mentor in the best of times, for Shadow and his older brother The Myth, whose wide open minds absorbed the early days of colorless programming that played host to game shows, soap operas, animated rabbits, talking cars, and wars among the stars. Although The Myth had been less swayed by an electric babysitter, Shadow spent his happiest days in front of a great white eye of wasted time, which taught him about the nature of things, in addition to something called a nuclear family, where stable taxpaying parents lived a seemingly normal life of togetherness and inclusion, and whom where always there to answer a child's questions in a loving home that was full and fair …unlike theirs, which was filled with yelling, and kneeling punishment.

But then, at the dawn of a technological age, a relatively new invention called a video gaming console was gifted under a tree, which suddenly opened a doorway to an entirely new world of electric sleep that saw two minds instantly hooked by the fact that they could race mice in a maze and experience trial and error without consequence, within a place called cyberspace that provided an escape from the belts and the beatings, where, moving the little squares upon the television screen in basic games eventually sharpened reflexes and the sowed seeds of frustration to overcome repeating patterns that gave rise to bouts of anger that was the stuff of legends, over the who made who of losing.

Obsessed with barrel tossing monkeys and invaders from space, Shadow soon got so good at gaming that The Myth finally threw down his controller and yelled, "You're a fucking vidiot!" before stomping off to find other distractions, thus leaving a child to drift alone within a two dimensional reality of bits and bytes, oblivious to time within a place of imagination and freedom, however, one day, whilst thumb mashing the single red button of an awkward joystick, Shadow suddenly heard odd noises coming from upstairs and with the curiosity of youth guiding him, an unwitting kid went to investigate these strange sounds, which he discovered was music coming from behind the door of his brother's bedroom.

Unlike the jailhouse rock or, the man in black that Mom and Father listened to on the living room stereo, this music was much more intense and chaotic than anything he had ever heard before, begging him to come on feel the noise. So, Shadow did what any kid would do, he opened his brother's bedroom door without knocking and was surprised to find The Myth standing there bobbing his head up and down to the brash musical tones, and playing ...an invisible guitar?!

"Don't you know how to knock!?" The Myth said standing up straight upon realizing Shadow was watching him. "Well... don't just stand there idiot! Hurry up and shut the door before Mom complains!"

"What is that?" Shadow inquired about the hard fast music tickling his ear drums, as he walked toward the mono cassette player on the bed without shutting the bedroom door, which annoyed The Myth whom went and shut it angrily.

"That, dummy, is heavy fucking metal!" *SLAM!*

Looking at the cassette wheels spinning into eternity, Shadow had no idea what heavy "fucking" metal was, as the incoherent vocals set to distorted guitars and pounding drums suddenly replaced a child's affinity for the video screen, with a whole new metal health of excitement that strangely compelled him to also bang his head and shake his brain to the point of concussion, which made The Myth laugh at first, but was eventually driven to shout at the devil thanks to a little brother constantly nagging and pestering to use a portable tape player, since the big stereo in the living room was off limits to a kid known for breaking things.

"Hey! That's my tape player…!" The Myth had yelled one day upon catching Shadow in his room using his stuff without asking, which led to fights between an older brother and his younger sibling in need of a metal music fix, "…And get the fuck out of my room!"

After that, The Myth no longer wanted to be around Shadow by letting him know in the most colorful ways… "No! You can't come in my room anymore!" and, "Quit following me!" …and Shadow's favorite, "Would you fuck off already!? I'm just going to fucking the bathroom!"

Yet, no amount of sibling rejection could deter a kid wishing to be just like his older brother, whom could fix any broken toy and figure out the most complex patterns, but when The Myth got his first summer job as a paper boy for the Home Town newspaper, you can bet your building blocks that Shadow wanted to be right there too, only The Myth refused to take his little brother along at first, leaving Shadow to remain stuck at home sad and sobbing, but then, on the eighth day, The Myth looked at his little brother and said, "…Yeah, sure, you can come with me!"

Upon hearing that he could tag along Shadow was overjoyed to follow his big brother, despite the condition that a naïve little brother had to run the paper to every doorstep while The Myth slowly pedaled his bike along the street with the newspaper bag, making promises… "I'll even pay you a dollar!" The Myth had said to sweeten the deal, but shiny coins held no value to a free bird living on the blank check of youth, whose only desire had been to follow his older self across the property line of adventure and begin exploring a monopolized society as a new token worker, whom was born to run the daily buzz to the doorsteps of subscribers upon a long route without a break, all the while The Myth calmly pedaled his bicycle along the streets yelling with authority, "Hurry up stupid… What the fuck am I paying you for!?"

By the end of the paper route, Shadow's little legs were on fire from all the running, and the next day, he could barely walk from the pain when The Myth announced, "Ok, slave! Let's fucking go!" leading a kid whom was drained by a physical strain, to begin questioning why he had it so shitty while another had it so easy?

"Because… I'm the boss! Now, do your fucking job …or, you're fired!" The Myth had said with an ultimatum that gave a kid his first traumatic lesson about duty for a dollar and suffering for attention, which, at wits end, had stirred something within young Shadow that he could not explain, something strange yet compelling that gave him the will to keep going, which soon found a king of pain capable of running the entire paper route without stopping, much to the surprise of The Myth whom ordered and commanded his little brother like a mustang sally from the comfort of his bicycle seat, which he never got off from until it was time to get paid.

Saturday was collection day for the newspaper subscription fees, so The Myth would get off his ass to go knocking on doors to collect, while Shadow stood back to observe in silence at the home of the nice granny with the freshly baked cookies, whom always opened her door to greet them with her usual warm smile, but when The Myth said, "Collection day!" the nice granny's face suddenly contorted into the scowl of a golem.

"Well, now you've gone and interrupted my show! I don't take lightly to being interrupted!" the old woman impatiently crowed, which frightened Shadow as the old biddy then stepped back and slammed her door shut in his brother's face. Stunned, Shadow wanted to leave, but was frozen by worry about not living up to his duty as they stood there wondering if the granny would return. Then, after an eternity of waiting, the old prude finally reappeared and paid The Myth in a lengthy complaint filled penny pinching count, which offered no tip and no quarter for two paperboys just trying to do their job.

When the old crow spat, "Now go away!" and slammed her door shut again, The Myth turned around with a sour look on his face and muttered, "Fucking old hag!" under his breath, before stomping away to leave Shadow standing there trying to understand the strange vibe whispering in his mind, telling him to not fear to the growls of a griping granny, which haunted his steps upon a blitzkrieg bop of collection attempts from cheapskates and delinquent subscribers, and that weirdo who always answered the door in his underwear and tried to lure them into his house for "cookies".

At the end of the day, The Myth had been left with only half the subscription fees, while Shadow had been left half traumatized after watching human beings transform into a monster mash of hatred and resentment at the mere mention of dollars and cents, however, dealing with a patronized public was child's play compared to dealing with Smug, the arrogant and mean paper route supervisor, whom made them feel inferior when he said, "I'm doing you a favor by giving you this job! So, if you don't get the subscription fees, you don't get paid!"

Watching Smug grow angry and impatient had scared Shadow at first, but then, once again, a strange vibe within him calmed his fears and gave him the courage to stand his ground, while his older brother The Myth, whom was fed up with the shit, told Smug exactly what he thought of a "favor" that was conditional of labor.

"Oh, yeah…? Well, we're not going to take it so, you can take this job and shove it straight up your ass because…" The Myth paused to take a deep flared nostril breath...

"We fucking quit!"

***REASON FOR LEAVING:*** Went back to being a kid?

# BIG BRO'S BICYCLE SHOP

## *Home Town, ~ 1984 ~ Shop Bitch*

After watching his brother abruptly walk away from his job, Shadow had been left troubled and confused by the concept of work and the notion of enduring misery for compensation, to which The Myth, upon seeing his little brother distraught over a dramatic scene, took it upon himself to explain the reality of existing within an economic society. "People will be dishonest and deceptive when it comes to money! So, watch your back!"

Tough love words spoken to an eight year old did little to quell Shadow's worries about one day having to enter a work force, which strangely left him feeling powerless and alienated by something called a job, where father went for long periods of time only to return unhappy when he got home from his big rig journeys, however, some questions from the crib would have to wait as The Myth again took it upon him to dispel any other illusions or funky fantasies that his younger brother might have had about childhood folktales and urban legends.

"Look, idiot… Satan can't fit his fat ass down chimneys! It's Mom and Dad putting the gifts under the tree… and, while I'm at it, rabbits don't shit chocolate and fairies don't steal teeth because they both don't fucking exist! Also, come here for a second and turn around…"

## Professional Shadow

When Shadow did as he was told, The Myth reached down the back of his little brother's pants and grabbed the elastic band of his underwear, then lifted up violently, *YANK!* thus picking Shadow up off his feet causing him to cry out in pain as he dangled in the air with his shorts wedged up his ass. "And that's called a Wedgie! It's what you get for always doing what you're fucking told so don't trust anybody!"

Upon learning the evils of humanity, currency and "wedgies", Shadow could no longer return to the blissful ignorance of youth that once filled him with a timeless innocence, which seemed like it would last forever only to suddenly vanish and leave him feeling older and unable to relate to his classmates at school, where the teacher asked the class what they wanted to be when they grew up. While the other students replied with generic answers like, "A Ballerina…! A Fireman…! A Policeman…! A Postal Worker!" when it was Shadow's turn, he could not see the future beyond the present and drew a blank, so he timidly said...

"I wanna be somebody!" …compelling the teacher and his classmates to begin laughing at Shadow, whom wondered if it was the corduroy pants that Mom had forced him to wear, or if his parents had made a tragic vocational error upon placing their sons in a French Catholic school system, when every facet their lives at home was in lived in, "Christian English?" leaving a kid to feel like a circle amongst a bunch of squares speaking a language of moving pictures, which were painfully long for some reason, within a simple life that got a lot harder after The Myth went on to junior high, and left his little brother at the mercy of an elementary schoolyard bully.

Crotte, the human turd, was like a barracuda preying upon the little fish in a pool of pre-pubescent mud suckers, whom enjoyed applying his own brand of catch, torture, and release upon any poor tadpole unlucky enough to get caught in his path. While on most days he was lucky enough to avoid being cornered and suffer the crapes of wrath at the hands of a big kid with anger issues, one day, Shadow found himself shit out of luck upon walking around the corner behind the school with his friends, and came face to face with the angel of death.

"Now I got you!" Crotte said as he grabbed Shadow by his shirt and dragged him out of sight from the watchful eyes of the school yard surveillance teacher, where kids once known as friends vanished to a safe distance whilst a brute had his way with a frightened kid. "You're nothing!" Crotte said with hatred and contempt before shoving Shadow down to the jagged gravel, which scraped his hands when he broke his fall. It had really hurt and he nearly cried out from the pain, but, just then, the same strange vibe within his mind prevented him from uttering the sounds that a bully so wanted to hear, compelling Crotte to get angry at a shit show of courage,

"Oh, a tough guy, eh?!" Crotte the human turd said as he moved in to unceremoniously pull Shadow to his feet, ripping his shirt in the process. "Let's see how tough you are!" Crotte said maniacally right in Shadow's face, whom was frozen in fear, but thought that he could hear something yelling from beyond, "Go fuck yourself!" just as a predator suddenly shoved his prey back hard into the wall of solid school bricks, whereupon impact, the side of Shadow's head hit the wall with a sickening, *KNOCK!* which sent a white light ripping through his eyes and caused his ears to begin ringing loudly, as intense pain unlike anything he had ever felt before began filling his skull with massive pressure, forcing him to close his eyes and grit his teeth from the agony, and then suddenly …fade to black.

The next thing he knew, Shadow was floating in a white cloud. There was no more school and no more bully. The pain in his head was gone as well as the ringing in his ears. It was very peaceful. "Where am I?" Shadow wondered as he looked around, but could see nothing except mist everywhere both above and below, leading him to assume that, "Am I in Hell…?"

"Don't let him do that again" Just then, an unknown, yet strangely familiar voice spoke up from behind him, which gave Shadow a start as he spun around to find no one there except for the clouds. "What?" Shadow wondered with a questioning look on his face, but before he could think of another dumb word, again from behind, the same voice commanded with a firmer tone, "Don't let him do that again!" Surprised again, Shadow turned around urgently, only to once again find nothing except a great white emptiness. "Who the fuck is talking to m…!"

At that moment, the pain in his head suddenly returned like an avalanche, followed by the loud ringing in his ears that made him grit his teeth in a tormented wince of anguish, which sent him falling back in black, and re-awaken back at school leaning up against the brick wall, where The Voice in the back of his head yelled, "LOOK OUT!"

Somehow, Shadow had survived the impact from hitting the school and had been left standing there like another brick in the wall and an easy target for an enraged Crotte, who, upon seeing that his victim had not gone down from his assault, had decided to come rushing in for a running tackle aiming to inflict maximum damage by crushing them into a school of hard knocks, however, just as Crotte the human turd was about to make his big splash, Shadow suddenly felt something take hold of his senses and at the last second, "they" stepped back out of the way to allow an unstoppable force of oppression, to crash face first into an immovable object of conformity, *BOOM!* which shook the entire school and sent Crotte, the human turd, bouncing off the bricks like the one that didn't stick, giving Shadow the opportunity to escape, only, they didn't.

While ninety nine percent of him wanted to run away to fear another day, the one percent that took control had other ideas... "This ends now!" The Voice in his head said with a cold calculating certainty, as Shadow felt their body suddenly move toward a battered bully, whom was stunned and wide open to receive the consequences of his misdeeds, when a hand curled into the tightest fist a scared little boy had ever made landed upon Crotte's already bruised up face, right to that soft spot between nose and cheek bone that would become known as Death Valley throughout a crazy story, which sent Crotte head over heels backwards to crash hard into the dirt in a knocked out, bloody heap and... "Hey! What's going on over there?!"

It was the schoolyard surveillance teacher arriving just in time to witness Shadow's violent act of self defense, for which he was sent to the principal's office to receive a lecture on tolerance followed by detention within an institution seeking to break his piece of mind and will, which evoked an angry and violent reaction from a road weary Father, but, from that day forward,

Shadow was no longer picked on by a human turd with a crooked nose, or anyone else for that matter, as "they" went on to be respected by the rest of the students, whom no longer laughed at them and suddenly sought out their protection against Crotte and the rest of the bullies terrorizing a public school system, but whom wanted nothing to do with that psycho crazy kid with "The Voice" in his head.

"What are you?" Shadow asked the entity now squatting in his head. "I'm you..." The Voice replied, but then corrected, "...Or, rather, the part of you that's without time." Feeling strange about talking to a voice no one else could hear, Shadow persisted, but cautiously... "Where did you come from?"

When The Voice explained how the impact had cracked their Pineal Gland and allowed it to leak into his head along with something called The Energy, Shadow's eyes grew wide at the thought of pineapples growing in his skull, but The Voice calmed his fears. "No! No, it's not like that! Just think of me as your other side, the one part of you that's always here if you need me... silly!"

Shadow breathed easier upon realizing that whatever was within him was a friend that would always be there to keep "Us...?" company in the lonely times, and keep "Them...?" safe in times of trauma, in a story of they, them, us and we pronouns, which would surely make "them" appear crazy to the point of rewriting the definition of insanity, which is what life was now all about for a kid with a concussion and quite possibly internal bleeding and cerebral hemorrhaging, which went unheeded and unnoticed by everyone including The Myth, whom looked at Shadow with wide eyes upon hearing their story, then said…

"Are you out of your fucking noodle?!" The Myth asked with doubtful skepticism, before then rolling his eyes and changing the subject altogether. "Look… stupid, how about you help me fix bikes in the basement, and I'll even pay you two dollars!"

When Shadow, ready to lick it up, immediately agreed, The Voice and one percent instinct in his head was compelled to protest, "He never paid you the dollar for the first job!"

Despite never getting paid for the newspaper gig, Shadow nevertheless jumped at the chance to be accepted within the circle of his brother's older friends, whom had begun coming over to hang out and trick out their bicycles for stunting.

First there was Meathead, the fat karate kid whom liked to fish and hunt, and had dirt bikes and snowmobiles, and was the obvious leader of the other two runts following him around, which included Rotten, as the skinny balding kid whom liked to make fun of everyone to the point of overkill, and was strangely full of tips on how to steal things? And finally there was Scruff, the kid with the full beard at fourteen whom was oddly silent all the time and looked like he wanted to kill everybody?

Together, they were a self-proclaimed shady bunch and a trio of trash talking pubescent shitheads, whom permitted Shadow to hang around on the condition that he not whine or talk about what went on in the bike shop, where they began to age faster among the elder kids, who, despite their egos and attitudes, accepted them as Shadow went to work for big bro bicycle shop as the parts bitch, tasked with keeping the basement workshop neat and tidy, in addition to cleaning and stocking the parts that The Myth and The Shitheads salvaged from old busted down bikes.

While at first, trying to recall all the many different types of components along with all the different tools to remove them, had been like a climbing a mountain of confusion for a kid barely able to keep track of time, however, with a little help from The Voice, which was like a second brain to remember things, Shadow was able to really focus on how The Myth and The Shitheads were performing their oddly hurried mechanical deeds, which taught a bewildered kid how things worked together in unison, eventually training a child's memory to remember not only the parts and the tools, but soon they became just as skilled as The Shitheads, in a matching of abracadabra talents that even impressed The Myth, who told his little brother in a rare complimenting moment, "You'll be a good mechanic one day!"

There, within a job role that held the potential to blossom into a career, the thought of knowing what the future held had been a comforting notion, however, when The Voice suddenly pointed at Fate and Irony laughing at them, "Don't you find it strange how The Shitheads keep showing up here with a different new bike every week?!"

*REASON FOR LEAVING*: Hot bikes and busted butts.

# 2

# *CHILDREN OF THE GRAVE*

# GREEN MILE GARDENING

## *Village of Barely-A-Choice, ~ 1987 ~ Gardener Guy*

"Keep your fucking mouth shut and I'll double your pay!"

When The Myth looked at them with narrowed eyes and vowed Shadow to a code of silence, all of a sudden a potential future career as a bicycle repair tech was replaced with a pretense for a preteen crime thriller, about a black market bicycle parts network operating out of the basement of unsuspecting and oblivious parents, which was destined for it's inevitable end since The Shitheads were stealing bikes locally and then selling the parts locally like morons, and it was here that Shadow learned the value of friendships when big bro's bicycle shop got busted and The Shitheads vanished, leaving The Myth to take the brunt of the punishment both legally and physically at the hands of an angry Father, which was a preview to Shadow's future, whom did not need The Voice to prophesize, "Here comes the pain!"

Ever since birth, Shadow had been scared of this ominous man called Father, whom was always smoking and drinking and waging an open war upon some invisible beast of burden, which often led to strange intoxicated rants about salvation, followed by random acts of violence upon a wife and two sons, whom endured the end of leather belts, blunt wooden objects and the occasional wall.

"We're ok!" The Voice had tried to reassure a sobbing Shadow, as he pulled their head from the hole in the wall of a broke and broken household, which was barely getting by and living on a prayer, in a place where knowledge was painful and love was something to be feared and respected in an era that condoned hits over hugs to instill family values, which saw beatings as a show of affection from an otherwise distant and drunken Father, but alas, those were the good times.

When Mom suddenly could no longer work her waitressing job due to severe arthritis in her hips and knees coupled by Father losing his truck driving job due to drinking and driving, it proved to be the final blow that shattered a family portrait when a hapless husband lashed out one final time, and was taken away by the police responding to a "till death do us part" domestic dispute call, which saw two people never meant to be together go their separate ways in a peace sells, but who's buying world of social assisted living that soon found a desperate Mom unable to care for her two wild boys, thus, The Myth was sent to live with Father somewhere out on the coast, while Shadow had remained as the fly on the wall, left alone to pick up the pieces of a fast fading youth.

"We need to get out and experience life." The Voice had whispered on the inside, which compelled the owner of a lonely heart to move on from childhood and begin his journey as a young teen before his time, leading Shadow to look to an older brother's friends, The Shitheads, whose rebel yell for all things rumored to be bad for one's health, soon found Shadow taking up smoking in the boys room, drinking, getting stoned, and getting their cherry popped within an initiation for the ages.

Caught in a mosh of prepubescent hormones, Shadow had tripped and fallen into Sassy, a hot tomboy girl whom was a few years older with the looks that kill, whom wasn't shy about taking the things she wanted, which, in this case, was Shadow virginity whilst her parents were away, which found them going in like a virgin and coming out like a country song when Sassy dumped their ass for a performance that was hardly chart topping, yet, made them go wild in the streets alongside a group of wiggers, preps and punks whose sole purpose in life had been to get fucked up, fight turf battles and commit wanton acts of mindless mischief.

"You're an idiot!" The Voice said after one too many police car rides home for breaking the law that found a problem child suddenly left facing the same penance as an older brother, when they were told by the social worker, "Its reform school or, you go live with your Father!"

In a repeat of history that sent tears rolling down the cheeks of a saddened Mom, Shadow rode away in silence seated next to a paternal stranger, who forewarned about the last caress of pain upon a journey toward an unknown place shrouded in mystery, within a sparsely populated seaside village located just outside of Odd Town, a coastal tourist trap of measured popularity, where a faltering Father had moved into a centuries old shanty at the edge of the ocean, with his salty sea hag girlfriend Hatchet Face whom looked like an old crow had applied makeup with an ax, and who's idea of parenting involved more death threats and a meat cleaver.

## Professional Shadow

"Maybe juvenile hall isn't such a bad idea after all!" The Voice reasoned about a reality of struggle and strife under the roof of a drunken duo, which saw Hatchet Face working at a seafood processing plant in the vicinity while Father limped on as a bitter logger with a bad back, eking out a living off of small time contractors whom were on the take and treated him with ridicule. Despite the growing pains, Shadow actually felt sympathy for the devil within a parent they had never truly known, as they moved into a drafty old seaside dive held together by antique wallpaper, where, any dreams about easy street were immediately traded for an existence of poverty and destitution that left them so far disconnected from reality that, not even a fated reunion of two brothers could cast a silver lining upon a welcome to my nightmare home setting.

"He's had it rough" The Voice had immediately spotted the subdued look in the eyes of The Myth, which painted a preview to a hair of the dog household, where Shadow realized that the only breaks in life would be when the stick of discipline broke signaling the end of another lesson in obedience and servitude. There would be no running bare foot in the surf, or sleeping in on Saturdays during summer break from school, quite the opposite, Shadow and The Myth were rudely awakened by a cleaver wielding Hatchet Face every morning, whom fed them both a dry peanut butter sandwich and a glass of smelly well water for breakfast, after which The Myth went to work with Father at his logging job while Shadow was put to work as the unwilling gardener and groundskeeper, tasked with maintaining a haggard homestead that found their days begin upon hands and knees within the large garden that Father had planted down the hill by the shore, where the seemingly endless rows of sprouting greens became Shadow's only mission as they weeded and plucked herbage in a scared frenzy amidst the bugs, sticky soil and brisk ocean breeze, all whilst under the menacing gaze of Hatchet Face, whose fox on the run facial features made her look right at home in that garden …as a fucking scarecrow!

After spending hours hunched over in a creeping death of mortal soreness, Shadow felt like an old man before ever escaping puberty, which had merely been a warm up for a harvester of sorrow whom now had to water their handiwork, which involved taking from two large barrels placed upon a pull cart that had to be manually towed up to the house for refilling, and then carted back again without any help from Hatchet Face, whom shouted at them, "Well, come on you little piece of shit! Get fucking going!" *WHACK!*

Hatchet Face whipped them with a thicket branch in a three times the torture task that found a skinny little boy straining every muscle to the point of burning and beyond, all the while feeling like a human pack mule without the benefit of the two extra legs, *WHACK!* "Ugh! Huff, puff…!" *WHACK!* "…Ok, huff, puff…!" *WHACK!* *WHACK!*

"This fucking sucks!" Shadow thought in their mind, while The Voice of one percent began imagining ways for Hatchet Face to have an accident, "Let's run her over with the cart!"

So mornings were a little rough at a job disguised as a chore, but through their dirty deeds done dirt cheap, Shadow learned to not only grow food, but also realized that they had the ability to endure anything inflicted upon them by the scarecrow management, whom told them that a bread and water break was over and the second half of a horticultural Hell had begun. From mowing a green mile of grass in a rubber booted relay race of busted heel blisters, to raking and bagging the clippings before they blew away like dust in the wind to hacking away at a battlefield of dead shrubs strangled by beach sand and sea salt, to pruning the trees in front of the house the hard way by climbing up to cut the branches with a hand saw, to chopping firewood that Father brought home from his logging job and then tossing said firewood into the basement to be stacked along the stone walls of their derelict dwelling, which was insulated with the smelly seaweed that Shadow collected from the beach at low tide, in a daily duty of responsibility that had begun to harden the human wheels of an unsung teenager.

*REASON FOR LEAVING:* "Work for it boy or, **stay hungry!**"

# LEGACY LOGGING

## *Village of Barely-A-Choice, ~ 1989 ~ Axe Murderer*

When it was time for school to begin, the thought of getting on a bus filled with short sighted coastal students was a claustrophobic sting to say the least, especially when Shadow was greeted by Jock-Strap and his strap-on crew of small minded village sport preps whom acted like a group of hanging tough guys, but whom were really just bunch of spoiled rich brats whom naturally thought them to be better than everyone else and whom became the welcome wagon of academic adversity that greeted the new kid on the bus with ridicule and rejection.

"Oh, look everyone! We got a new bum on the bus!" Jock-Strap openly taunted about Shadow's dirt stained jeans and faded jean jacket that The Myth had passed down to his little brother, which garnered everyone's attention for the wrong reasons as a sad teen was made the fool by a familiar bully type, to which The Voice swiftly took exception... "Let's knock him the fuck out!" Although Shadow knew the only way to gain respect and not be viewed as a pushover by the other students was to smash a bully's teeth down his throat, however, the south of heaven beating they would surely receive from Father if they got into trouble on their first day of school had compelled Shadow to do nothing about it.

## Professional Shadow

"What? You can't be fucking serious!" The Voice screamed with disbelief between Shadow's ears, just as a foreign object bounced off the back of their head thanks to Jock-Strap at the back of the bus, which made Shadow angry in silence, while on the inside, The Voice wasn't about to let go of the sticks and stones of disrespect being tossed at them by assholes, "Alright, have it your way then… but sooner or later, it's going to be you, me, and mister fucking bully …savvy?"

Uncertain about the intentions of an inner self, when Shadow arrived at Father Saul's French Catholic Junior High School, they discovered that a long name belied a tiny brick institution, where self-righteous teachers preferred to inflict their instruction via the meter stick upon a classroom of placated pupils, whom were being held beneath the wheel of conformity within a place that refused to acknowledge individuality or, for that matter personal talent, like Shadow's proficiency at writing essays for which they had been denied a perfect score by the tubby, pastry eating principle whom claimed to have scored ninety eight upon his literature exams to become a teacher, and who, as a matter of principle, could not give a higher score to a student?

"The principle is an idiot!" The Voice affirmed in response to being held back by someone with obvious inferiority issues, which only helped to cast them further adrift upon a solo social raft that found Shadow lingering at edge of the schoolyard at recess, from where they kept an eye on Jock-Strap and his strap-on gang, in addition to that group of black leather jacket wearing punks over by the baseball field, whose greaser type appearances had been a reminder of a previous city life. There was something about their togetherness that had drawn Shadow's attention and envy, while sadly, they lacked the courage to go over and get to know these "rocker" looking kids whom looked like they might kick their ass if they went over there and said something dumb, so, Shadow stood unmoving and merely watched, until one of the black jackets began to walk this way!

Unsure what to think, they were a little nervous to meet this teenager with the mullet, the acid wash jeans and the stud in his left ear, whom greeted them with a sly pretty boy grin that was deceivingly captivating. "How's it going…?" Pretty boy asked without looking for a reply, "We saw you looking us and I want to know… what, are you looking at?"

Shadow didn't know how to answer the somewhat dumb question, so The Voice within offered, "We can knock him out!" but just then, within a split second eternity, Shadow thought they sensed something within Pretty Boy they could relate to… "Well, you all look way cooler than Jock-Strap and his crew of fucking tampons over there!" Shadow said with a hand gesture toward Jock Strap and his strap-on crew, whom were running around the soccer field like a bunch of fairies, compelling Pretty Boy's face to sour into a spiteful gaze that confirmed a previous notion that the black leather jackets hated the preps, as Pretty Boy then looked back at Shadow and suddenly smiled wide.

"…Yeah? Well, fuck them! Hey, you wanna join my gang?"

For the first time in their life, Shadow felt accepted within a group of friends their own age they could relate to, as they traded a blue jean jacket for a black leather one to become the newest member of the Black Jacket Society, which was an eclectic group of anti-establishment teenagers whom were feared by the other students along with most of the faculty at Father Saul's French Catholic Junior High School, in addition to Jock-Strap and his strap-on posse whom kept their distance in the school yard, but on the school bus however, it was a different story.

"Just let me do him! You won't even have to do anything!" The Voice pleaded as Jock-Strap continually pushed his knees into the back of their seat… *KNEES* *KNEES* *KNEES*

Fearing something even worse at home, Shadow did their best to resist The Voice inside, all the while fighting the urge to climb over the seat and rocking a jock into a fucking coma because of his… *KNEES* *KNEES* *KNEES*

"Where are your buddies now, huh? There's no one to save you here!" Jock-Strap threatened as he persisted… *KNEES* *KNEES* *KNEES* …causing Shadow to become flush with embarrassment and rage, in a slowly we rot moment that got noticed by a strap-on crew, whom began teasing and chiding, "Oh, look! I think he's going to cry!"

"You can't let this asshole keep disrespecting us!" The Voice to flat out scolded, but Shadow remained ever still, until… *KNEES* *KNEES* *KN…!*

"That's fucking it!" The Voice had snapped within an episode that most medical professionals would call a psychotic break, which had seen them wait for Jock-Strap to push his knees into their seat back one last time that would find a bully in a prone position and wide open, as a kid of questionable mental stability swiftly bolted around behind their seat in a lightning fast move, which culminated in hard right fist landing within Death Valley between nose and cheekbone upon Jock-Strap's stunned face…

"Thought you were tough, huh!? Guess you've got another thing coming asshole!" Shadow screamed echoing The Voice, before then glancing over their shoulder to glare at the surprised strap-on crew to see which one of them would be next. When none of them moved, Shadow knew that a fight with a bunch of fakes had ended, along with their bus ride home when the driver pulled over and kicked only Shadow off the bus like nobody's fault, just as Jock-Strap came to and began to snivel at the sight of his own blood.

"He won't be messing with us anymore!" The Voice reassured as they walked home toward an unknown parental reaction that would no doubt make Jock-Strap's bullshit seem trivial, however, when a so-called tough guy whined to his wealthy mommy and daddy whom in turn pressured a pastry eating principle into permanently expel an "undesirable", the loss of a new group of Black Jacket friends seemed like the least of their worries compared to a father's wrath …that never happened?

"At least I know I didn't raise a fucking pussy!" Father had stated with pride, which had left Shadow thunderstruck by a rare showing of kinship, however, "But… if you pull that shit again at your new school next year in Odd Town, you'll wish you had been born dead!"

For a moment there, they dared to believe that a coma of souls could actually begin to call themselves a family, however, their beliefs had been misplaced when The Myth suddenly ran away to Tower City with some blonde bimbo he had met through some secret friends, which found a kid brother losing a part of himself all over again whilst now having to fill the vacant boots of a logger's helper, "You're coming to work with me in the woods boy! Or, the consequences will involve a piece of wood!"

They had loved playing in the forest as a child, but going back to nature to chop it down somehow felt wrong as they trudged through the thick brush wearing steel-toed boots two sizes too big for their feet whilst carrying a chainsaw, a gas jug, tools and drinking water to some over the hill and faraway place, where Father, with a cigarette in his mouth and a smoking chainsaw in his hands felled tree after tree in a path of manmade devastation that found a kid struggling to keep up in a hard labor of sweat, sticky tree sap and flying buzzards.

"If the trees are the lungs of the world and we're cutting them all down, what the fuck is tomorrow going to be like?" The Voice wondered, leading Shadow to pause and look back upon a graveyard of stumps left in their wake, which left them stumped to envision the critical mass of an uncertain future, all the while stacking junked up logs that were three times their size.

"Keep up boy! Or, some pain will last!"

At fourteen years old, it strangely wasn't the danger of being crushed by a falling tree, or the risk of amputation by chainsaw that troubled Shadow the most, but rather, getting whipped by a half-crippled, chain-smoking alcoholic Father struggling at a go-nowhere job that presented the most turmoil, which ultimately invoked pity within Shadow toward someone whom seemed all but guaranteed a future involving more pain and struggle for an aging, poorly educated man, whom had to labor solo when it was time for his son to go back to school, where, they no longer wanted to be. In many ways, Shadow felt worse about leaving Father to his fate than they did about showing up at a new school in sap stained jeans and a tattered T-shirt, where a rough boy had to endure the down nose stares from the snobby students wearing all the latest vogue fashions, all the while trying to believe that an education and a chance at good life was possible for a teenage metal head with long hair and a black leather jacket.


***REASON FOR LEAVING:*** All for one …and justice for all.

# 3

# *PARANOID*

# PATERNITY SEAFOODS

## *The Village of Barely-A-Choice, ~ 1991 ~ Fish Fucker*

Since day one, the home room teacher, Professor Tapette, had openly used Shadow as the daily class example of what not to become, which had effectively pissed them off in a seemingly forsaken in a life that did not feel like their own.

"Why me...?" Shadow asked the universe without expecting an answer, but then The Voice pointed out the obvious, "It's because they're afraid of you or, rather, The Energy we carry."

Shadow was confused by "The Energy" revelation and merely rolled his eyes at the obvious that wasn't, which Professor Tapette had mistaken as an act of defiance to his authority that led him to triumphantly impose detention upon a rebellious teen trapped within a classroom of dorks, which in turn finally compelled Shadow, whom could no longer tolerate being oppressed, calmly stood up and walked to the front of the class, where they looked down at the feeble little man shouting his displeasure and simply told him, "You... can go fuck yourself!" Shadow then turned to the rest of the class and gave them all the finger as well, before walking out forever as a sixteen year old dropout.

Standing just beyond the edge of the school yard with their back turned to, "Not-Even-Going-To-Attempt-It" Junior High School, Shadow couldn't help but feel like a tiny speck of dust in a greater war ensemble of ancient agendas, while The Voice tried to look on the bright side, "It will be worth the beating for quitting school just for never having to listen to the bullshit anymo...!"

"Hey, you!"

Just then, a voice arose behind Shadow and it wasn't the one that usually followed him to the bathroom, and when they turned around, Shadow stood looking a big bald kid wearing a muscle shirt, camouflage pants and high laced combat boots.

"Holy shit... He looks crazy!" The Voice exclaimed within, as the unknown teenager covered with many home made tattoos peered at them a moment before introducing himself... "I'm Tattoo Terry... I see you're the new Guy here, what's your name?"

When Shadow said nothing and merely sized up the imposing brute standing before them, Tattoo Terry suddenly began getting angry and went to persist, "I said...!" however, to avoid making his day worse than it already was, Shadow raised his hand and revealed their name, before clarifying, "...and we just quit!"

At that moment, an evil grin suddenly appeared on Tattoo Terry's face, who looked around quickly before asking them bluntly... "Wanna do some acid?"

Now, they had gotten stoned before, but never in their life had Shadow ever been... "Holy fuck we're high!" ...after quitting school and dropping two tabs of LSD with his new friend Tattoo Terry, whom was also known as "The Acid Man", who sent him on a trip at the brain unlike anything they had ever experienced before, as Shadow gazed upon the world through a purple haze of infinite realities, hidden within the mind of a kid flying high again and again in a place where, for the first time, he could actually see The Voice in his head, which started off as his own reflection, but then took on different shapes… "Ha! Ha! Ha…!" Shadow laughed with a glazed third eye, "You look like a white rabbit!"

"The fuck did you say!?" The Acid Man said in sudden surprise, which pulled Shadow from the far reaches of their mind, where they had been lost to illusions and forgotten that Tattoo Terry had been tattooing a skull, dagger and snake upon Shadow's left shoulder using a homemade tattoo contraption involving a guitar string, a bent spoon and a small electric motor from a portable CD player, which hurt like Hell, but was just as quickly forgotten thanks to the acid orgy in their system.

"When I'm done tripping out here, I'm going home to tell Father that school's out for us and that we're going to continue helping him with his logging gig until we can get a legit job to help everyone out… or, something like that, I think?" Shadow nodded with blind confidence, while Tattoo Terry, whom was also high on LSD, dipped the crude guitar string slash tattoo needle in ink and said, "What the fuck are we talking about?"

At that moment, they could not remember either what Shadow had been saying, leading them both to begin laughing for no apparent reason, in bouts of laughter that came on in ever increasing waves until their faces hurt, only to catch their breath and then laugh more.

## Professional Shadow

After spending the night high as a kite and playing video games in The Acid Man's bedroom in the basement of his exasperated, yet, very liberal parent's place, Shadow walked home the next morning sporting a new tattoo, fully expecting Father to be at his logging job and Hatchet Face to be sitting in the kitchen waiting for them with her meat cleaver, but, upon reaching the house and seeing Father's car still parked in the driveway, a feeling of terror was delayed when they spied the other car parked beside it... "That's Grandpa God-Finger's car!"

Still feeling the effects of the LSD lingering in his eyes and tickling their senses, Shadow opened the door and stepped into the kitchen of the old house, where they were certain that a "Hell awaits" sermon of was forthcoming upon seeing Father sitting at the kitchen table next to Grandpa God-Finger. "Sit down" Father had instructed in a cold tone that gave them the acid chills, as Shadow sat at the far end of the table hoping to be out of reach of violent hands and close enough to the door should a troubled Father or an overtly religious grandfather choose carnage in the temple of the damned.

As the captor of sin and aggressive perfector type, it was inevitable that Grandpa God-Finger would begin preaching via bulging neck veins and the great index finger smash upon the table, about one thousand days of Sodom and the demons within a last child, as though driving home the nails within a family crucifixation, yet, strangely, no Hatchet Face?

At first, Shadow merely figured that she had been hiding in the bedroom to avoid having to listen to Grandpa God-Finger's crazed rants about miracles unseen since before the creation of time, but when it was revealed that she had moved out the day before upon finding out that Father had been cheating on her with some other woman in Odd Town, whom he planned on moving in with? "Well, so much for good intentions!" The Voice ceded, as a Father told his son that they had until the end of the month to figure out a path in life, which to them, seemed to contradict the houses of the holy theory being spewed by a burning bush of conformity, whom showed no remorse for the plight of a grandson, whom had just received the last rites of a dead family.

After some much needed rest and a day to get their mind straight, Shadow sat alone in a has-been home, facing the post mortem reality of finding their first real job so they could pay to survive somewhere else, which left them facing a mountain of uncertainty with a severe lack of comprehension concerning their immediate future. "What the fuck are we gonna do?" Shadow asked The Voice in his head, which had unwittingly become a career guidance councilor.

"How about going into business for ourselves and doing landscaping... We have intimate experience with that!" The Voice offered in reference to the whippings they had taken at the hands of Hatchet Face. Although it had been a great suggestion in light of all the forced experience they had gained whilst maintaining the yard and garden of a drifty property, all Shadow could do was raise their eyebrows to the obvious, "We're barely sixteen candles over here genius!"

Placing face to hands and closing their eyes, Shadow wished upon the universe for an answer to appear from the darkness, but when none materialized, Shadow opened their eyes once more in despair and glanced around the old weathered kitchen that was in a state of disarray from not having been cleaned since before Hatchet Face departed in haste, leaving dirty dishes piled up in the sink, empty beer bottles haphazardly strewn about the grimy floor, and the stack of old newspapers by the back door? At that moment, the memory of delivering the paper with The Myth came flooding back, reminding them of a time when a kid just learning how to read, had flipped through the sections glancing at the articles that had included the sports section, the cartoons, the crossword and…

"…The fucking want ads!" Shadow exclaimed as they leapt from their chair and hurried over to the stack of outdated newspapers, whereupon grasping the most recent volume Shadow pulled out the employment for hire section and then simply dropped the rest on the floor before going back to the table, to glance through the available jobs with a breath of anticipation, "Garbage man? Nope. Hairstylist…? Nope. Truck driver…?" Shadow lingered for a moment upon the industry of a family legacy, which had only led to misery for a failed Father, "…Nope!"

When a previous breath of anticipation was exhaled in disappointment, Shadow could feel the hopelessness of the future blob begin to crush them between the hammer and the anvil, but just then, down at the bottom of the column, they suddenly spied a heading that read… *SEAFOOD PROCESSING LABOR NEEDED*

"You think so?" The Voice wondered at the three days old job ad, but Shadow was nonetheless compelled to jump on their ten speed bicycle and pedal their ass over to the seafood processing plan, which was located at the edge of a rocky coastal bluff of crashing waves, where, the riptide of desperate hopes found an adolescent filling out an application for a night shift position, which saw most of the experience sections on the application left blank. Despite a lack of work experiences, the manager seemed nonetheless interested in hiring them however; he could not sice they didn't have any identification.

"What the fuck does a plastic card have to do with proving were alive!?" Shadow exclaimed with determined exasperation that compelled the night manager to reveal another option, "You have ambition kid so I'll tell you what… Bring me a letter from your parents proving who you are and I'll hire you!"

It was a tiny ray of hope that lifted their spirits until Shadow suddenly remembered that Father was spending all his time getting drunk at his new girlfriend's place in Odd Town, and the house phone had been disconnected for nonpayment. "Fuck!" Shadow cursed as they rode away in disappointment from an opportunity rooted in brain damage, after having salvation dangled before them like a carrot on a string, only for it to be held forever out of reach for someone deep in the hole of…!

"Ah, shit!" Shadow said with compounded despair, when the front wheel on their bike suddenly went flat, spurring a fit of rage that momentarily made them hate everything including a shitty old bicycle, which they picked up and heaved into the ditch with a firm, "Fuck you!" before beginning to stomp away, only, they didn't get far when a big grey sedan suddenly pulled up beside them with a middle aged man and woman inside… "We saw the great bicycle toss back there…" The man behind the wheel revealed, "…Need a lift?"

With their broken down bicycle locked in the trunk of a car, Shadow rode along feeling dejected over their last few turbulent days, which had been noticed by the man driving whom inquired about the visible turmoil gripping a young backseat passenger, to which Shadow, with nothing to lose, proceeded to describe all the events leading up to their presence in the back seat of a strangers car that left the married couple visibly stunned as they looked at each other in wide eyed shock, before the man looked at Shadow once again in the rearview mirror…

"You know, *we* work at the seafood plant that you just tried applying at…" The man paused for a second to glance at his wife before continuing, "…and we have extra space at our place..."

A sudden rush of intrigue gripped Shadow as Douggy, the husband driver, quickly looked at his wife Georgina again with a sly grin before looking over his shoulder at Shadow, "…And I can write that letter for you …son!"

Standing upon a damp processing line alongside fifty men and women wearing hairnets, smocks, rubber boots and rubber gloves, Shadow felt ridiculous, but was nonetheless happy to be earning a real paycheck at a job that offered a green teen's first glimpses into the organized chaos of a processing industry, which they were now a part of as a seafood processing employee, tasked with unloading the many trucks arriving with countless vats filled with fresh daily fishermen catches, followed by the endless gutting and boning of fish upon long conveyor like tables that reeked of fermenting innards. Never before had Shadow considered all the steps that a fish and chips diner went through before reaching their plate, until they witnessed firsthand the entire labored process within a job made possible by Douggy and his wife Georgina, the married couple whom had quite literally saved the life of a stranger teenager by quite literally adopting an unknown kid off the side of a gypsy road, and giving Shadow a shot to prove their integrity at overcoming a dire situation that, despite the smelly setting and monotonous repetition of their labors, found them nevertheless putting a best foot forward like a killer of giants, whom was just as capable and could keep up to the adults they were working with, whom had been impressed by the drive and determination of a fortunate son, working hard to measure up in a young man's pursuit of prosperity, which compelled the elder veteran workers along with the alcoholic night manager sneaking sips of whiskey in a jar in his office, to confirm something The Voice had previously mentioned, yet Shadow still did not understand, "That kid's got The Energy!"

***REASON FOR LEAVING***: A last minute life.

# THE SCHOOL OF S.T.F.U.

## *Home Town, ~ 1992 ~ Work Whore*

To them, Douggy had become like a Father figure in a crazy reality devoid of family, which had been a comforting notion for someone feeling snowballed by a ready or not destiny in a young life without a clear path, as they awoke each day before noon to face the responsibilities of adulthood that first began with breakfast compliments of Georgina, their surrogate mom, before heading to the beach to spent their afternoons smoking hashish and tripping on Peyote with Douggy, whom told hilarious tall tales of his adventures as a youth, which had them in tears from laughing so hard, before going in to do their night shift duties at a workplace that saw most of the employees getting wasted on breaks given the absence of management brass and the food inspectors, whom only worked the day shift, thus leaving every night wide open for drugs, alcohol and horseplay to run rampant on company time.

With newfound layers of cash piling up in their pockets, the necessities of life along with complacent luxuries had suddenly become accessible to a backstreet kid raised within the struggle of poverty, which had instilled no concept of financial foresight beyond the notion that currency was merely something people used to pay rent and buy shit with, leading to a measure of smells like teen spirit spending upon trivial possessions and items of a hallucinogenic nature thanks to The Acid Man, Tattoo Terry, whom they had remained close friends with and who introduced Shadow to a whole new crowd of people like The Goblin, The Acid Man's supplier of LSD, whom was much older and the classic hippie type that hosted stoner parties, where they met passing faces in a psychedelic flash of fast friendships, which included Skinny Jesus, another aspiring tattoo artist whose home made ink needles also touched Shadow skin.

There was Cousin Evil, Bird-Brain, Tiny and Scrapper, all of whom were older and paid no heed to the unknown teen standing unnoticed in the corner, in an era when it was all about the musical energy and the fight for your right to party, which found them going to many open house festivities that either ended in the destruction of a dwelling, or someone getting kicked in the teeth, and it was at one such demolition party that Shadow met James, a long haired hippie whom was the lifelong friend type worthy of a mention in a future biography.

Of course, hanging around with older friends brought about the nightclub scene, where Shadow followed despite still being too young to legally enter drinking establishments, which they dealt with by assuming a confident scowl of unimpressed maturity at the club entrance to fool the low wage doorman, whom probably knew they were too young, but never gave another a second glance to a cotton eye Joe ready to dance on a floor of fun and frolic within a totally new electric avenue of pulsing beats, which inadvertently found them bumping into Lust, a heavy metal bad girl type whom was a year older using a fake ID to get in bars, and whom immediately felt an attraction toward Shadow that saw her become their first real teenage girlfriend, whose affinity for cocaine and oral sex had blown more than the wad in their wallet.

"If she keeps this up, she's going to suck me right out of you!" The Voice had worried, but Shadow could only grin like an idiot in a youth gone wild that found them so entranced by a girl that aspired to be a cycle slut from hell that was built for speed and a total distraction from reality as they never stopped to look down the country road to the end of a fishing season, which suddenly spelled the end complete to an illusion of prosperity, not-to-mention a loyal relationship, when Lust, whom had only been with Shadow for the fringe benefits, swiftly dumped their ass for some other mutt whom immediately got her pregnant, in a double whammy of Fate and Irony they had been too high or too hung to foresee.

"Now that was thinking with the wrong head!" The Voice had tried to deflect responsibility for the in-a-gadda-da-vida of a near miss, however, Shadow was in no mood to argue with inner demons, "Well, I didn't hear you complaining when Lust turned her throat into a thrash zone! So, if you want to fucking stay in my head you'd better make yourself useful and come up with some ideas, because it's going to be a long cold winter if we don't figure something out, fast!"

Looking for a solution to problems with an unpredictable outcome, Shadow was left with options that were as nonexistent as the fair-weather friends they had so foolishly spent their earnings with, which now found them in a precarious situation to pay their dues to the family whom had opened their home to a homeless kid. The thought of freeloading until the following year's work season had been neither a real option, nor an appealing notion for someone that had been shown respect for who they were and not what they could buy with a now dwindling bank account.

"Too bad The Acid Man is going to Tower City to be a skinhead..." The Voice had pointed out in hopes of tripping over blind inspiration, "...we might have been able to bunk over at his parents place!" compelling Shadow to merely shook head at the what ifs and maybes that were never going to happen, just like finding another job in a small religious tourist trap that would completely shut down during the winter months, meaning that they were ultimately screwed, until The Voice said something ever so simple, but suddenly earned its keep between Shadow's his ears, "...How about we call, Mom!"

It was a shot in the dark, but it was the only one they had that held the most promise of not spending the winter outside in a freezing snow drift, only, they did not have her number and could only guess blindly that she still lived at the same place, as Shadow packed their things and got Douggy to drive them to their childhood house in Home Town, where, with fingers crossed, they began knocking on heaven's door, hoping for a sign that would offer salvation to someone that had almost forgotten what it was like to be the son of the woman whom answered in surprise.

Upon seeing a long lost parent with a hobbled leg that was bent at the knee in a way it should not be, they felt a profound sense of pity for a frail looking mom they barely recognized, whose back story they had learned from Father whom had told a grim tale about a third born daughter growing up in a large family, which had shunned an innocent mind and treated her as the fool for being born on April Fool's Day?

"I hope we never see our self righteous, asshole fucking relatives ever again!" Shadow vehemently vowed, as they aimed to do whatever it took to be a better son that was going to get it together, by first getting a job that would see the return of an income to support their broke ass, which would in turn help out the one whom had granted them life, and quite literally, had just saved it. Thus, at the risk of repeating a fateful first job experience, they once again turned to the newspaper want ads that once again offered the same out of reach and otherwise unwanted employment opportunities.

"Let's see here… Garbage man… Nope. Hairdresser…? Nope. Truck driver… What the fuck?" After spying all the same jobs as before, a notion that a city should behold more industry than a comatose coastal village was left trapped under ice in a frozen, jobless landscape, which found Shadow teetering on the edge of hopeless anxiety, until, suddenly, The Voice saw the plot of a new adventure.

"What's that?" The Voice had nudged their attention to the heading about some government funded program, which had been created to help drop-outs get their high school equivalency, "And they'll even pay us for it!" Suddenly, with hopes pulled back from an overly dramatic precipice, a second chance to salvage a crash and burn education seemed like a fateful godsend upon a road to nowhere, compelling Shadow to take the bus over to the School of S.T.F.U., where they signed up for a curriculum that beheld a little more than the simple ABC's of indoctrination when it was revealed that other learning modules were being instructed like cooking and life skills, basic computer skills, carpentry and woodworking, resume writing and…

"Job exposure?" Shadow questioned warily, which suddenly made the nice administration lady with the bright smile look at them with a cold dark stare that erased all confidence in a karma chameleon on a government salary, whom said… "As a condition of your attendance in the program, you also have to participate in our employment placement segments, where you'll spend two weeks working for one of our sponsors over three separate placement intervals and…"

Shadow barely heard the rest after their mind stopped at the word "condition", where The Voice attempted to crunch the numbers behind a godsend that suddenly didn't seem like such a good deal upon realizing they would actually have to physically work for their diploma. "Hmm… three months of Fate divided by two weeks of Irony, times three, equals… fucking bullshit!"

The thought of literally having to sweat for an education instantly removed any notion of something for nothing in a hard fought chance at a better life, which clearly would never anything for free in a reality that was strangely more difficult than it had to be, leaving a no-choice applicant to sign upon the dotted line of a loaded contract that placed them within a haphazard classroom along with a generation landslide of dropouts whom were the epitome of social issues notably more serious that a split personality.

From criminal delinquents concealing weapons to pregnant teenage moms seeking a career receiving monthly child benefits, to that homeless addict whom was merely there for the free change and free food in the Home EC class, Shadow never imagined they would find themselves in a curriculum of insanity, but, there they were, watching the paper planes fly over a cuckoo's nest of modified morals wondering if they would last in a classroom that was prone to projectiles and potentially violent student outbursts. Surrounded by an expendable youth, they eventually made threadlike friendships with the likes of Stinky Carl, the kid that looked and smelled like he never bathed. Stinky Carl wasn't very bright, but otherwise an innocent soul to talk to, unlike Marie, the very hot and very pregnant seventeen year old wannabe gangbanger, no pun intended, whom had gotten knocked up simply for the government child benefits she would receive upon bearing a child into a ride or die world of hardships, which made Shadow wonder what a young girl had been through to make her see the price over a life.

And finally, there was Pigeon, the hopeless stoner with an eagle tattoo on his left shoulder that looked more like, well, a fucking pigeon, whom became a friend in need that led to drug hookups and the eventual distribution of LSD compliments of Shadow, which Pigeon sold to the rest of the classroom dope heads, except for beautiful pregnant Marie of course, which helped to finance a struggle to survive until their once a month program payment came in. Although Pigeon was kind of an idiot and essentially an aloof moron, he was of acceptable mental capacity to least become someone else to talk to within an otherwise solo life of conversing instincts, which had led them to begin hanging together outside of class in a sort of bond formed between two dropouts left to die upon the road of life, which for Shadow, was someone other than The Voice for company and conversation, until suddenly, one day Pigeon disappeared without a toxic trace.

"He's probably in jail!" The Voice reasoned when Pigeon suddenly vanished their life and from a classroom curriculum, just before the start of the work exposure segment, which made them quickly forget all about Pigeon and focus upon their first two week stint working for a sponsoring business that specialized in heating and air conditioning, where Shadow was paired up with Stanley, the lead technician at the company whom was a certified professional at his job, and whom explained every detail pertaining to all things HVAC, in a communication breakdown of technical information that fast fried a teenaged stoner's mind, however, with the help of The Voice, eventually the concepts and theories of a certifiable industry soon began to make sense, making Shadow feel like it was something they could do for a career, especially after they found out how much it paid.

***REASON FOR LEAVING***: The fine print of sweating bullets

## THE BEAVER FACTORY

### *Home Town, ~ 1992 ~ Window "to the future" Maker*

With their diploma only a few months away, it seemed like Fate and Irony had just dropped a golden egg in their lap, however, upon showing up at the sponsoring company on week two, the expectation that they would continue working and learning with Stanley, the lead technician at the company, found Shadow mistaken when they were instead paired up with Mr. Brownstone, another HVAC technician who just happened to be one of the biggest drug dealers in Home Town.

"First of all, you can call me Mr. B! Secondly..." Mister B. paused to pull out a big bag of weed upon driving out of the company yard, "...roll a joint so I know you're not a fucking narc!"

Upon returning to class, Shadow's put on their best fake smile when ask to recant their experiences working with a covert professional who had permanently distorted a theory of nine to five living for an aspiring HVAC assistant, whom had just learned new plaster caster ways to make fast cash involving the nasal candy upon accepting Mr. B.'s one way offer to take up a lucrative side hustle that paid far more than a technician's salary, not-to-mention a meager monthly payment that barely fed a hollow stomach. When faced with getting thrown off a rooftop, a decision to take up dealing had been a no-brainer for a kid of two minds hoping to help out a tired Mom whom was saddened to see her son suffer the hardships of Fate and Irony within an unprepared life, to which The Voice felt obligated to point out the obvious... "You know what will happen if *you* get caught dealing that shit!"

"Oh, shut up! You love it here! I know you're hot for teacher!" Shadow said to silence The Voice's territorial pissings, which were casting a golden shower upon a fantasy of taking extracurricular lessons with the hot jobs councilor from resume writing class, whose number one rule when it came to writing that perfect resume or curriculum vitae was simply, "When in doubt ...lie!"

"Ask her if she wants to do rails after class!" The Voice hit back sarcastically, which killed Shadow's boner for a Bachelor's Degree in bed based ergonomics that...!

"Holy shit...! Did you see that!?" Shadow exclaimed a loud when Stinky Carl, whom had brought his pet Chinchilla to class for show and tell and had set it loose in the room to during his enthusiastic presentation, accidently stepped on the poor thing with his big clumsy winter boots whilst trying to collect a jittery animal, effectively crushing a hapless creature and snapping its neck with a sickly *SNAP!* before watching it die a horrible, convulsing, blood puking death right there in front of a shocked class.

"Uh, can we take our diploma exams now please?" Shadow thought with raised eyebrows, while on the inside, The Voice was busy whipping the idiot buried in the backyard... "Knock,

knock... Who's there?" Shadow felt the twitch of laughter and despair tickling the corner of their lips, "Dead Chinchilla!"

"What... Too soon...?"

When they got home that day, all Shadow wanted to do was forget dying rodents, crying classmates and time crunched careers that were too far away to be worth anything yesterday, however, upon discovering that a physically impaired Mom was moving to an assisted care home in Odd Town due to her debilities, a plan that had been set in motion before the unforeseen arrival of an estranged son, they were left to find alternative accommodations.

"I didn't know how to tell you" Mom had said with regret, but they could not blame her and only them for being such a failure, as they contemplated their options, or rather, a lack thereof, which found Shadow pursuing the only option they had by calling up acquaintances met though their helter skelter side hustles, leading them to move in with Finch, a phony gangster and mid level street dealer whose drug operation had been funded by the inheritance of passed away parents that had also bequeathed a home, where Shadow took up residence downstairs in the separate basement suite that did not require a deposit or credit checks.

"Great way to honor your parents" The Voice had remarked despite a steal of a deal that offered an entire flat to them with the exception of one room, which was to remain under lock and key and off limits to everyone, "You know what will happen if..." The Voice had started about the off lease rental stipulations, which would not bode well should the law come kicking doors down at some drug dealing, gun toting egomaniac's place, whom was known to draw unwanted attention to himself, but alas, with hope at the end of a rope, Shadow had no time to worry about when the hammer falls as they merely resolved to maintain the status quo in a strained situation, and continue... *SNIFF!* ...going the distance... *SNIFF!* ...in hopes that everything would all work itself out... *SNIFF!*

"Are you always going to be this fucking stupid?" The Voice said rhetorically and with annoyance, as Shadow sat in class rubbing their eyes in an attempt to alleviate the sinus migraine left behind by the disco dust they had done the night before, which had become an all too common occurrence within a snow blind reality that soon began questioning the merits a minimum wage education, especially when they could make way more selling blow at high dough to the masses.

With no answers or fucks given, dissecting dusted theories would have to wait until after another two week job exposure at a different sponsor, which found them sent to a window manufacturing business and placed upon a production line, where it was their job to install the same boring hardware into the same boring window frames all day long, in a repetitive eight hour duty spent standing next to a group of time clock laborers whose lowered life expectations made the task as monotonous as it sounds, yet, somehow...

"I actually like this" Shadow said of an easy gig that, when compared to the HVAC place and its overload of information, wasn't that bad for an aging teenager with a keen video game reflex, which had taught them to master their hand and eye coordination that proved especially useful during the handling of power tools used during an assembly task.

Overall, it was an easy does it job exposure that was mercifully free from trauma based learning, which had been a surprise upon seeing the company manager, The Beaver, whom showed up each morning looking like can of smashed assholes in an obvious reveal of late night boozing and other questionable habits, but whom had noticed an energetic and otherwise profitable new young tool within his midst that had compelled The Beaver to offer Shadow a permanent position upon the production line of his company…

"When that course is done, come see me and I'll hire you!" The Beaver had told them, which had been not only encouraging, but also a reassuring confirmation of their abilities at barely eighteen years old, however, the fact that Shadow was now fixing up the boss after hours upon learning that their employer had a thing for powdered supplements, yet again found them omitting details of their job experiences upon returning to class, where they chose to leave out the master of puppets payoffs that had seen Shadow snorting lines and getting fucked up with The Beaver during solo "overtime" at the factory, where they would be going to work upon getting their diploma and…?

"I'm sorry, what the fuck do you mean we can't go work there?" Shadow asked the program administrator with a look on his face like they had just stepped on a dead Chinchilla! When the lady administrator suddenly turned into a demented hobbit forbidding them from permanently working for a sponsor… "It's in your contract!" …Shadow, came up with their own stipulation.

"Well then, screw your fucking contract because we quit!"

Aware that The Beaver would choose the blow over the black betty bullshit, they went to work at a guaranteed job despite the guilt of failing to get their diploma that somehow, from the beginning had felt like it was never going to happen anyway, however, the fact that they didn't need the diploma to get a job had led Shadow to quickly forget about cruel schools and focus upon a normal taxpaying life by day, whilst by night, they were an uncertified Dr. Feelgood of the underworld, moving large quantities of drugs in a high stakes cat and mouse game of profits and misguided morals, which got a lot riskier after Finch, their landlord, got caught in a parking garage with his loaded hand gun.

"Hey, stoopid! It's time to move the fuck out of here!" The Voice advised, to which Shadow was in full agreement as they began looking for another place to live that would enable them to continue Shadow's illicit activities, however, everything got sidetracked when a phone call from Mom suddenly announced the passing of their …Dad?

The news had hit them like a train of consequences, within a world that suddenly felt a lot smaller for a son wishing they could have had more time with a simple man whom had succumbed to lung cancer at forty eight years old after falling ill to a stage four sickness that had been soothed by a morphine induced coma from the pain, and reduced a human being to a nearly unrecognizable alien state within a coffin of sorrows, at a funeral service of unfamiliar faces and disconnected family relatives whom they barely knew, and sadly, had no will to know beyond the symbolic handshakes of empty condolences.

In a time of tragedy, the only silver lining had been the return of The Myth, which had rekindled a link to the only one capable of understanding a little brother's hopes and dreams within a live and let die existence that, despite the immediate need to survive, was still without a future goal or a clear vision of purpose beyond the certainty of physical labor and the late night coke sessions with The Beaver, whose obsession with Lucy in the sky with diamonds was providing much needed profits for someone stuck in a heart shaped box of lost time and never realized moments.

***REASON FOR LEAVING***: A friend in need is no friend indeed

## R.I.P.

**DAD**

# 4

# *THE HAND OF DOOM*

# BIG RED CONCRETE

"When you don't have any enemies left, the only people that can hurt you are friends and family."  Big Red

## *No Fun City, ~ 1993 ~ Concrete Survivor*

"I'm tired of just being 'The Voice'! I want a real name!"

Still feeling the effects of the synthetic icicles in their skull from the party they had attended on a week night, Shadow was in no mood for an alter ego seeking an identity, as they pedaled their bicycle home from work on that rainy Monday. "Ok, how about... Norbert!" Shadow said in a mocking tone whilst avoiding large puddles of muddy water.

"Fuck you! Drugs are turning you into an idiot!" The Voice replied flatly in reference to the reckless life they were leading which had seen Shadow's consumption of drugs and alcohol increase ever more in a ghetto boy lifestyle living for the hustle and the party, all the while hiding behind the strange feeling that everything was not meant to last. "We'll go look at that place tomorrow..." Shadow confirmed, "We'll rent it and move in with Pigeon!"

While The Voice had been pleased about the first part of a relocation plan, the addition of Pigeon created a sense of unease upon coming home from work one day to find Pigeon hanging out upstairs with Finch their landlord, in a small world scenario that had seen the reunion of two friends that had seemed innocent enough to Shadow, but stranger than fiction to a one percent instinct.

"Something is weird about all this!" The Voice had cautioned, but Shadow had been looking at the profit of a friend in need, whom revealed that his absence from class had been due to some gimme a bullet story about an ill fated warehouse job followed by countless moves in a hard luck life, which Shadow figured was probably bullshit… "And not even a phone call?" …but otherwise harmless.

Looking beyond the despair behind the details, Shadow had decided to use their essentially homeless friend as an excuse to escape a hot environment, where the addition of a roommate and runner to move product while they were working at a legit job, seemed like a fated move in ironic times that…!

"What the fuck…!" Shadow suddenly exclaimed upon veering onto their street and spotting the flashing lights of police vehicles parked in front of Finch's place. Slamming on the brakes, they stood motionless in the pouring rain, watching from a distance as uniformed officers entered the house they once called home, only to exit a short time later carrying bags of items in a search and seizure they knew damn well wasn't sugar.

"I think we're being raided!" The Voice said of the obvious scene, which felt like they were watching a crime movie only the script was being written right before their very eyes, leading to questions to begin flooding their mind… "What the fuck happened? How much did they get? Did they get what was in that locked room? Where's Finch...? And, Pigeon...!"

They might have stood there forever waiting for ninety nine answers were it not for a one percent instinct that slapped their brain into action. "Let's get the fuck out of here!" The Voice yelled between Shadow's ears, compelling them to fast trek it out of there and high tail it over to an older brother's place, whom no one except for Mom and the Shitheads knew that The Myth had resettled in Home Town after Father's funeral, and where they went to lay low until the damage could be assessed.

"It's not good!" Finch had informed them upon meeting up later at an alternate location, where Shadow learned the world eater details that had seen Pigeon turn out to be an informer for the police.

"I fucking knew it! The Voice screamed on the inside, as their now ex landlord explained how he had been arrested for possession of a small personal quantity of drugs and released to appear in court on his own recognizance, however, when the cops went downstairs and kicked down the door to a locked room... "What did they get?" Shadow didn't really want to know despite a part of them desperately needing to.

"About a kilo and a half" Finch replied with a measure of disgust, which made Shadow sick to their stomach for other reasons, when Finch said, "They're looking for you!" However, what almost made them puke up regurgitated giblets, was the revelation that Pigeon was a snitch who, they learned through Finch's lawyer, had vanished from the School of S.T.F.U. not for a job and homelessness, but rather, the fucking little kike had been arrested for burglary and theft, and had been offered a deal to become an undercover mole in a drug sting operation on Finch, and, by association, his tenant and expendable friend Shadow, all in exchange for a suspended sentence.

"He's a fucking squealer!"

No matter how many different ways Shadow repeated it, it would not change the obvious behind a non coincidence, which had left them holding the bag both figuratively and quite literally that now found them a fugitive of the law. Despite Finch losing product, the fact that the separate basement suite had been in Shadow's name had denied the authorities the catch of a "bigger fish", leaving them to take the fall when the weight comes down upon a now homeless teenager on the run from the law, with no help or good advice from Finch's lawyer except for... "Good luck!"

Completely fucked, Shadow knew life in Home Town had just been reduced to two choices, prison, or the horizon, where, after a lot of soul searching and some "Shithead" networking, it was decided that they would start over on the other side of MY-BIG-HOUSE in No-Fun City, after Meathead from The Shitheads, whom had been chumming again with The Myth, revealed that he had a friend over the mountain on the western shores whom could set them up with a place to stay and a job …if they could make it there. The thought of leaving their entire life behind instilled a deep sense of loss that was made worse when Shadow called their now former employer, and told The Beaver they would not be coming back. "What do you need?" The Beaver had asked in solidarity, to which Shadow laid out their plan to escape a bad moon rising by collect the last of their earnings and purchase a ticket for a one way trip to the farthest place they had never been, where they hoped to start a new life.

On the day of the flight, Shadow was nervous at the airport, where even The Voice had been certain they would get nabbed before boarding the aircraft, "We're going to get popped!" However, upon making it to their seat and experiencing the rush of takeoff, Shadow breathed a sigh of relief at thirty thousand feet upon their first ever ride in a jet airliner, which hopefully, was flying them toward a better future filled with bright new beginnings that would see a the turning point leading out of and away from a fruitless history, within a simple plan to hook up with The Sandman whom said that he could set them up with a place to crash and a job, which had all sounded great to a desperate ear over the phone, however, upon landing in No-Fun City, The Sandman, whom was supposed to meet Shadow at the airport ...was nowhere to be seen.

A sudden twitch of anxiety began to stir in the pit of their stomach as Shadow they picked up the pay phone receiver and called the fateful number, which rang and rang ...and rang some more, until The Sandman finally answered sounding irritated and intoxicated.

"Who!?" The Sandman questioned when Shadow said who they were ...three times, which was followed by disbelief that they had made the trip, before finally giving up his address with instructions to call him from a phone booth at corner of 18 and Life Street, where he would go meet them.

"Something is very off about all this!" The Voice warned, but Shadow really didn't want to hear it after such a long trip, which still required a lengthy journey upon a disorienting elevated train and multiple transit bus rides that eventually placed them at their destination, within maze big city maze of streets and high rises unlike anything they had ever witnessed before. The hour was late Shadow didn't own a watch, so they decided to ask the big guy jogging past them… "Hey… Mister! Got the time?"

When the large jogger suddenly spun on them and yelled in their face, "Don't fucking talk to me man!" Shadow took a step back and reached for the blade concealed under their black leather jacket, ready to fight off an attacker with glazed eyes and …multiple puncture wounds visible upon his bare arms?

"Whoa... That's a big junkie!" They thought in panic as the large jogger merely stood there looking at them for a moment before running off, leaving Shadow to breathe a sigh of relief, while The Voice eschewed a silent greeting, "Welcome to the jungle!"

Upon reaching the payphone they had been told to use, it took three separate tries before some woman finally picked up, whom at first did not seem to know who The Sandman was, much less some strange new-in-town teenager, only to then say that The Sandman wasn't available, which stoked another flame of panic within Shadow, until finally, the woman sighed with annoyance and said that she would be right along. When nearly an hour passed, they began to wonder and worry whilst standing there in a rough looking neighborhood late at night, and were just about to lose hope when suddenly some tiny native woman approached them and motioned for Shadow to follow without saying a word, which had been hardly reassuring as they were led to some large apartment complex of questionable livability, where an image of salvation and some much needed rest filled the mind of a weary traveler seeking to stop a roller coaster ride of insanity, however, upon entering a tiny bachelor apartment and seeing a big native man sitting at the kitchen table doing the spoon man thing …with heroin, and seeing a man lying on the floor knocked out and bleeding in a pool of his own urine…

"Enter Sandman, we presume", The Voice said in silent defeat, when Shadow was informed by the tiny native woman that the white devil sleeping on the floor was the one they had been supposed to talk to about a new life, leaving Shadow to suddenly realize the grave error they had made after escaping the frying pan back in Home Town, only to jump in the fire four thousand eight hundred and sixty miles away.

"He had it coming…" The big native man suddenly spoke in reference to The Sandman's unconscious state, without ever taking his eyes off his illicit task. "I'm Big Red… Have a seat"

After sidestepping their would-be host whom was still snoring through blood bubbles on the dirty kitchen floor, Shadow sat before a "this is your life" moment, where they learned two very important things about their new environment with the first being that The Sandman, had been full of shit with all his talk about a new life and a great job, since it was Big Red whom was the one with a small time primal concrete sledge business that was nowhere near as grandiose as a had been claimed by a drug addict, leading to the second point, which now found them in the company of intravenous drug users.

"That's for you if you want it!" Big Red said upon placing a loaded syringe on the table in front of Shadow, whom knew if they took it that it would lead to certain death, so they chose to avoid dialing the number of the beast and refused the loaded syringe. "Good choice…" Big Red nodded as he tied his arm off with a piece of stretchy hospital tubing and then grasped the syringe with the golden liquid within, "…More for me!"

Although they didn't want to watch, Shadow sat unmoving as Big Red shot the vile substance into his veins and then untied his arm, allowing the malicious mixture to circulate within his bloodstream that caused his body to go limp as he teetered in and out of consciousness as Shadow looked on unblinking with their life flashing behind regret filled eyes. When The Sandman finally stirred back to life, Shadow wanted to put him back under for being such a lying piece of garbage, who had baited them into a move and a scam that was seemingly worse than prison …maybe.

Lost to a land of confusion, they endured the illusion of freedom by sleeping on the floor of an empty bachelor apartment along with three other people addicted to crack and heroin, which didn't exactly inspire visions of a long term career upon learning that Big Red was a certified concrete finisher doing "light" commercial concrete jobs around the suburbs, where Shadow learned how to work with a heavy, society building substance by a functioning addict whom gassed up his old beat up pickup truck and then drive off without paying.

"You just gotta make it out of the zone and the cops from other zones won't bother with a petty gas and run!" Big Red and The Sandman had claimed triumphantly, with Shadow stuck in the middle, fully aware that their employer's "it ain't a crime" outlook was not their way of life, however, without resources or anyone to guide them, they knew that a new life awaited them not and that sadly, prison was a far better Fate than dying on the streets of Irony in the company of people whom used Shadow's for their fresh credentials to scam a then loosely regulated social welfare system, to which The Voice had enough sense to guide a ninety nine percent discouraged teenager to quietly purchase a one way plane ticket back to Home Town, before the junkies could hustle and steal the rest from a sleeping mark, whose instinct of survival had been dialed up to eleven in a constant readiness for the world to come crashing down around them at any moment.

"Hold steady, we'll make it out of here!' The Voice reassured, as they waited for that economy flight to arrive, when Shadow suddenly vanished with their travel bag that had been picked through by drug fiends, to board a plane of salvation and doom all over again without knowing what the future held for a lost soul and a lamb to the slaughter.

***REASON FOR LEAVING:*** ...Don't fear the reaper

# THE ZOO

## *Dark Wall Hamlet, ~ 1993 ~ "Nanny?"*

"Yep, you're wanted dead or alive!" The legal aid lawyer had replied, after Shadow called the courts to find out the extent of their legal troubles. "This legal aid clown is a real fucking comedian!" The Voice spat without a sound, about a duty council with terrible humor, whom failed to lighten the mood, as the lawyer continued… "You should turn yourself in. They will arrest you and maybe release you until your court date to secure legal counsel and we'll see then once we know all the charges!"

Despite getting lucky to not end up prison bound the moment they had landed back in Home Town, Shadow did not need a law degree to know that "release" wasn't going to happen for a flight risk, not-to-mention the owner of two equally shitty choices… "Do I take the risk of turning myself in and they hold me, or, do I stay on the lamb and try to survive until they catch me?" With neither option sporting a positive outcome, they settled upon the second choice, and remained at large, languishing between hideouts and sympathetic acquaintances in a hard living scene that sang the ballad of a thin man, which had seen them become skinny and drawn from not eating. Shadow knew they could not keep it up for long and that it was only a question of time before they got picked up by the police.

"Freeze...! Get on the fucking ground now! Hands behind your head! Do it! Do it now!"

When they were finally caught and arrested in a dramatic scene of flashing lights and guns for hire, one nightmare had ended and another one began, as they were taken to the station and processed like a gutted fish by the enthusiastic officers, whom acted like they had collared a celebrity cartel boss as they took mug shots and fingerprinted the king of Sodom and Gomorrah, whom would be forever branded as an outlaw by a black and white system...

"And most of the shit wasn't even ours!" Shadow thought with regret, yet never revealed a crucial detail to the interrogators that might have saved their ass, but would have surely sunk Finch in the process. While they owed nothing to their former drug dealing landlord, the notion of going out as a fink like Pigeon was not a path either of them were willing to take. "We're fucking no rat! We put us here, now we'll deal with it."

"We...? Oh, now you're going to start listening to me?" The Voice inquired with fake enthusiasm, as the thick steel door to their first ever jail cell closed behind tightly them in a loud *CLANG!* that continued to echo in their mind long after the world with all its hate, misery and lies suddenly ceased to exist, leaving only a sad but true reality to bear when the out for blood prosecutor made it clear that they were going to make an example out of Shadow and seek the maximum sentence for someone whom could not afford to defend themselves within a courtroom circus act of supposedly blind justice, all the while being represented by a yawning duty council whom cared not for the Fate and Irony of some lost teenager facing a terrible certainty.

"Fuck it... Guilty your honor!" Shadow said with defeated resolve to deny a system the pleasure of pouring salt in a gaping wound that had been their life. "We rather be locked up in jail than listening to his bullshit!" The Voice said with contempt when the mortal wearing the black robe denied their request to be sent to the military.

"I hereby sentence you to three years of incarceration within a federal system of institutions, to be carried out immediately and without delay!" While they took it like a man, a verdict within a tragic moment sent tears down a sad mother's face, whom had been sitting in court watching her son transition from innocent civilian to a convicted felon, whom was led away shackled and drawn into an era when criminal legislation for convictions related to drugs stated that, Shadow was classed as a non-violent offender to be sent to a minimum security facility for the duration of their sentence.

"We'll do easy time!" The Voice had said with fragile confidence, which was immediately shattered when they were sent to a super max slam located deep in the forest some five hours north of Home Town. "Ok... That's not good!"

From the moment they disembarked the inmate transport, the glint of sunlight refracting off the scope lenses of the rifles trained upon them by the tower guards was a vivid reminder that life could end at any moment as they were led inside the electric circus of a world they might never leave.

Upon being led chain gang style into an armored complex that housed psychopaths, murderers and the most vile humans that society had to offer, the guards, also known as the "Screws", forced everyone to strip off their clothing and their dignity, to be searched again before being made to shower in a room full of unhappy convicts, after which they were all given nothing more than a jumpsuit to wear and shoes without laces, followed by more mug shots and fingerprints to ensure an accurately infamous record. Then, everyone was given a serial number that would forever bind their body to an invisible straw man of limits and controls... "Inmate, 9-4-1-9-9... 1-C! Front and center for your effects!"

Carrying a small bag of toiletries that was rumored to be currency in a place where the very air a person breathed had value to the right bidder, they were led through a series of gated hallways and security check points staffed by guards standing in bulletproof glass control rooms known as "bubbles", until they arrived upon the reception range where new fish were held, and shown to the cell that would effectively trap a wild spirit inside a tiny concrete room with nothing in it except for a metal sink, a metal toilet, a metal bunk bed ...and the other guy whom looked about as cheerful as a hammer smashed face but, mercifully, did not appear threatening.

"He better not try to pour some sugar on me!" Shadow thought as the heavy steel door slammed shut upon a journey that had suddenly, if not mercifully, come to an end in a fall from grace two times the tragic, which suddenly, albeit it strangely, felt as though a massive weight had just been lifted from their shoulders at no longer having to be a slave to the grind of human society with all of its taxes, time clocks and some imaginary burden of debt, leaving just them to exist in belly of the beast, where, they were very aware of being a teenager in a big man's prison.

The thought of ending up as someone's unwilling sex toy didn't not appeal to a boy suddenly become a man, whom put on their hardest scowl to appear older and hopefully meaner, all the while making peace with the fact that they might have to fight to the death to keep their integrity, not to mention their anal virginity, in a place where everyone and everything, including time was the enemy. For those first few nights, Shadow lay awake in a heightened state of awareness, staring at the ceiling two feet from their face upon the top half of a bunk bed that contained a snoring human upon the bunk below, where, in the absence of societal noises and distractions, they could feel the very essence of a place filled with so much pain and misery, which enabled leading Shadow to sense the presence of another entity within the room?

"What is that?" Shadow wondered in a state of reanimation, to which The Voice casually replied, "That's just The Energy." Frowning, Shadow questioned this entity The Voice had hinted to a few times in the past. "What do you mean …The Energy? What the fuck is it?"

A split second eternity passed before The Voice answered, "It's the spark behind all things living and beyond, and it's been with you since before you were born and…!" Shadow suddenly shook their crowded head, "Whoa, whoa… You mean to tell me 'The Energy' has been inside us all this time? Is that what I've felt all my life?" Another moment passed before The Voice answered, "Yes, everyone has it. It's what we feel when we are awake, when we're near people, like captain snore-a-lot below us."

Suddenly, they could feel The Energy of the man sleeping below, and sensed that he was in prison for sex crimes, which left Shadow momentarily worried, but more angered than anything else. "You mean to tell me that The Energy enables us to read other people ...and you never told me!? I thought you had our back!"

At that moment, there was no more "they", "them", "us", "we" or fucking maybes as Shadow lay at the edge of madness, pissed off at his inner self for not revealing an important detail that might have saved them from ending up in their current predicament, however, The Voice harbored no retribution for the dead. "You were too young and too naïve ...and you never let me finish that day when I arrived in our head!"

Just then, they felt something in their mind snap that sent them free falling ever deeper into the crypts of rays, until they had reached that room beneath Hell, where Shadow wished to remain forever locked away within the emptiness, never to return to a world that had caused them so much pain in such a short life span, which would forever remain as their social scars to bare for the rest of an unnatural life.

But, The Voice could not permit this to be and pull Shadow back from the frayed ends of sanity, whom lay there behind a dead skin mask day after long day, until the steel door to their concrete cage finally opened about two months later, and the guard told them, "Inmate 9-4-1-9-9-1-C! Pack your bags lamb chop! You're going to The Zoo!"

"The Zoo", was a minimum security installation about an hour south of Home Town in Dark Wall Hamlet, which they had learned was a place where thieves, snitches and rapists were sent to do their time because they could not placed in higher security prison populations, which found Shadow not really wanting to go despite the need to leave a shared cell that had forced them to witness another human being defecating into a toilet barely four feet away. Upon arriving at Dark Wall Farm, aka, "The Zoo", which sat in the eternal shade of Dark Wall Penitentiary next door with its tall, black stone walls. There, they were immediately informed that the livestock being raised in the pens were worth more than the "residents" being held within a fenceless maze of torment, which was nothing like the hell hole they had just emerged from, thus distorting a notion of doing "hard time" upon seeing that everyone slept in their own bedrooms within brand new six bedroom condominiums that had all new furnishings, and were equipped with all the amenities of outside living, complete a fully functional kitchen and access to all the best foods, in addition to a weekly pay that found everyone walking around with cash in their pocket?

"Ok, what?!" Shadow couldn't believe their eyes as they moved into a place that felt more like a resort for rejects than an actual prison, which, whether by Fate or Irony, turned out to be the best housing they had ever lived in. "This is fucking crazy!" The Voice said of their incarceration, leading them to think they had seen it all, only to be proven wrong when The Zoo warden told them that all the new fish had to assume a caretaker role within their respective housing units, which found them suddenly, and quite unwittingly hired as… "We're a fucking nanny to a bunch of scumbags?"

Initially, Shadow had feared having to fend off fatal violence for refusing prison sex from some large convict named Susan, but given they were doing time for a dope rap involving someone else's drugs, and the fact that they had not snitched to get out of serving their sentence meant that they had been deemed solid by an unspoken convict code that made the "I am the law" courts on the outside seem like a Broadway play by comparison to an eye for an eye inmate justice system, especially when it came to certain crimes such as snitching and the raping of women and children, which was the one thing that made doing time at The Zoo the most difficult to endure, as they were forced to live in a retreat for the rotten, whom sought not rehabilitation and instead openly bragged about their life shattering exploits that had given them such a rush, all within the safe confines of a minimum security institution that was hardly a slap on the wrist for monsters doing time for the atrocity of destroying a mind.

"A fucking pipe to the face and death is what these pieces of shit deserve!" The Voice re-sentenced the skinners and the "diddlers", the name given to child molesters by the skeletons of society, as Shadow watched the scum walk around without fear of retribution, all the while planning their next infanticidal acts without a care of being heard.

**REASON FOR LEAVING**: Worth it.

# THE ABYSS

"Beware my friend, as you pass by, as you are now, so once was I…

As I am now, so you must be, prepare my friend, to follow me."

Author Unknown

## *Hopeless Ville, ~ 1994 ~ "The" Janitor*

Lying on the top bunk of the reception cell at The Abyss Medium Security Institution, the writing on the ceiling was a bit of finger to the obvious and a daily reminder that they should accept responsibility for their actions, but by no means, did they have to regret their actions after tossing a pot of boiling vegetables into the face of a diddling piece of shit, whom had entered their housing unit and begun boasted about how he had stretched that little girl until her pelvis broke and…

*SPLASH!*

Although a molester would avoid permanent disfigurement, an act of street justice on the inside had found Shadow swiftly transferred to a higher security prison facility, where, despite avoiding charges of bodily harm and time added to a sentence when a child rapist refused to reveal what happened to him in a flicking moment of guilt for his misdeeds, their chance's for early release had suddenly evaporated, thus assuring a lengthy stay within a place that looked more like the first slam they had been sent to, with its steel cell doors and concrete walls, not to mention the crepitating bowel erosion of another human being relieving himself upon a toilet of mortality, which had once again become a stage for psychological torture that, in the end…

"Fuck him! It was still worth it" The Voice stated adamantly, which, for a fleeting second, permitted half a smile to appear on Shadow's face, whom had no excuses for the unknown realities they would now have to face within in a prison society, where, a simple glance at another inmate could get a person killed by death… or, worse. Thankfully, albeit sadly, they were already institutionalized into the prison system, which meant they were fast tracked off the reception range into the general population, where another top bunk in the cells next to the showers at the beginning of B range within housing unit E became their new home and final resting place, where Shadow did not move from except to line up for headcounts and take the long walk to the prison mess hall for meals of mass produced prison food, which they ate in the most inconspicuous manner possible to avoid any unwanted attention, all the while subtly studying the many different walk of life seated around them in a tense tablespoon truce that could explode into a violent body count at moment with merely a glance.

Watching without looking, it was easy to identify the prison hierarchy among the inmates, which saw the lifers and those serving the longer sentences seated at the row of tables at the edge of the kitchen with their backs to the concrete window slots, while their enforcers sat in the row in front of them to create a human barrier separating the real convicts from the short timers and the skinners, whom Shadow had avoided by choosing to sit alone at the risk of being singled out in a dining experience that was as real as it gets regardless of race, creed, color, religion or sexual orientation.

Having grow up in an era that had forbade any mention of homosexuality, Shadow had never met a truly gay man before going to prison, but upon meeting Homo, the gay inmate chef placing the sausages upon his plate in the breakfast line up, whom said to him with a wink, "I've got another sausage I can serve you!" even The Voice had been lost for words on how to respond to the advances of another man without diving over the counter to stab him with a butter knife, which had seen Shadow say nothing and merely shuffle along trying to avoid eye contact. Luckily, Homo wasn't the violent or threatening type, except perhaps for the fact that he seemed to know an awful lot about the circumstances surrounding their recent transfer.

"I've been watching you…" Homo had told them one day whilst putting mass prepared macaroni and cheese on their plate, "I know why you're in here, and for the record, that piece of shit deserved it!" With the mess hall known to be the central gossip hub of the prison, Shadow figured that Homo had learned about them through the other riff raff, or the Screws, however, the idea that they were being watched by another convict did not sit well with a freshly turned nineteen year old, whom worried about being cornered in a cell with little elbow room to fight off of potential attackers.

Thus, they decided to begin going to the prison gym, where the open space of the weight pit would at least provide room to move in the event of an altercation, as they began pursuing a fitness training regimen that firstly simply involved doing cardio via the heavy punching bag far removed from the exercise equipment, where Shadow stealthily observed the training schedules of the other inmates and more importantly, the workout routines of the long timers and lifers, whom took precedence over the fitness equipment and whom held zero tolerance for those dumb enough to break an unspoken rule, like that one new fish in particular, who was using a bench press during a particular lifer's time slot and told Homestead, a man doing life for killing a man he caught in bed with his wife, to… "Go fuck yourself!" …resulting in Homestead dropping a forty five pound barbell plate on the face of the new fish, whom was lying on his back upon the bench, half way through a press.

"Nothing beats a broken nose, missing teeth and a flat face to teach an idiot some manners!" The Voice had cheered, but Shadow wasn't laughing as they began taking fitness training seriously within a den of wolves, which found them working out every evening in the pit and then pushing out all the remaining painful memories through more pushups, sit ups and triceps dips back in their eventual single cell down the range next to the lifers, which had seen the return of a semi decent night's sleep without hearing another man snore, not to mention the ability to take a private shit.

There, Shadow made unhurried friendships with dangerous people all the while pursuing a newfound fitness obsession, which had seen them build chiseled gains that helped to piece together a once shattered self-esteem, which occasionally compelled the other inmates in the weight pit to break the unspoken stare rule by watching them perform their sets, which did not bother Shadow, whom had slowly earned their place within a weight pit training curriculum, however, during one particular evening's workout, they noticed three individuals staring at them from across the gym that even made The Voice nervous, since one of them was Homestead, the lifer whom had drop the weight on the new fish.

"Are we using his stuff?" The Voice wondered as Shadow showed no signs of their awareness until The Voice exclaimed, "Oh shit! They're coming over here!" which led them to quickly look for potential weapons without appearing obvious, as the fearsome trio stopped a few paces from them and simply stood there watching Shadow do their shoulder sets, in an awkward moment that compelled the convicts working out nearby to quietly get up and leave. Unsure what would happen next, Shadow was surprised when violence never erupted and the man doing the life sentence asked a rather odd question… "Do you know The Bad Man?" …to which Shadow merely shook their head in silence, leading Homestead to pause again and peer questioningly at them, before saying something that left Shadow confused by what had just taken place.

"You should drop by my house later, there's something I want to talk to you about…" Homestead said as he and the other two inmates, whom were obviously his enforcers, turned to leave. "And you can relax…" Homestead added sensing the tension within them, "…you're under my protection here, which means you work for me now!"

Wondering what "under his protection" actually meant and what it would demand in return, the thought of befriending a group of stone cold crazy killers whom could have very easily ended their life in a place with nowhere to hide, which quickly made Shadow forget about this "Bad Man" character, as they went to work for a …convicted employer?

"And now were working as an enforcer for a murderer!" The Voice said leaning heavily upon the Fate and Irony of a killer reality, which saw them being paid in contraband to maintain a prison contraband hegemony that, had earned them the title of "The Janitor", tasked with cleaning up the delinquent debts from those foolish enough to default on a transaction with known killers, leading a mama's boy whom never wanted to hurt anyone, to change in the house of flies and become one of the hardest and meanest S.O.B.'s upon the old cell block, whose take no prisoners outlook left them immune to the pleads of the fallen and the screams of the damned begging to avoid destiny.

After spending seasons in The Abyss, they had grown cold to the thought of some goof getting stabbed in the showers or some piece of shit child molester getting the blanket treatment, which was the act of covering someone with a blanket to blind and disorient them while a second attacker came "runnin up on ya" with a blunt object, to begin installing dents into a victim's head, within the madness behind these walls, where a person was real …or nothing at all.

***REASON FOR LEAVING***: The end of eternity?

# 5

# *AFTER FOREVER*

## ROTTENWOOD FURNITURE

### *Home Town, ~ 1995 ~ Convicted Laborer*

Aside from watching the occasional new fish whom lost their grip on reality and got taken away in a padded suit and placed on the bug juice in the psyche ward, most days were all about the art of killing time by working out, watching television, listening to their favorite Prince of Darkness cassette, speed reading through books, playing in prison card tournaments that saw cheaters nearly getting killed and winners hustled out of their prizes… However, the one thing they perhaps enjoyed the most was playing rounds of chess against Mr. Thompson, a criminal mind whom was essentially a genius and a psychopath crazier than a conspiracy.

Mr. Thompson was doing time for having evicted someone's soul from their body and quite literally impossible to defeat at a game of chess, or rather, make that a thousand games of chess, of which Shadow lost each and every round, each and every evening after their workouts, to a lunatic of god's creation, whom began offering prizes to taunt and tease them such as tobacco, hashish, and those little blue sleeping pills that were coveted like gold and considered to be an inmate's best friend in a constant war against of time within a sentence that was best served behind the wall of sleep.

"If you can ever win before I get paroled that is!" Mr. Thompson teased, aware that his humorous jabs were an added distraction upon an opponent using two minds to try and outwit a thousand, but failing miserably to find cracks in a seemingly impervious game defense…"Maybe get The Voice in your head to help you out!" Despite being a ball breaker and, a murderer, Mr. Thompson had been the only other person aside from their mother to have been capable of sensing a nameless alter ego, which in a big way had been strangely comforting, while in a small way, a little disturbing to be told that they were not crazy by someone that was essentially crazier than they were.

"So it's like that is it?" The Voice said in defiance. "Well then, can I play with madness? Shadow, look for The Energy inside him and you'll see his patterns and his strategy!" Confused, Shadow had no idea what that meant as he tried looking at Mr. Thompson without lifting their eyes from the board, but The Voice, clearly annoyed, clarified, "No, dummy… Look at him without using our eyes!"

"Sigh…" Shadow took a frustrated breath and exhaled slowly to find a center, which made Mr. Thompson snicker at their discomfort as he sat arms folded across his chest, rubbing his pudgy chin as he peered down at the checkered board between them. At first, Shadow felt nothing and was blind to a husk of flesh and fatness, however, just then, they caught the notion of a faint aura that seemed to become visible around Mr. Thompson, that caused Shadow to feel a rush when they were suddenly able to see within their opponent and sense The Energy inside the fractured mind of the mad man sitting before them, which not only revealed how crazy their opponent actually was, but also…

his next moves! It was here that Shadow began to tap into The Energy, which led them to realize they had been trying to beat the wrong game the entire time... "We...?" The Voice corrected, as Shadow suddenly began to focus upon Mr. Thompson's bait and switch game strategy, thus granting them foreknowledge of things to come, along with the ability to counter a seemingly unstoppable adversary, whom had the potential to kill again.

All but certain they had gone insane in the brain, Shadow suddenly began initiating a persecution mania of game pieces that not only turned the tide of a mind game, but against all odds, a queen took a rook and a knight took a bishop, leaving Mr. Thompson's king to finally fall...

"Checkmate!" *COUNT TIME!*

It was the nightly head count before lockdown interrupting their chess session, to which Mr. Thompson told Shadow, "You're playing me again tomorrow, or, I'll fucking kill you!" as they walked away with a victory and a fistful of little blue sleeping pills, not-to-mention a newfound ability to wield The Energy both within them, and to look within others, which led Shadow to finally understand the gift that had always been there inside them, "If only I had discovered The Energy sooner I'd have...?"

"Don't do that" The Voice quickly dispelled them part of them that was ninety nine percent regretful, "Don't beat us up over what is and what should never be! Fate and Irony always had a different plan for us, and...!"

"There you go again about Fate and Irony…" It was Shadow's turn to cut in, as they walked into their cell that had been left open without fear of anything being taken by a prison population that knew better than to steal from The Janitor, "What is the fucking deal with Fate and Irony? Why are 'they' constantly involved in seemingly every part of our life?" When The Voice did not answer, Shadow was left to consider the obvious that isn't alone, but then suddenly remembered what The Voice had just said about Fate and Irony's "different plan".

"So… we're meant to do something with our life when we get out of here, check… Any idea what it is?" When again The Voice between their ears never answered, Shadow suddenly felt the weight of regret return upon their shoulders, as the mechanical steel door to their cell began to close upon another day of insanity within a human animal house, however, now it was on… "Things are going to be different when we get out of here!" Shadow said aloud whilst staring at four concrete walls without looking, "We're going to claw back time any fucking way we can and find a purpose in this forsaken life!" They looked down at the little blue pills in their hand, "…and if it's a fight Fate and Irony want, then a fight they are going to get, because we're going to use The Energy to become more than what they intended for us, so we never have to come back here!"

Thanks to The Energy, Shadow had seen the envy hiding within Homestead's voice upon finding a condemned man standing in the doorway to their cell on the day of their release, whom roused them from a pill induced coma… "Get up! It's time to go!" Although they could not change their friend's reality or destiny, Shadow at least took consolation that everything in their "house", would go to Homestead, since the prison would not allow anything to leave that was not officially registered upon their inmate cell card, which merely stated the items they had upon getting arrested. "A portable cassette player and a Prince of Darkness cassette…" Shadow said taking one last look at a hole that had been home, a fully furnished cell with two televisions, two video game consoles, a stereo, a kettle, a toaster, and a host of other luxuries not on the cell card and not including the one hundred and fifty pouches of tobacco in their cell locker and the quarter pound of hashish hidden in the walls.

As other enforcers and faces they hoped to never see again cleared out their former a cell, Homestead walked with Shadow to the guard bubble leading to the front gate and on to freedom, where a twenty year old already hardened by time and trauma was strangely nervous about leaving the comfortably numb confines of a dangerous place that, strangely made them feel safe. "You're young and got caught in a bad rap, but, you never belonged in here…" Homestead told them in a moment that seemed almost fatherly, "…however, if I ever see you in here again… I'll fucking kill you!"

A fond farewell via death threat from Homestead, had been a fitting knock em dead send off for someone hoping for the best, but fearing the worst as they boarded the bus headed for Home Town, which reintroduced them to the feeling of motion sickness after being locked up in a maggot colony for so long, but after a few minutes that of nearly colored the upholstery, the experience was soon therapeutic again for someone driven to move forward in life, and begin a new story after taking up residence with their older brother The Myth, whom was living in an unremarkable two bedroom apartment with his girlfriend Skanky, whom was rumored to be wanting a baby, thus the plan from the beginning had been for Shadow to impose until the expiry of a lingering sentence, by which time they would hopefully be self sufficient enough to set off upon their own quest for a purpose unseen, in a land of measured opportunities and freedoms that would forever haunt their steps, starting the moment they walked into a new home sweet home, where The Voice immediately sensed that something was not quite right with the universe, not least because of the weird vibes they felt upon learning The Myth had taken up selling hash oil to supplement his income, in much the same way they had done years prior that had netted them a now "prior" criminal record for their efforts of stupidity, for which they had done the time and were now on parole for, which included curfews, no alcohol, no drugs, and no association with…

"A drug dealer you say bro? That's …great!"

In the span of just one breath, Fate and Irony had taken over the lease of a distorted living arrangement that instantly shifted a happy reunion and the promise of a bright future, right back into an old lifestyle that had found them caught between honor and a death sentence should they return to prison, which left Shadow wishing they had smuggled out a few of those little blue pills to put their lessen a sleepless anxiety as they lay there that night in a strange bed wide awake, fully expecting a SWAT team to kick in the door and send their ass back up the river faster than they could say… "You're crazy!"

Having to accept a precarious reality simply because there was no other choice, the line between right and wrong had already begun to blur not even twenty four hours out, as a parolee mandated to visit a coyote ugly, beach ball body, crew cut, flannel shirt wearing dike parole officer, whom looked like an ogre shat out a troll that puked up a dead coyote, and whom ordered Shadow to attend a substance abuse program that the system had failed to administer on the inside, but was now compulsory under pain of re-incarceration, which found them fatefully having to show up to a room filled with the very same criminals and drug dealers they were ironically forbidden to associate with, in a weird rekindling of old faces caught within a similar predicament as them, whom had the potential to restart a journey into a world that was addicted to chaos, especially when they took a seat within the circle of sharing, next to a stranger with his back turned, whom turned out to be none other than… "Oh, hello Mr. B… what brings you here?"

"You think we should share our home life with the group?" The Voice wondered as they sat listening to the hard luck stories of uncaring ex-cons, many of whom were stoned and already back into the same habits that got them there in the first place, in a scene reminiscent of a hooligan's holiday for someone without the luxury of "time off". As another condition of their release, a born again tax slave was to be immediately re-assimilated back into to a working system designed to trap a human being into a sentence with the potential of being worse than prison, which was swiftly facilitated by their lock stock and teardrops parole officer, who directed them to a manufacturing company that hired ex-convicts to make wooden patio furniture, and it was there that Shadow got their first taste of outside life as an employed felon the moment they walked in the door at the lawn furniture company, and were given the scourge of the earth treatment by the administrative staff whom spelled out the one way rules... "Disobey our orders, or give us a hard time in any way, and we will have you thrown back in prison faster than you can say...

***REASON FOR LEAVING***:  The expiry of a lifetime.

# SCAB WINDOW

## *Home Town, ~ 1995 ~ Window Faker*

"Well, this sucks!" The Voice repeated about a droning duty of forced labor, as Shadow placed a wooden lawn chair leg into a wooden lawn chair seat bottom for the millionth time, in a repetitive, mind numbing task that had burned an image of chain gang slavery upon their psyche by the end of the first day.

"Yeah…" Shadow agreed with focused regret and resentment, at being trapped in a last minute life that had led them to dark places they were never meant to see, only to end up working for a felony company using freedom as blackmail to exploit its labor force that was viewed as nothing more than human capital stock for profits. "…I think I'd rather be in jail than put up with The Rash."

While going back to prison was not high up on their to do list, it seemed a far better Fate than putting up with the teenage, arrogant, acne faced production line supervisor, whom was like and a rash on everyone's ass, hence the name, by continually sneaking up on convicted felons to rudely ask… "How many have you got done convict?!" Although no one spoke their minds, Shadow could hear the thoughts of the other convicts, whom visualized ninety nine ways to die for a pimple faced peon holding his clipboard like some biblical tablet of commanding self interests.

## Professional Shadow

"No talking when working!" The Rash barked anytime anyone dared to engage in camaraderie or show any signs of humanity, leading to an atmosphere of silent rage that was constantly aggravated by a walking skin tag with a death wish. "You go to the water fountain when I say so, because in here... I'm God!"

"Who died and made you god?" Shadow wondered whilst watching The Rash run around the production floor staffed by violent offenders believing that he was untouchable simply because of a job title, which really put into perspective the inequality of a labor system created by the man who sold the world in the name of greed and profit. "He would be someone's bitch in prison!" The Voice noted solemnly about a young and dumb kid who was oblivious to how fast he could be popped like a pimple, leading Shadow to ignore the inevitable by their imagination to escape an hourly sentence much like they had in prison, which gave rise to thoughts of the one place they could escape to, where the future and a world of technology, stopped at the door.

For them, it was comforting to know that Mom lived a simple life that was mostly devoid of all the electronic gadgets that kept a person plugged into corrupt agendas and bulls on parade, making her place a rare haven of serenity in a world dominated by the media telling people what to buy, what to think and how to feel. There, it was a place to recharge The Energy they had recently discovered, which helped them to weather a precarious existence until the expiry of a conviction, when they quit the shitty lawn chair job and told a rude, overbearing, gender mixed parole officer to... "Go fuck yourself!"

## Professional Shadow

On that day, they chose to enjoy the illusion of freedom away from big bro's girlfriend Skanky, whom had been acting strange of late, especially when Meathead and Scruff from The Shitheads came over to buy dope when The Myth was away. "You think she's screwing around?" The Voice questioned, but Shadow didn't want to think about it as they sat in the food court at the Home Town mall, which had been renovated too many times since their childhood to be familiar anymore. There, they glanced at the want ads for available jobs, which might offer a new direction beyond unemployment... "Garbage man... Nope. Hairdresser... Nope. Truck Driver... Nope...! What the fuck!"

All of a sudden, Shadow felt caught in a loop that distracted from reality, leading them fail to notice the unknown figure whom had just approached their table, and when they glanced up to the mystery individual standing there, whom Shadow realized was The Goblin, the pusher man whom they had met through Tattoo Terry, aka, The Acid Man, both of whom they had not seen since before getting busted in a previous life chapter.

"I heard you got busted and went away... welcome home." The Goblin had said with a wide smile that bespoke of sincerity, yet, hinted undeniably at old ways, which compelled Shadow to smile out of instinct as they relived a recent eternity behind their eyes. "So, are you playing again?"

The Goblin had popped the inevitable profit driven question, which created a sudden twist of Cain moment that could go in any direction, but, when Shadow merely shook their head in honor of a promise to a man doing life in a vow to never deal again, they figured a chance encounter would end there, but, when The Goblin invited Shadow to attend his private garage parties that he held every Friday night out at his place on the outskirts of Home Town, Shadow was hesitant at first, until The Voice played to the obvious.

"It's no different than being at home…" The Voice mentioned their fatefully ironic living arrangement, "…and, it's better than hiding in our room away from Skanky!" Shadow knew his one percent was right. "Besides, we're not under conditions anymore, meaning we can do whatever the fuck, you want!"

And so, they accepted the opportunity to properly celebrate a release from a rusty cage, and showed up at The Goblin's place that Friday night, where they were reintroduced to faces from a blurry and faded era, as distant characters returned into focus in the form of renewed friends such as Cousin Evil, whom was related to The Goblin and was only "evil" by name to make him sound fearsome. In truth, Cousin Evil was really just a mild mannered person worthy of a mention in a future crazy memoir.

There was Scrapper, whom was strong with The Energy in the life of a bar fight enthusiast, whose fists were counted as separate patrons whenever he walked in at Home Town night clubs, compelling the bouncers to question whether the pay was worth the pain. Scrapper was very energetic to say the least, and always had some thrilling tale about fisticuffs that often ended in handcuffs.

Then there was Tiny, the obese wannabe entrepreneur with a barely relevant steam cleaning business, which he used to hide the income from the dope show of an illicit, nickel and dime enterprise. Tiny was really just a petty dealer whose equally petty morals reflected The Energy of a man constantly conniving and plotting, and whom would take advantage of friends if given the opportunity… "That fat fucker is persona non-grata" The Voice fatefully confirmed about Tiny, whose ironically thin credibility was somehow still of use to a crazy corner of burnouts, where Bird-Brain could often be found getting intoxicated as a human melting pot of ingested drugs, which could put a normal person into a coma.

Bird-Brain was also engaged in the street trade by night, where he used The Energy to peddle his wares to support his habits, which Shadow was about to dismiss until Bird-Brain revealed that he also held a day job …as a supervisor at a window making company? "Uh, excuse us, what did you say?"

Although it was difficult to imagine a stoner like Bird-Brain as the manager of anything beyond his drug consumption, when a walking, talking dead embryonic cell described his job, the hints of opportunity were suddenly echoed by The Voice, "Do it!" which, compelled them to play a game of chess with destiny by nonchalantly revealing their industry experience, leading to a surprisingly quick job offer from Bird-Brain.

"We're always looking for bodies that aren't scared of a union!" Bird-Brain had said with contempt, which Shadow found strange, but nonetheless accepted the production line position and agreed to show up the following Monday to work, despite the feeling that something was off.

"That was two easy… Don't you think?!" Shadow was about to pick apart the obvious that wasn't when the door to the garage suddenly opened, and in walked two characters who immediately shifted The Energy in the room to higher ground. The first to enter had been Tombstone, a long haired biker type whom was a builder by day for a construction company owned by his parents, and by night, a two wheel man of mayhem engaging in activities best left unwritten and unspoken. Given Tombstone's wild side, he was in tune enough with The Energy to spot the prison bars still visible in Shadow eyes, which made them instant friends capable of understanding their separate histories of crazy. And lastly, they met Crippled Crab, the care free semi-amputee with the bum leg, whose long hair and goatee gave him the appearance of a front man in a death metal band, or that dude with the crooked cross whom had worn The Energy upon his sleeve, just like Crippled Crab, whom could resurrect any crucified party and was a master at all things fishing, drinking, bread breaking and, being an all around good soul whom made most everyone he met feel welcome, including Shadow, with whom they quickly developed a bond as they got drunk with cheers until dawn.

"Wasn't that a party!?" The Voice commented about the weekend festivities with the Brotherhood in Rage Wrecking Crew, a self imposed title upon a group of guys that mostly wrecked brain cells. "Yeah…" Shadow acknowledged as they rode the bus toward a new job on Monday morning that had been guaranteed just by showing up, where the plan was to use their previous experience to excel at a job that would put them on their feet again and…!

"You should give me a name!" The Voice suddenly interjected in hopes of catching Shadow off guard in a state of altered consciousness thanks to the lingering migraine in their head, which felt like the icing on a cake of omens, leaving Shadow in no mood... "Oh, were on this again!" Shadow said with an annoyed smirk, "Ok, how about... Roberta!"

A tense moment passed before The Voice replied, "Fuck... y...!" Just then, the bus suddenly stopped right in front of a shouting crowd holding signs, whilst standing in front of the place they were going to work, and when Shadow disembarked, the crowd of disgruntled union workers began shouting at them, "Get the fuck out of here scab!"

"We're going to work as fucking scab labor?!" The Voice questioned with alarm, which immediately began canceling any thoughts of a lasting career, as they pushed their way through a mob of angry again employees, voicing their displeasure to Shadow's presence via colorful obscenities... "Loser!", "Ass kisser!", "Brownnoser!", "Corporate cocksu..."

Once inside, they were surprised by how much the negativity had affecting them, as they met up with Bird-Brain, whom seemed oblivious to the mob rules outside, and whom swiftly put Shadow to work in somewhat familiar job role that found them standing in one place on the assembly line, installing the slightly different hardware into slightly different window frames, in a repetitive routine that gave them flashbacks of The Beaver's factory prior to prison, where Shadow had thought about returning to were it not for the stigma surrounding their abrupt departure, which had compelled them to leave sleeping dogs lie.

**REASON FOR LEAVING**: Army of one, savior of none.

## TOMBSTONE ENTERPRISES

### *Home Town, ~ 1995 ~ Prospect Laborer*

In a first that saw their assembly skills and experiences carry forth into a similar position, they had easily outshined the rest of the scabs, whom mostly comprised of drug clients that Bird-Brain had bribed or threatened to fill a labor void left behind by a union gone on strike, resulting in a coked out, crash and burn crew of drug addicted junk heads trying to work together in a serious work setting beset by horseplay and flying projectiles of various dimensions.

Truthfully, Shadow had weighed the specter of poverty and starvation versus getting injured at a low wage job that essentially amounted to fucking bus fare. Yet, in another strange way, they felt right at home in a manufacturing madhouse, which was really nowhere near as crazy as the places and things they had seen before twenty years old. "Oh, how I could just kill a man" Shadow whispered in reference to the murderous many they had called friends, whom they would have preferred as co-workers over the crap-manship crew they had to endure.

"At least those guys were solid, unlike Skanky!" The Voice had observed, which led Shadow to wish for cell-phone technology to be more advanced, so everyone could have one and they could call The Myth whilst at his long haul job, to tell him their suspicions about his ol' lady...

"We'll tell him when he gets back" Shadow concluded, as they disembarked the bus for another day of rinse and repeat within the life of a production peon and labor ...slave? The noticeable absence of loud picketers had been a relief for just a moment, until it occurred to them, "Where's the human capital stock?"

Inside, the obvious was revealed when Bird-Brain informed them the unionized employees were back to work after reaching an agreement with the company, which had effectively seen most of the scab labor let go, including Shadow, whom was suddenly out of a job and without an income ...and had to wait a fucking hour for the next bus home.

"Yeah... Sorry dude, but you're done!" Bird-Brain's remorseless words echoed in their mind upon the bus ride home, where Shadow would hide in their room slash prison cell, to contemplate the pretty noose of Fate and Irony chocking the life out of their hopes and dreams, however, when they reached the apartment building and got off the bus, Shadow felt a twitch in their gut and a tingle in their forehead, "Maybe I'm just being too dramatic about everything and we should just relax!"

It was a feeble attempt at finding an emotional ledge after accepting another job loss that had just put them back to square one, so The Voice attempted to fill the gaps, "So *you* screwed up a few times!" Shadow rolled their eyes as they walked in the apartment building, "All me huh? Mister can't see the fucking obvious either!'"

Climbing the stairs to the third floor, The Voice tried to deflect, "Look, are we going to keep repainting a portrait of shit for the next millennia, or find our fucking key already!?"

Fumbling for the apartment key, Shadow didn't think their day could get any worse, however, just as they unlocked the door and went to step inside, The Voice tried for one last silver lining, "Look at the bright side; at least we're not in jail! What could be worse than…!"

"That!" It was all Shadow had to say upon walking into his brother's apartment to find Meathead and Scruff from The Shitheads, spit roasting Skanky in a torrid threesome right there on the living room sofa, causing everyone to scramble for their clothes in a state of haste and shock upon seeing Shadow standing there in a conspiracy turned into reality, which had suddenly shattered like glass as The Voice suggested, "We should fuck them up!"

"Yeah…" Shadow agreed, before dismissing the entire scene fully completely, aware of what the aftermath was going to be when The Myth eventually came home to a heartbreaking tragedy. Before anyone could say anything, they turned around and simply walked away from three stunned pieces of cheating shit, whom had not been expecting anyone to arrive home from a job loss upon a shitty day, which ultimately turned into a nuclear nightmare when The Myth finally arrived to find out that his girlfriend had been cheating on him with not one, but two of his so-called friends, which resulted in a trio of turds being dismissed by a scarred and disconnected brother, whom decided to abandon a dejected life in Home Town along with the useless expense of an apartment, which found The Myth liquidating everything and going to live on the road never to be seen or heard from again, which left Shadow essentially…

"Up shit creek without a fucking a paddle!"

It had been the most obvious way of explaining their situation to The Goblin without mincing words, upon that Friday night at the garage party where the reaction had been… "Man, you're life is crazy!"

The Goblin had replied with stoned, narrowed eyes, which had beheld no answers for someone looking for a place to happen without the benefit of money and resources, however, before Shadow could wallow deeper into their own misery, The Goblin told them something that not only changed the subject of the conversation, but it made Shadow quickly forget the trivial problems of a mortal reality, when his friend announced the death of another. "Remember Tattoo Terry, The Acid Man? He's dead! O.D.! Well… at least that's what they say, anyway." Suddenly, the vinyl record in the jukebox of their mind scratched to a halt as Shadow processed the passing of someone whom had been too crazy for his own good in a short life spent walking the left hand path of an intravenous drug addict, which had left them stunned, however, "Wait, there's more!"

When The Goblin shared how Tattoo Terry had been heavily indebted to some nasty people and it was rumored within the addict circles that someone had injected The Acid Man with a speedball containing an added air bubble that stopped his heart, all Shadow could do was shake their head in shock and raise a drink in tribute to a suffer the children tale that was the bitter icing upon a cake of crappy events, which still did not present any options for the homeless man taking shot after shot from Fate and Irony.

*GULP* "Sucks to be him!" *SLAM!* Shadow slammed the shooter glass down on the old garage coffee table and looked at The Goblin, "But that still don't help our situ…!"

At that moment, the door to the garage suddenly burst open to reveal Crippled Crab and Tombstone, whose loud entrance immediately turned the attention upon them, leaving Shadow to stew in silence whilst nodding and smiling at a gathering that had just gone from idle to let's get crazy shitfaced.

"Man, you're life is crazy!" Crippled Crab had echoed The Goblin's opinion upon hearing Shadow's troubled tale, but then unexpectedly, a real friend offered a faint glimmer of hope within a crazy train life seemingly at the end of its tracks again, when Crippled Crab said, "Don't worry, you can crash at my place on the sofa until you get figured out, and Tombstone here will hook you up with a job on his building crew!"

Shadow couldn't help but feel small about needing saving by someone whom had so much taken from him in a motorcycle accident as a teenager, which ripped up a right leg and left a young man to limp on as an eater of the prescription painkiller for the remainder of his days, destined to live on a meager disability benefit that all but guaranteed a struggling reality, which they were no stranger as Shadow moved to a sofa at Crippled Crab's place, and there, they rediscovered the tones of home.

## Professional Shadow

There we just something about sitting in a place that looked like a fourteen year olds bedroom to make the world seem less serious and therefore less threatening, as they gazed upon rock posters and whiskey flags pinned all over the walls of a hippie's hideout, whom lived a simple life with The Energy discovered after tragedy, to see the good in everyone and to idolize his favorite music groups and singers, whose songs and sounds always made "most" of the pain go away. Gazing upon all the memorabilia and The Energy it represented, suddenly took them back to a simpler time, when they collected albums of their favorite bands and singers, whom inspired them to dream and push boundaries, and…!

"Fucking computer bullshit!" Crippled Crab suddenly exclaimed and then threw his video game controller down to the floor after losing at his favorite aggravation racing game, which made Shadow laugh upon listening to their friend and brother go on about how… "That fucking game is aware! It has it out for me… it has to cheat to win… Fuck this!" At that moment Crippled Crab hobbled to his feet and limped over to his pride and joy, a multi thousand watt stereo system upon which he popped in a Prince of Darkness and the Godfathers of Metal CD.

To them, Crippled Crab was the wizard, a veritable rock and roll doctor whom was capable of prescribing just what The Energy needed to recharge, and the soul needed to feel fucking better about a shitty situation that found them existing somewhere between heaven and hell upon a worn sofa, as they went to work with Tombstone to build barns and structures out of wood, which had revealed a hidden talent, as well as a fondness for building something out of nothing.

"We're just a couple of 'thugs' you and me" The Voice sang in their mind as Shadow labored away at a physical job that was tedious, yet, rewarding to be active and moving to maintain their physique, which enabled them to handle the load of their new career as a carpenter's apprentice, in a trade that had been challenging at the start given their lack of hammer wielding skills and a dropout's level of education with fractional numbers, however, over the weeks, and with a little help from The Voice counting upon metaphysical fingers, the clarity of understanding soon came to be, thanks to Tombstone and the positivity from working with his crew, whom, Shadow knew had their back.

To be certain, working alongside a band of merry bikers all carrying guns under their vests, had put a different spin upon doing a good job, as they quickly learned building plans and the concepts of construction within a building career they actually considered fun, even though their employer had the power to make Shadow disappear, leading The Voice to quietly resolve, "If we start building coffins we're quitting!"

However, Shadow had a slightly different take on their crazy employment situation, "…Quitting on these guys!? Yeah… you just remember hot shot, whatever kills you …will kill me first!"

*REASON FOR LEAVING:* …**Brothers in arms**

# 6

# *JOHNNY BLADE*

# TRASHED HOPES WASTE DISPOSAL

## *Home Town, ~ 1995 ~ Garbage in ,garbage out Man*

Over the weeks, they had slowly and cautiously saved every penny without denying themselves of too many of life's little luxuries …like eating, which finally led to the acquisition of a long overdue driver's license that was quickly followed up with their first ever motor vehicle purchase, in the rough shape of an early eighties sports car, slash, fixer upper that, truth be told, was on its lasts miles due to the deep rooted rust in the car's body in need of extensive repairs at a professional shop in order to pass a mechanical fitness inspection.

"Good thing for friends in low places!" The Voice celebrated, when Tombstone hooked them up with someone whom could help with such matters, which, coupled with some crafty backyard ingenuity that revealed a surprising ability to improvise with little to no resources, and placed Shadow in the driver's seat after so many years of having to run like hell to get anywhere. Now, no fishing hole was too remote and no friend lived to far to visit, like the weekend parties out at The Goblin's Corner, where they toasted their newly found independence in moment with substance that actually felt like they were on the road toward beginning a long delayed life.

"Just keep punching forward!" Scrapper had told them while recanting one of his street fighting man stories which had seen

Scrapper chauffeured home many times by the police, a home that just happened to have a vacant room in the basement, where the opportunity to go from a sofa to a real bed in fully furnished bedroom suddenly arose, which was a great idea that was sadly oddly not shared by Crippled Crab, who made a fuss about losing access to anytime rides and the rent money he was receiving, which had threatened to cast a friendship to the dark side of the moon, however, given their bond with The Energy they could not stay mad at each other for long, as Shadow moved into Scrapper's basement to get a good night's sleep… on weekdays, at least.

Living after midnight in the basement of a weekend party house had given them a front row seat to a whole new theatre of debauchery, within Saturday night celebrations hosted by a human firecracker that saw no sleep till Sunday, thanks to all the chemical stimulants in his body courtesy of The Goblin, which made The Voice remind them through a nervous shakedown. "You know what happens if!" But, Shadow was too preoccupied with enjoying their life for the first time since being born, in addition to enjoying the benefits of having a room at the most happening party house in Home Town, where, "Big bang baby need to sleep somewhere!"

"So… getting laid in like fore-never was nice" Shadow thought calmly upon waking to a run of good fortune, which seemed to indicate they had finally found a footing, and could begin building toward a future of unknown destinies they could only feel… But then, Fate and Irony decided the party was over.

"Yeah, sorry bro, but I'm leaving the construction biz to focus on club business!" Tombstone had told them right before winter, which had not only slammed the brakes upon a free wheel burning lifestyle, but also thrust them back into survival mode within a coastal career landscape that was about to roll up the sidewalks for the season. While being unemployed again was an annoying inconvenience that sucked ass, kissing ass however, was not going to happen when Scrapper came looking for the rent of friendship to pay off his powder habits, meaning that coke would come before camaraderie.

"You didn't happen to say the word "happens" with the "shit" in front of it …did you?" Shadow asked The Voice with a measure of dread over a celestial one-two sucker punch that rang more than their financial bell. "You know what 'happens' if we say those two shit words in order!"

"No, I did not! Can we focus please?!" The Voice snapped back with annoyance, as they sat looking in the jobs obituary, where the death of someone's career was an open casket opportunity for an uncertified dropout, whom was certifiably fucked to find another job. "Truck Driver… Nope. Hair Stylist… Nope. Garbage Man…? Ugh!"

Another feeling of dread gripped them when Shadow envisioned riding on the back of a smelly garbage truck out in the cold. "You can't be serious!" The Voice said upon feeling their pride shatter into confetti. "We'll cover our face and hope we don't work the neighborhoods where our friends live!" Shadow offered as counter weight to a rock and a hard place situation, "What other choice do we have!" But, The Voice was already far beyond driven within its opinion... "I say *you,* don't make it through the week!"

Shadow felt queasy when they drove out to the waste disposal company to fill out an application, and nearly threw up when they were hired before they could leave, "We're not telling anyone about this!" At least they agreed on something as Shadow reported for duty the next morning in a dirty, noisy shop, where need not smell the dilapidated garbage trucks, nor see the haggard-looking staff to know that the place was going to be a shit show, especially when they met their driver Ramrod, whose social demeanor was as bad as his driving, resulting in a death grasp for dear life as they rode on the back of the truck in the freezing cold.

"This asshole is going to get us killed!" The Voice warned each time Ramrod made a hard turn that flung around a hapless helper all day long in a job duty that quickly became a daily drain of courage and stamina, rewarded by endless bags of household refuse and various junk, which they physically tossed, heaved or lobbed into a compactor of crushed material dreams... "I can't believe *we,* made it two weeks!"

The lack of confidence within The Voice had Shadow on edge that morning, as they drove to work under overcast skies that seemed to predict a day of mandatory suicide they could not shake, despite dangling off the back of a garbage truck, where they kept looking over their shoulder in hopes of outrunning Fate and Irony. Stepping off at the next stop, Shadow nearly lost their footing on the ice and twisted an ankle, which caused them to curse profusely whilst tossing bags of reeking trash into the compactor opening at the back of the truck, after which they angrily grabbed the lever to activate the compactor and... *POP!* *PFFT!*

When a hydraulics line running down the truck's steel body suddenly burst next to them, The Voice reacted faster than Shadow could think by turning their head away to avoid catching a big time spray of hot acrid fluid to the eyes, which thankfully had been blocked by the hood they were wearing, however, with their clothes now soaked in hydraulic oil and the truck essentially down, Ramrod, whom had stomped to the back of the truck in a fury over a mechanical breakdown, began telling them... "You fucking idiot! You just fucked up our run! Now I'm gonna have to work extra time, you dumb fuck!"

At that moment Shadow no longer felt the cold when their pulse suddenly quickened to a boil with every verbal spear flying out of Ramrod's mouth, which sank ever deeper into their thick skin of tolerance until... ""You're not riding back to the shop in the truck! You're riding back on the tail of the truck ...you fucking piece of shit!"

They had been standing at the rear of the truck in front of the compactor opening when Ramrod, whom was gone shooting with trigger words, evoked an equally reactive response with a touch of extreme aggression that saw Shadow grab a belligerent and stunned mouthpiece by his belt and shirt collar, and then heave Ramrod into the compactor like the sack of human waste of that he was, which, unsurprisingly, infuriated the little prick even more as he began to frantically swim his way back through the bags of trash and rubbish, all the while cursing like mad as they stood there without emotion, waiting for Ramrod to reach the threshold of the compactor opening, which would find an irate little man's contorted face at just the right spot to receive a power slap of old school proportions that sent Ramrod sprawling back into the garbage, where he lay unmoving and finally fucking silent, thus granting Shadow a moment of peace to reflect upon an employment position that made them feel less than trash.

"Too bad the compactor is down!" The Voice quipped, as Shadow leaned up against the side of the truck and waited for Ramrod to come to, which he did a few moments later, and clambered out all red faced and flustered, but said nay a yakety-yak as they drove back to the shop with Shadow sitting the passenger seat.

***REASON FOR LEAVING***: Took out the trash

# D.A.R.K. TATTOOS

## *Home Town, ~ 1996 ~ Vampire's Apprentice*

"I'm getting a different helper" Ramrod announced upon arriving at the shop, but Shadow no longer cared as they simply walked away and punched their time card of turmoil for the last time, before leaving for good an employment position that had literally found them down in the dumps.

Left with a paycheck of meager earnings, strained finances and friendships would be all but assured on rent day, when Scrapper came looking for his money and they came up short to pay a drug addicted landlord whom was adamant to get what he was owed because he owed for outstanding drug debts to The Goblin, whom was also adamant about getting paid, leaving Shadow struggling to fee the "brotherhood" as they sat at The Goblin's garage party, lost in a haze that had nothing to do with smoke on the water.

"The world's greatest burden" Shadow thought whilst trying to not appear depressed, but clearly failing when Tiny suddenly came over to ask… "What's eating you?" …leading The Voice to reply, "If this was the apocalypse, probably you! You obese motherf…!" When Shadow suddenly shook their head to cut off The Voice, Tiny mistook the move as a punk off and began acting offended, with an agenda for profit, "I know you're not working and need a job..." Tiny said with fake concern. "...But, you can work for me as my helper with steam cleaning ...bro!"

The fact that Tiny had never called them "bro" before was the first hint to an opportunity that was anything but, since Tiny was known for giving people he owed the run around, which compelled The Voice to pick apart the shortest straw of false chivalry. "Bro our ass... That chunky chump is going to screw us over the first chance he gets, because that's what guys like him do to people he does not respect ...and he don't fucking respect *you*!"

For the sake of avoiding an argument, Shadow simply faked a modest smile and then looked at the floor to ponder their next move, but The Voice wasn't finished. "...And furthermore, the fact that Tiny just tried to take advantage of us whilst in a compromised situation makes him a human piece of...!"

When Shadow chuckled and nodded at inner thoughts, Tiny mistook the move as acceptance of a loaded job offer and immediately began dictating duties right there at the Friday night garage party, which caused them to look at the piece of human cholesterol with a "what the fuck" look that Tiny took personally and reacted like a text book bully, in his attempt to establish dominance based on the size of his ego and the dimensions of his ass. "Well, you nodded your head!" Tiny said attempting to make a nonexistent problem into their fault? "Do you want the fucking job or not!?" Tiny was getting close to crossing a thin red line, which found Shadow's one percent begin charging up... "Careful you fat French fry... Or, we will rock you!"

Shadow simply clenched their teeth to a personal point of view, which of course was noticed by Tiny whom began stoking the flames by speaking in a condescending tone, "You know, you're lucky I even offered you a job! I can hire anybody I want and don't got to do you any favors... You should be fucking grateful!"

"That's fucking it!" The Voice said no longer tolerating being treated like an idiot by a fucking idiot, compelling Shadow to take a breath of good luck, and stand up to face the undertow of confrontation against someone three times their size. Naturally, this move surprised Tiny, whom hesitated and swayed backwards ever so slightly, revealing a chicken hiding under all the pork about to become hamburger, however, just as time began to slow to a split second eternity, at that moment the man door to the garage opened, and in walked the second craziest looking son of a bitch they had ever seen.

"Is this a hit?" Shadow wondered, as the large stranger in a long black leather trench coat entered to a suddenly muted and still room, which created the appearance of some mafia enforcer until The Voice did a double take using The Energy, when they noticed the multiple facial piercings embedded into the man's face and the tattoos stamped on either side of his head, leading Shadow to ascertain... "He's either really good at fights with all those piercings in his nose and face ...or, he doesn't fight at all!"

"He's no threat..." The Voice concluded, and neither was Tiny, whom was now standing two paces outside of striking distance... "Because he fucking knows better!" ...and just then, another stranger walked in and stole the show.

At approximately five foot six inches tall and roughly two hundred pounds, the stranger had the build of a fighter and looked even crazier than the first, but it had nothing to do with the piercings and tattoos as they watched everyone nearly stumble over each other to go shake the hand of a freaky looking man they could tell just by looking at was powerful with The Energy.

"He's strong with it…" The Voice whispered in Shadow's mind about a freakish character that had a definite presence about him, which was unlike anything they had seen or felt before, as they merely stood firm and unmoving, while The Goblin, Scrapper and Bird-Brain ran to him like a bunch of groupies clamoring for a celebrity's photograph.

"Pussies…" When The Voice echoed the word, the short freaky stranger suddenly turned his attention toward them as though he had heard their inner thoughts, and at that moment, with just one look, the stranger spoke to them… "Who the fuck, are you?!"

"What?" Shadow wondered upon hearing the stranger speak through his eyes, whom suddenly ignored the others and began moving toward them with a noticeable grace that confirmed a fighter theory, as the tattooed dancer casting the illusion of barely touching the floor, floated up to them, and there, they held each other's gaze in a moment that traded The Energy in a way none could understand but them, leaving the rest to look on within their schism of suspense.

"You know who I am?" The stranger and freak of nature, asked without using his vocal cords, which was again strange for Shadow, so The Voice replied for him...

"You're The Freak."

It was the first time they had ever encountered someone whom could talk to them on a level that rivaled Mr. Thompson, the chess playing psychopath back in prison, which enabled them to use The Energy in a way Shadow never realized they could, or even thought possible, when, all of a sudden, they could suddenly hear the thoughts of everyone else in the room...

"This should be a pretty good fight!" thought Tombstone whom was present, which made Shadow's eye twitch in surprise while The Freak merely smiled slyly as they sized each other up.

"Ah shit... they're going to wreck my garage!" The Goblin fretted, which made both The Freak and Shadow grin slyly.

"The Freak's going to kill him..." thought the metal faced stranger, and obvious ally to The Freak, whom merely rolled his eyes annoyingly at the unspoken comment, which broke the ethereal ice and took the threat out of their encounter when The Freak momentarily broke character and revealed his true brat... "That's The Squid... he's harmless."

"I bet I can take them both!" Scrapper then thought with arrogant overconfidence that was reflective of his character, which made The Freak's left eye twitch at the challenge, however, it wasn't until Tiny wished... "I hope The Freak fucking kicks Shadow's ass!" ...that Shadow's eye twitched when The Voice lit up again, "These boots are made for more than walking!" When The Freak peered at them with a questioning look, Shadow explained without using words, "That fat fuck is trying to con us into working for him so he can rip us off later, like the cheapskate everyone knows that he is!"

The Freak nodded slightly to the obvious as they stood within a room that was a powder keg of tension, which seemed like it could explode at any moment compelling Crippled Crab, whom was also present that night, to make formal introductions, "Ahem! Shadow, I'd like you to meet..."

"...The Freak." When they finished Crippled Crab's words, everyone was surprised except for The Freak of course, whose boyish smile exposed dentist implanted vampire fangs that gave him the appearance of a demon child living within the warrior, who extended his right hand to Shadow, whom grasped not the hand, but rather, The Freak's forearm in another exchange of The Energy that marked the beginning of a bond no one standing there had anticipated would happen, especially when The Freak finally spoke up and asked Shadow, "You guys want a job?" which they accepted without knowing what the job was exactly, as The Freak then looked at Tiny with contempt... "So, they work for me now!"

Compared to the crazy shit they had witnessed in twenty one years of breathing, going to work for someone whom looked and acted like a nosferatu was both crazy ...and a breath of fresh air to a boring and predictable Home Town life, as Shadow began showing up at The Freak's dark tattoo shop at noon every day, to perform his duties of dealing with the daylight mortals, while The Freak slept in his makeshift coffin in the back room.

"The mortals... Ha!" The Voice laughed on the inside each time The Freak used the term to portray the random humans coming in for a tattoo or piercing, which had offered Shadow their first taste of customer service within a hardcore setting unlike anything they had experienced. "I never thought we'd be working in a tattoo parlor!" The Voice admitted, as they began learning about the art of stabbing the people for profit with laser sharpened instruments, in The Freak's place of business all painted black.

*REASON FOR LEAVING:* Someone... didn't pay the rent.

## THE BEAVER FACTORY pt.2

### *Home Town, ~ 1997 ~ Quality Control Freak*

"It explains the studio name" Shadow reasoned at first, but was corrected when The Freak said he had named the shop after his son, whose initials spelled the word D.A.R.K., where, despite the "dark" atmosphere that was tough to keep clean, cleanliness and sterility were of the utmost importance for The Freak, firstly to prevent cross contamination and spreading the disease, and secondly, and we quote… "So I don't get fucking sued!"

Before meeting The Freak, whom had just return from a last minute runaway adventure in No-Fun City on the other side of MY-BIG-HOUSE, they never imagined that The Energy within them could be used for more than explosive fights and predicting movements, as they got to know their new nocturnal friend, whom had not only mastered The Energy, but could use it to quickly see through people's bullshit and influence "the humans" to his will.

"Pretty sure that's got something to do with your martial arts training since four years old!" The Voice telepathically, as they watched in silence while The Freak expertly pierced a human tongue with the speed and precision of a samurai surgeon, whom had mastered his senses and trained his body to become the ultimate weapon that none dared go up against, including the Home Town police, which were rumored to be under orders to not approach The Freak under any circumstances in the event of an incident, and to instead place two phone calls, one for back up, and the other…

"They call the fucking chief?!" The Voice roared on the inside while Shadow shook their head in amazement that Fate and Irony had led them to discover someone with a "you can't bring me down" personality, which was not only a comfort to know they stood next to someone whom could back them up in any fight, but through The Freak, they were inspired to become something greater than what Fate and Irony seemingly intended, by seeking out a purpose in a roller coaster life that now found them getting paid to implant surgical steel into human beings.

It was a rush every time they pierced someone and the client slash victim went stiff from the pain for that split second eternity, only to relax a split second later once the piercing spike had exited the other side, in a procedure and experience that changed people forever both inside and out. Afterwards, they repeated the aftercare speech and thanked them for the business by telling them… "Stab you later!"

Speaking of stabbings, when it came to fringe benefits arising from working in a tattoo studio, the witching hour ink sessions were perhaps the most valued and cherished, as The Freak began to cover up the atrocities that had been sliced into their skin by The Acid Man, Tattoo Terry, which placed new images and visions over the blurred and distorted memories. If The Freak was known for one thing it was his speed and finesse that was both incredible to watch and incredibly painful to endure at times, especially across certain sensitive areas that forced them to become one with The Energy in order to block out the agony of a mortal reality, but, at the end of the day, it was worth it to feel a bond with someone whom wore The Energy on his sleeve, like the live undead with whom they were capable of sharing thoughts, dreams and ideas with, whom was a friend to the needy, a teacher t the wayward and a bro to the true at heart.

"Bro... That's what Tiny said to us! " Shadow told The Freak, as he tattooed a big dragon cover upon their broad chest.

"Tiny is a fat, lazy piece of shit!" The Freak replied with a defiant frown, "I would knock him out with one punch..." The Freak paused to dip the needles of his tattoo machine in the small cap of ink on tray next to him, then continued, "...And as for Scrapper, he would find out the hard way that he isn't the hot shot fighter he thinks he is, after I break his arms and legs in three places!"

They could feel The Energy within The Freak begin to surge at the thought of confronting adversity, which had inspired Shadow to confront their own fears, doubts and disbeliefs, but also, it reminded them to not make the tattoo artist angry during a session, whose tattooing hand began pushing the tattoo needles down further into their skin, "Too deep... TOO DEEP...!"

Through it all, working with The Freak was an experience that went far beyond a meager apprentice salary that barely kept them flush with the rent during the slow winter months of small coastal city, where, the rest of the career prospects that paid more demanded a blood blind certificate of perfection to acquire, but did not foster personal creativity and growth using The Energy, which led them to seriously consider a future as a tattoo artist whom might one day run their own studio, however, there were two things in the way of that dream with the first being a serious lack of artistic ability that had never been developed as a child and the second …was The Freak.

If The Freak had one vice, it was his impulsiveness when it came to getting something he really wanted that not bills, rent, or the reaper himself, could prevent The Freak from buying that authentic katana sword down at the pawn store, in one of many last minute and albeit poorly timed purchases that had often left The Freak short to cover commitments and expenses, which he always somehow managed to square up …eventually, however, this time, things didn't work out as planned when bad weather and a shittier than usual winter economy caused The Freak to fall so far behind that he had to shut down his studio and return to tattooing from the kitchen of the apartment he shared with The Squid, the larger pierced stranger from the garage party whom had been supposed to work for The Freak.

"The Squid is a lazy piece of shit!" The Freak had explained one night, which had been the fateful reason for their ironic hiring in a tattoo studio that was D.O.A., leaving Shadow to sit in their basement room over at Scrappers place wondering how they were going to pay the rent to a cokehead whom would surely get angry upon learning they did not have his money for next month, leaving them basically one option… "You can crash on the couch here and if Scrapper has a problem with that, you tell him I said to shut his fucking mouth or I'll put my fist in it!"

There had been no hesitation and no fear within The Freak when they suddenly moved out Scrapper's place and took up residence over at The Freak and The Squid's trash apartment, where, upon a tattered sofa they could at least exist in a place that was free of conditional friendships that left no one surprised when Scrapper turned sour over the loss of a rental income, only to quickly drop the matter in light of whom they had moved in with, confirming The Freak's previous opinions about a powder head with diluted honor that was tough yes, but not crazy enough to fuck around and find out whom was the greater skilled fighter.

In a same as it ever was scene of penniless pockets and self preservation, at least they were in a cleaner environment as far as drugs and booze were concerned, given that The Freak did not drink and hated anyone doing hard drugs, while The Squid, whom was also against drugs, merely drank his preferred Vodka, which had been a strange feeling for Shadow, after being around the shit for as long as they could remember, however, when it came to keeping a tidy place…

"You can't judge a book by its cover!" The Voice had joked about two individuals whom were the epitome of a white trash bachelor lifestyle known for remodeling previously pristine rental properties via indoor throwing knife practice and discarded waste, much to the chagrin of other tenants in the building whom dared not protest. Without a doubt, The Freak and The Squid were the reason why rental references and damage deposits were fast becoming standard upon lease agreements, making them a landlord's worst nightmare on a good day.

Faced with frequent eviction notices and utility disconnects for nonpayment, The Freak and The Squid moved twice before springtime had even arrived, which had seen them get away on empty promises to pay compliments of The Squid, whom was a master at bouncing rubber checks signed with good intentions off the foreheads of the naïve and the unsuspecting, in a borrow now pay you never lifestyle within an era with no shortage of gullible humans dumb enough to lend or give anything to someone preaching a lie cheat and steal gospel.

"That's not our gospel" The Voice's affirmed as Shadow tried going the slightly more honest route by looking for another job position in the jobs obituary, aka the employment hiring section of the Forgotten Times newspaper, because the internet was still shit back then, however, the same worrisome lack of career entries meant that a belt would grow tight from hunger, which did nothing to lessen the weight of a financial crown of thorns upon a life running on fumes over at the gas station, where Shadow pumped their last thirteen dollars into the tank of their old sports car thinking… "What the fuck are we going to do now?"

"Hey! How's it going?" When Shadow turned their attention in the direction of a vaguely familiar voice, they had been surprised to find that it was The Beaver, their old boss from before going to prison, whom was looking as rough and unkempt as ever in a clear indication that he was still engaging in old habits, which initially compelled Shadow to merely smile and wave and drive away when The Beaver dropped the inevitable ask for a hookup of past conveniences, however, just then…

"Ask him for our fucking job back!" The Voice suddenly shouted in their head, which led to an all or nothing shit toss at the wonder wall of fortune, where, at first, it didn't seem like anything was going to stick when The Beaver replied…

"Well, things are slow right now you see, and I don't really have a spot for you at the moment…" Unlike before, Shadow could now see The Energy within The Beaver, which revealed someone with easily swayed morals stalling for what he wanted, which led Shadow to convince The Voice to swallow their own morals, as they fixed up a previous employer with nostril grease on the condition that they get their old job back …and a raise.

In the game of golf, it's called a Mulligan when a player is given another attempt to make the same shot count, but in life, being given a second chance to immortal rites had been nothing short of a miracle, when The Beaver rehired Shadow and stationed them within the quality control department with that pay raise, where, given their previous experience and keen eyes for details, they were the perfect fit within a rerun career come full circle, which, strangely, made the last five years of their life seem like it had all just been a bad dream.


***REASON FOR LEAVING:*** Fate, Irony and a bloody Beaver

# 7

# *DIRTY WOMEN*

# THE DIRTY C…

## *Blink Hamlet, ~ 1997 ~ Doormat*

Through a bond based upon one for all and fuck all for anyone else, it seemed inevitable that a third musketeer would begin dressing like their compatriots of chaos, which found a trio of long haired, trench coats wearing tattooed bad boys whom were like a terror in tinsel town, going around scaring the humans, and terrorizing the mortals to incite predictable reactions from people with patterns, regardless of where they were whether it be a corner store, at a shopping mall, a funeral home, since The Freak was into coffins, or their favorite restaurant, The Angina, where they went for cheap steak and cute waitresses, whom were mesmerized and enthralled by the immortals eating their steaks bloody rare, whilst glaring at the wide eyed patrons seated nearby, whom tried to not appear frightened despite being inexplicably drawn by The Energy that everyone in the place had felt the moment they walked in, including The Rodent, whom was the rat faced owner of the restaurant and a real cheese eater type whom openly massaged egos and kissed asses to get what he wanted, and when that didn't work …he bribed people.

"Poor *and* respected…? Yeah… right!" No one needed to see The Energy to see the comfortable liar lurking beneath The Rodent's façade of chivalry, whom was dangerously at ease with bending morality to achieve selfish ends, which had instantly instilled a sixth sense of silent disdain within The Freak and

Shadow as they merely smiled and nodded at The Rodent and his agenda based extravagances, while The Squid, well, he seemed right at home in the presence of the fakes and the phonies in his bid to capitalize upon anything that might render a table scrap of opportunity, which no one gave a second thought to until a few weeks later, when The Squid called them one evening requesting that they meet him at The Angina for evening dinner ...his treat?

"The fuck did he do, rob a bank?" The Freak questioned with puzzlement as they drove over to the restaurant in Shadow's old sports car, whereupon their arrival, they expected to find food and roxy-roller waitresses, only to discover that the serving girls had morphed into strippers baring it all upon a newly built stage, while the kitchen had been replaced with private back rooms that now offered full nude shows, in Home Town's first exotic entertainment club.

For someone used to living on the edge, watching women take their clothes off within the world second oldest profession really wasn't a big deal, however, what really blew their minds wasn't the sight of tits and ass, but rather, finding out that The Squid...

"You actually got a fucking job?" The Freak said in shock when The Squid revealed that The Rodent had hired him to be the head of security for the club, compelling Shadow to glance around the club, "Where's your crew?"

When The Squid replied, "I am the crew!" The Voice called the obvious, "So... he's a bellhop in a booty bar!" while Shadow replied, "So... you're just a fucking doormat!"

## Professional Shadow

From out of nowhere, The Rodent had placed Pandora's box upon a pedestal and spread her legs for all to "bare" witness, in a move that saw hoards of horny hillbillies come rushing out of the woodwork to drool over the naked female figure, causing religious leaning law makers to enter into a frenzy of limp dick politics and presumed moral values, upon a quest to censor something as trivial as the attraction to exposed skin that backfired when they slandered The Rodent upon the six o'clock news, in a failed attempt to breed contempt amongst the locals that instead served as free publicity for a previously unknown sin city factory, which resulted in every sexual deviant for miles around to come stampeding into Home Town seeking the illusion of flesh for fantasy that produced a tsunami of unregulated profits for The Rodent, whom sowed the seeds of a sexually driven expansion that soon saw the erection of another strip club just minutes outside of Home Town within a tiny place called Blink Hamlet, where The Squid again floored everyone…

"Get the fuck out of here! The Rodent made you the manager of a strip joint!?" Such was the rapid and recurring response The Squid received upon announcing that he had been tapped to run a new skin dive some fifteen minutes south east of Home Town in Blink Hamlet, where, The Squid was basically the manager of himself, tasked to run a defunct restaurant turned into a derelict love shack that found him bartending and doing the D.J. thing, all the while babysitting a troupe of annoyed strippers making zero money in a place located upon an abandoned highway that no one remembered, leading The Voice to think, "What a fucking shithole!"

Glancing around at the weathered establishment Shadow had to agree, as they sat at the bar sipping their free drink whilst surrounded by a flock of hungry stripper vultures eying a piece of raw carrion, whom tried to fathom why The Squid had summoned them there to begin with. "So since nothing is free in life... Why are we here?' Shadow asked The Squid, whom revealed that he needed their help to spread a quiet word about a new naughty hideaway, to which they were hesitant to get involved beyond a drink and a private dance, but then figured, "What can it hurt?"

When they went to work Monday morning and saw The Beaver whom looked like he had been though a tornado of souls, Shadow figured their employer was the perfect fit for the stripper setting so they revealed the existence of The Dirty C... in a moment of chivalry that felt like they had just done their duty and honored their word to The Squid.

"Better than snorting coke in his fucking closet all night!" The Voice had resolved about a "what can it hurt" theory, however, when The Beaver did not show up at work that Friday, which didn't seem like too big a deal at first, things began taking a strange turn when Shadow got home after work and their flip phone suddenly buzzed and when Shadow answered, they were surprised to hear The Squid telling them flatly, "Get out here now!"

"Maybe, we'll be able to afford fixing up our old sports car after all!" Shadow thought out loud as they drove out to the Dirty C..., where auto repairs were the last thing on their mind upon pulling into the club parking lot and spotting The Beaver's company pickup truck, which was why The Squid had wanted them out there so bad. "You think it's that bad?" The Voice wondered.

"I fucking hope not!" Shadow wanted to deny as they walked in the club and discovered a busy place, which they quickly scanned for their employer whom they spotted sitting at a corner table with one of the dancers. "He looks sloshed" The Voice quickly pointed out simply by studying The Beaver's body language, however, before Shadow could reply their attention was drawn by The Squid standing behind the bar.

"His shit is on you!" The Squid's first words did not inspire happy tidings as they learned how The Beaver, whom was trashed, had been acting like a pervert to the girls in the back. "He's a fucking idiot!" The Squid continued, "…but, he's got money to spend and we need the sales, so handle it!"

Aware of The Beaver's chemical romance, Shadow walked over to his employer's table hoping The Squid had been overreacting, only to discover otherwise when their boss greeted them with an obnoxious rant… "Have a drink on me! Blah, blah, blah…" Given the loud music and the ballroom blitz going on around them, it was all but impossible to reason with their stoned and drunk employer, whom they tried to convince had consumed enough and should perhaps let them drive him home, despite The Squid's quest for profits at the cost of morality. But, alas, The Beaver didn't listen, and Shadow eventually ended up back at the bar, where they agreed with The Squid…

"Yep, he's an idiot!" Shadow confirmed, while The Squid looked at them like it was their fault, leading The Voice to protest, "What? Hey look, you said spread the word and Shadow figured what could it hurt?"

"Thanks for the help…" Shadow thought sarcastically as The Squid turned to the coolers to fetch them a beer, however, during this time, unbeknownst to them The Beaver had gone to the back rooms with his private dancer during their conversation, and just as The Squid was about to say that he was going to cut off Shadow's employer, they heard a primal scream coming from the back, "Ah! Help…!"

When a fast glance over to The Beaver's table revealed empty chairs, they already knew what the problem was as they rushed to the back close behind The Squid whom burst into the tiny private room and the source of the screams, where, they discovered the dancer cowering in the corner and The Beaver standing over her …trying to shove his junk in the poor girl's face?

"Ah shit" Shadow muttered under their breath as The Squid moved in to break it up, however, upon grabbing The Beaver's shoulder from behind, Shadow watched in amazement as their employer suddenly threw his elbow back and caught The Squid in the face, which sent him stumbling over the empty chair beside them and crashing into the wall in a funk phenomenon of events set to the bouncing club beats. "Hey! Knock it off!" Shadow yelled in hopes that they didn't have to get into it, but when The Beaver paid no heed to their commands and kept trying to force feed the stripper, Shadow felt a one percent instinct take over as they moved in to handle the situation.

Between their experience with prison violence and the martial arts training they had been undergoing with The Freak, whom taught them to be like water in a fight and to flow with an opponent's strikes, Shadow became the eye of the tiger upon stepping up behind The Beaver, where they simply touched his right shoulder that compelled their intoxicated employer to repeat the same elbow back smash that previously got The Squid, a move they deftly avoided and quickly countered by leaning back and then slipping forward under an opponent's raised elbow to grab an opponent by throat, all the while planting a right foot behind an adversary and in one fluid motion, Shadow pulled The Beaver back violently by his throat in a Judo hip toss, which sent their employer flipping over in a near complete pirouette, before crashing hard to the floor on his face and erect penis.

"What the fuck you doing... I fucking pay you!" The Beaver screamed at them, but Shadow stood silent and without emotion as their boss pulled up his pants, during which time The Squid had gotten back up and moved in to manhandle The Beaver to his feet. At that point, they figured it was all over, however, the next thing Shadow knew, all hell was breaking loose when The Beaver suddenly exploded with a powerful forward shove that sent The Squid stumbling back over the same chair and into another wall, this time leaving a large depression in the broken plasterboards.

"Wow..." Shadow admired as time suddenly slowed to a crawl and a great debate took place within a split second eternity... "He's right you know, The Beaver does sign our paychecks at a second chance job!" Shadow presented the facts despite already knowing what a one percent instinct was going to say, as their right arm began loading up with The Energy.

"Don't excuse the crime when it comes to honor!" The Voice replied in preparation for the coming altercation. "Yeah, I know…" Shadow agreed, "…I was just hoping that Fate and Irony would let us keep this job. I fucking hate looking in the jobs obituary!"

After shoving The Squid, The Beaver had begun turning to confront Shadow, but they were already delivering a Death Valley shot to their soon-to-be ex-employer's face, which instantly stopped the fight as The Beaver crumpled to the floor in a bloody semi-conscious state. "You're fucking fired! You don't work for me anymore!" The Beaver had yelled after The Squid dragged him outside and cast him down to the dirt followed by a complimentary kick to the balls. "Fuck him'" The Voice had resolved as they left an ex-employer to rise up from the dust and peel away half drunk in his pickup truck. Back inside, Shadow sat at the bar feeling like a born again idiot for allowing Fate and Irony to cancel a second chance career, which at first had seemed to all have been for nothing, until the dancer later followed them home to reward her rescuer through another type of physical altercation, while The Squid, impressed by their acts of bonehead bravery and trusted back up, told The Rodent what had transpired, whom in turn hired them on as club security.

*REASON FOR LEAVING:* The voice of tomorrow?

# THE ANGINA

### *Home Town, ~ 1997 ~ M.C. Energy*

"On the bright side, we can put off doing laundry for a few days!" The Voice quipped with humor, compelling Shadow to look down at their new staff shirt as they stood by the entrance of the Dirty C..., in their first ever security role as a doorman that left them vexed over previously breaking The Squid's balls about his security role. Despite being thankful to simply be employed, it hardly felt like a grand career move to be the lone karma police tasked with taking care of business if trouble should arise within a seedy strip joint filled with drinkers and naked strippers looking to take advantage of any opportunity.

"Oh, come on, this isn't that bad!" The Voice protested without fear of violence, which always held the potential of turning people into agents of chaos during fights, where the risk of weapons being involved was ever present in the form of broken bottles, hidden blades ...or sharp nails.

"Know your enemy!" Shadow remembered The Freak's teachings on how to quickly recognize the mortal patterns that hinted to forthcoming dangers within altercations, which required them to remain one step ahead of a generation swine at all times lest they get their ass handed to them for an off-the-books pay that was barely half of their previous earnings, leaving Shadow skeptical about a rock and roll duty that more like a sentence given their hard rock history, which thankfully found them in peak fighting shape to deal with arguments and physical disagreements that, were mercifully a rare occurrence leaving boredom as the true adversary within a job role that required remaining irrelevant until needed.

Yet, it wasn't all stand and deliver, as they sometimes had to cover for The Squid at the bar whenever he stepped outside to talk to someone about a horse, meaning the purchase of methamphetamines in a side hustle to satisfy the needs of addicted dancers and pill popping patrons, which enabled Shadow to learn the workings of a cash register while making cocktails for the downtrodden drinkers as well as the strippers, to whom they became the house psychologist offering insights about life theories. Overall, being the one that everyone turned to in times of need and trouble made Shadow feel like they were the only one in the crowd capable of tapping into The Energy, however, when they had to take up The Squid's slack with the D.J. slash Master of Ceremonies' duty during those busy times, suddenly, they found the outlet that permitted them to connect to everyone in the house, where, despite being told they had a radio voice, Shadow's favorite part of the M.C. gig was without a doubt playing the music, which enabled them to control the tempo of the room using the power of sound and song, which included a healthy mix of heavy metal to break up the droning club thumpin beats. Sadly, they could not overdo it since the dancers in the back had a hard time doing a sexy lap dance to thrash metal.

"This is wild!" Shadow thought when they picked up the microphone for the first time and cast their essence over the air waves, which suddenly enabled them to share The Energy on a new level never before experienced… "Alright everybody it is show time once again out here at The Dirty C…, where our smoking hot ladies up on stage will tempt your every fantasy before taking you for a private dance that will have you begging for more…"

Shadow took a deep breath, "…and speaking of more, don't forget our drink specials going on all night long to fuel the fire of temptation, which is what you're about to get when this next sexy kitten does her stray cat strut up on that stage…" They took another good inhale, "Gentlemen… and ladies, let's hear you make some noise for the wild and savagely sexyyyy… Quela! The tempting Tequila Tigress!"

As improbable as it seemed, the Dirty C… had gone from an unknown piss-hole to a premier hot spot for exotic entertainment, which not only defied expectations, but soon began outpacing The Angina back in Home Town both in popularity and in sales that eventually found all the dancers wanting to work out at the Dirty C… to make fast stacks within a jumpin-jumpin scene, while The Rodent was left in limp limbo, unable to find girls willing to strip in his floundering flagship club.

"Getting paid to party…" Shadow thought with amusement one night whilst standing by the entrance of the club, watching over a body count of aroused Acadians spending their hard earned cash for a tease and a lasting hangover, "We've been through worse!" Although The Voice was in agreement, they couldn't shake the notion of a greater purpose beyond spending the rest of their life as a mere bouncer in a back road peeler bar, but just then, The Energy in the air tonight suddenly changed to a foreboding feeling they could not shake, one that always preceded the arrival of The Rodent whom suddenly entered the club with his weasel demeanor and dark aura they had learned to sense from a distance. Although The Rodent occasionally ventured out to the Dirty C… to keep a jewfish eye on his profits, seeing the boss out there at such a late hour was unusual and immediately placed them on their guard when The Rodent stopped before them and asked, "How are you?" in a question of false chivalry.

"To what do we owe the pleasure?" Shadow asked skipping the dishes and getting straight to the point, in a smoke screen of authority and control reflective of their job position, which The Rodent cast aside with one statement. "I'm replacing you here at the Dirty C… with someone else because I want you to be the M.C. at The Angina!" At first Shadow wondered if they were being punished for having sex with some of the dancers when The Rodent expressly forbade anyone getting involved with the would-be talent, a cardinal rule they had broken the first night they were hired, but just then, it occurred to them that word of their skills on the microphone had echoed beyond the walls of a backwoods booty barn, in a mildly flattering revelation that failed to justify the fact that The Rodent had left out any choices in the matter.

"And if we can't do it?" Shadow explored the alternative to which The Rodent, whom was aware of holding all the cards, merely replied without emotion, "Well, then I have nothing for you!"

## Professional Shadow

"Fuck you liar!"

With three words, The Voice had summed up a lifetime filled with dishonest people seeking profit, which belied The Rodent's dire need for a Master of Ceremonies at The Angina, since the current one was an unreliable junkie with the personality of a necrophiliac and clearly half the reason a show palace was struggling at a time when exotic entertainment was the slice of everyone's pie.

"This is bullshit!" The Voice remarked as they sat in the cramped D.J. booth at The Angina, after Shadow accepted the "offer" to be the house M.C. in a bid to salvage a feeble financial situation, and to avoid testing the resolve of a man clearly incapable of guilt or compassion. Unlike the Dirty C… with its slow ride atmosphere that cared little for professionalism on the microphone, working as the house M.C. at The Angina was an entirely different ship to be playing the captain howdy host to a much larger capacity crowd, which created higher stakes that left little to no room for error whilst conveying The Energy over the airwaves in a "thrown-under-the-bus" job that was comparable to jumping off a cliff, forcing them to their fears head on and simply hope to be good enough to meet a challenge unlike any they had ever faced. "I'm the man…"

Presiding up high above the private rooms at the back of the club, where it was also their job to keep an eye out for girls performing extras in the stalls below, thus ensuring that The Rodent was squeezing every dime out of an employee, and an enterprise that fed upon The Energy of the used and the abused for profit, whom were now their burden to entertain.

## Professional Shadow

Looking down the cross of mortal sin from their position up in the east wall, from their vantage point they could see every corner of an open concept drinking lounge beginning with the stage straight ahead all the way across to the west wall, which seemed stupid to have the D.J. so far away from the action. To their right, the serving bar stretched along the north wall, where no barstools had been placed in order to keep the perverts corralled at the tables in the center of the lounge, where they could be glared at by the large knuckle dragging bouncer standing at the entrance within the south wall.

"Sigh…" A slow breath to steady them as Shadow cued up the microphone. "We got this…" The Voice reassured, as they found courage and then, stepped off a precipice into...

"Good evening to all and welcome to The Angina, the only place in Home Town for heart stopping action that could melt a pacemaker…!"

Goosebumps suddenly appeared all over their body as The Voice rated their pitch on a scale of one to ten, "I give it a six!" while Shadow took another breath before taking another leap of faith…

"…But heart don't fail me now because we've got cold drinks and all the hot girls, girls, girls you can handle, whom are just dying to show you what they are made of both on stage, and in our one on one private back rooms, where your pulse will rise along with something else…"

The Voice gave it a seven for effort. "...when you gaze upon our beautiful ladies in all their glory, 'cumming on you live here every night of the week..." They took another deep one...

"This next performer needs no introduction, as you all have "cum" to know her as one of Home Town's very own homebodies, returning to you here *each* and *every* night of the week ...all month long? To kick start my heart and hopefully yours..." Shadow breathed a last dying breath, "So let hear you love it loud and make this beauty proud... Get your hands together for the lovelyyyy ...Bertha?"

While it had taken a little time for Shadow to master their tone and tempo to fake enthusiasm night after night, not even their best efforts could prevent the patrons from getting up and leaving during stage acts, especially after witnessing a living dead girl up on stage with no theme, or personal hygiene, or seeing the same junkie jitterbugs with scratching sores and single moms with stretch marks slinking around upon a stage of scrutiny and broken dreams all nightmare long, where survival after tragedy was on full display to make spectators go limp and liquor sales to crater, in a flaccid scene that hardly inspired the image of love in an elevator and gave rise to a condition known as the "marriage effect", when the allure of attraction gets replaced by apathy for the scar tissue hiding beneath the remains of those once full of The Energy, but now forgotten.

***REASON FOR LEAVING***: A death in the family

## GHOST CHAPERONE SERVICE

### *Home Town, ~ 1998 ~ Lucky S.O.B.*

"The Rodent has to hire real dancers!" The Voice said barely able to look at the girl on stage, whose cellulite between her shoulder blades and electrocution hairstyle stole the show, but in a bad way, in a serious quality control problem that could be squarely placed upon the shoulders of their employer, whom only cared about profits and little about anyone else, especially when it came to vetting the talentless slither showing up to crater the profit margins, which finally pushed a cheap strip club owner to open his checkbook to pay for a ghost booking agent.

Hailing from Mob City about eleven hours to the west in the French Lands of MY-BIG-HOUSE, when The Ghost arrived with a troupe of fresh features and fat-free backsides, a bootylicious theme was saved from castration by women whom could actually fucking pole dance, not-to-mention work a sex type thing to convince not only the lonely to part with their entire paychecks, which suddenly breathed new life into a heart attack and put The Angina back in business, as Shadow cued up the microphone one once more and inhaled truly, madly, deeply, ready to lead the charge with another hook in mouth sermon tailored to inspire …a happy ending?

"What do you mean? We were there first!" Shadow said to The Rodent upon being passed over for the manager position out at The Dirty C… after The Squid had been tapped to go manage The Stroke, The Rodent's newest porn star dancing venture down in Stink City a few hours south west of Home Town, which effectively found The Squid moving out on them and The Freak in a "what the fuck" moment they had been certain would have provided an escape from claustrophobic confines of a tiny D.J. booth, but more importantly, would have been their chance to prove that they had what it takes to run a night club…

"No, I'm keeping you here at The Angina!" When The Rodent denied Shadow's request and instead gave the job to Bonehead, his dumb nephew with zero social skills and the personality of a brick, Shadow thought they felt Fate and Irony brush past them as they walked out of The Rodent's office.

"What a fucking asshole!" The Voice spat in resentment, "We would do a way better job than Bonehead!" Whether or not The Voice was right about Fate, it seemed like the future was locked in Irony for someone whom was being held back from bigger and better things due to their own fucking talents, which had begun stirring anxiety from feeling trapped in a never ending loop of lost opportunities. "Well, looks like it's just you and me again!" Shadow said a loud, to no one…!?

"Who are you talking too?" Startled by someone behind them, Shadow quickly glanced over their shoulder, but when they saw no one, a flashback of the day The Voice had been granted the ability to come out and play led them to believe that perhaps the job was taking more of a… "for whom the bell tolls" …than previously thought, as Shadow turned forward again to look out upon the lounge…

"Ah!" When from out of nowhere they suddenly noticed The Ghost standing next to them, a jolt of surprise that sent their heart racing and left Shadow flustered, as they greeted a pale, hairless man with an amiable disposition, whom was a cancer survivor that embodied the most out of a second chance at life, by having created a successful talent booking agency that catered to an exotic entertainment circuit spanning multiple cities across MY-BIG-HOUSE, which specialized in feature entertainers whom were provided a chaperone service during their rotations.

"Hey, keep this quiet, but..." The Ghost said in a lowered voice, "...would you consider being a Chaperone for my girls?"

The sudden offer caught them off guard, leaving Shadow at a loss to reply despite The Voice screaming... "Fuck yeah we do!" ...to a hail to the king opportunity that included a better off-the-books wage, a new suit, a new rental car to drive, an expense account ...and a gun? Obviously Shadow was interested, but the position sounded intense and prone to certain risks that an ex-con fearing a return to prison was hesitant to accept, which The Ghost immediately picked up on and then dropped the subject altogether.

"It's ok! No pressure. Just think about it." The Ghost said with a smile, as Shadow quickly glanced at the timer and saw that it was almost time to announce another stage act, however, when they looked back to where The Ghost had been standing, he had vanished? "...So that's what that feels like!"

"Are you fucking kidding me!?" The Voice started right away, "I can't believe that after the whole crying over you for being denied career advancement, we're not taking the chaperone job!

It's right up our alley! Imagine the fun we could have!" While it did seem like a wicked cool job role, Shadow did not make the attempt to escape the job they had, which was at least some form of financial security to support a reality of bare bones survival.

"Chicken shit!" The Voice ended with disappointment as Shadow continued to bark praises across a gorilla radio that served up the sexy sermons and the poontang pitches of a career destiny that seemed like it would never change, until it did, about a week later, when the sudden news of the passing of Quela, the tempting Tequila Tigress, crumbled everyone's reality in a scene straight out of a horror movie, when it was revealed that she had been found dead, apparently murdered by The Ripper whom was a client she had been doing private home shows, and whom had buried her body in his basement to hide his crime that left everyone stunned in disbelief.

"Wow..." It was all anyone could say at the thought of a bright light being so brutally extinguished like a candle in the wind, whom would never again share The Energy she carried with the world, including them, given they had been more than close friends with benefits, leading Shadow to give a second thought to The Ghost's previous offer of chaperoning...

"We'll do it! Shadow told The Ghost before giving their notice to The Rodent, whose anger over Shadow's departure and absolute lack of remorse for dear friend whom had met tragic ends, only made it easier for them to leave and take on the role as a private chaperone, tasked with escorting feature performers around Home Town and vicinity in a brand new rental car, whilst wearing a brand new suit that had instantly transformed them into a sharp dressed man, whom turned heads everywhere they went including those of the women Shadow waited on hand and foot thanks to an expense account that covered everything within a duty of companionship and protection, within a silent vow to prevent anything from happening to the clients on their watch.

"The weight of that thing…" The Voice noted about the hand gun resting heavily in the shoulder holster strapped to their chest, "…I suppose we can always pistol whip a fool if it ever jams!"

Indeed, the weight of an instrument of death and the power to take away someone's life was an eye opening experience within a fast paced lifestyle that brought them into close contact with all types of people harboring questionable morals and motives. All of whom did not realize how quickly the illusion of invincibility could expire at the hands of a handsome reaper. "I hope we never have to use it" Shadow quietly asserted as they focused upon their chaperone duties with professionalism and utmost sincerity.

From holding her bags while they shopped to holding their hair when her cookies dropped after too many free shooters bought by adoring perverts, the chaperone role seemed like a perfect fit to their naturally accommodating social disposition, which found Shadow become a confidence man for their clients, whom was capable of entertaining any hope, dream or idea that was bounced off their ear, which often led to something else bouncing upon them afterhours.

Pillow talk psychology sessions aside however, Shadow never forgot the most important reason they were in the bodyguard business, which at times wasn't always a bed of roses given their client's line of work, leading to one particular event that had seen them working against the odds to earn their pay when things got heated at a bachelor party.

From the moment they had walked in that old barn on some remote farm, The Voice had sensed the evil intentions behind The Energy of the twenty plus frat boys gathered to celebrate their friend getting married, whom all got upset when they realized that no one was going to be running a train on the entertainment, leading to a standoff that found Shadow using the bachelor as a human shield with a big gun pointed at his head, in a skin o my teeth scene that found them barely escape being taken apart piece by piece by a group of knob slobs whom pelted the rental car with rocks as Shadow and the feature performer sped off in haste.

After that shit show, it was decided they would take a more direct approach by purposefully leaving the empty gun holster exposed at stag parties, where they claimed it was all part of the act, however, just the sight of it strapped to Shadow's chest was enough to serve as a silent warning that they were not in the business of playing games, and that the gun, probably wasn't far away.


***REASON FOR LEAVING***: The Rodent strikes back.

# 8

# *SYMPTOM OF THE UNIVERSE*

# THE SEXY SURF

## *Home Town, ~1998 ~ Doormat 2.0*

In the absence of legislation and big worded laws, everyone and their dog wanted to jump onto a-lap-dance-is-so-much-better-when-the-stripper-is-crying bandwagon, which soon found many ragdoll strip joints popping up everywhere in hasty attempts by misguided entrepreneurs looking to cash in on a skin and sin trend, only for them all to fail except for one other place, which actually became stiff competition for The Rodent and his clubs.

Like The Angina and The Dirty C..., The Sexy Surf had seen its beginnings as a restaurant, until the rich Pasta Papa whom owned it and the city block upon which it sat, converted the place into Home Town's second premier exotic entertainment establishment, much to the chagrin of town council since the club was located right across the street from Home Town High School, where Meatballs, the eldest of two pasta siblings was in charge of operating a den of decadence, while his younger brother Dimwit, had been made the slumlord of the shanty house on the corner behind the club, where the dancers stayed on their rotations.

Unlike The Angina however, with its high vaulted ceilings over an open concept lounge of grand panache, The Sexy Surf had a much lower ceiling that gave the place a laidback almost cave like atmosphere filled with dark corners, which eventually became the preferred getaway for the staff of other drinking establishments, and where Shadow could also be found haunting the chapel of hedonism at their reserved table, after Meatballs also became a client of The Ghost, whose talent services permitted The Sexy Surf to compete with The Rodent in an open war of pink and provocation, which often led Meatballs to approach Shadow in search of juicy tidbits of information about the competition… "So what's new in the exotic scene?"

"Nice try noodle nuts!" The Voice quickly dismissed, while Shadow entertained their host with omitted details, whom had even tried recruiting them for the house M.C. position, where, it didn't take a drug councilor to see that the current M.C. was a drug addict whom was hardly a shot of epinephrine on the microphone. While the offer should have been flattering, they knew that it wasn't really their audible skills that Meatballs was after, but rather, access to Shadow's social network that would greatly benefit a bottom line of profits should that friend's network begin gathering at The Sexy Surf.

"You'd be an idiot to quit the job we got for this clown!" The Voice protested after everything they had endured, to which Shadow confirmed, "Nothing is going to make us quit this job!"

Well, at least that's what they thought about a career that seemed like it would ride on forever into the land of bright lights and beautiful people, which suddenly all vanished when The Rodent started his own booking agency and stopped using The Ghost and his services, which resulted in a restructuring of operations that left Shadow, suddenly unemployed …again.

"Great… we're fucked again, and not even a courtesy spit!" Shadow said about a job loss for which they could not blame The Ghost, however, the ominous reality of going back to some shitty labor job in a local economy that was comparable to a vasectomy, found Shadow enable t focus on the game at hand.

"So, you gonna go work for Meatballs?" The Freak's question had snapped them out of a career fog just in time to watch their brother from another mother clear the backgammon board and win the round within a wagered best out of three challenge, which was a fleeting priority in light of a bright future suddenly gone dark faster than The Freak could roll double sixes, immediately giving him the lead and another turn.

"We don't have much choice at this point" Shadow replied as they rolled the dice for a combined "five" and limped their game pieces ahead. Despite making good coin working for The Ghost, the off-the-books nature of the job had yielded zero financial fall backs, thus leaving their suddenly strained cash reserves as the only thing left to get them by in a get's me through world of recurring bills and expenses. Aware that they were not going to get far on empty pockets Shadow hated being an outcast of a black or white society that beheld no mercy for the struggles of an uneducated ex-convict searching for a normal life and career, but seemed destined to be thwarted at seemingly every turn by fatefully ironic events.

"You know Meatballs is probably going to fuck you guys over, right?" The Freak had a point out as he rolled double sixes again, leaving them far behind to imagine how it was going to play out when they crawled back to The Sexy Surf looking to get hired in the M.C. position they had once turned down…

"No fucking doubt" The Voice answered as Shadow rolled a shitty seven draw, which left them trampled underfoot both in game and in career, but alas, what could they do? With no other job in Home Town that could even come close to being as rewarding as the chaperone gig, their obvious next choice had been returning to an M.C. position that would somewhat salvage a social image, and illusion, of prosperity. Shadow struggled to smile at both their situation and The Freak's apparent magic touch, when the lucky brat rolled the dice and hit double sixes for the third fucking time, granting him a sizeable lead…

"Knowing that you have these abilities thanks to The Energy, do you ever get the feeling like you're meant for more than Home Town …than this shit?" Shadow suddenly asked his best friend, which made The Freak take a deep breath as he rolled those damn double sixes again, which saw many of their game pieces get knocked off the board and have to start all over in a repeating example of their life.

"I just want to start a chain of tattoo shops across MY-BIG-HOUSE, so I can spend my life travelling shop to shop in every city and just collect the profits!" The Freak had dreamed, which Shadow couldn't argue was a nice dream, but, it still didn't answer the question leading to more uncertainty about a burning notion of purpose, as though the universe was trying to tell them something beyond the fact they were wasting time laboring for someone else. The war of attrition must have been apparent on their face, leading The Freak to suggest they should relax, as the fucker rolled double sixes again! "Forget about it man, you're gonna drive each other insane!"

Shadow could only smile at the comment while The Voice replied, "Too late!" ...leading the both of them to accept their Fate that they would most likely go insane before figuring out their true purpose, all the while trying to deny the Irony of a repeating dice roll.

Sitting at the bar at The Sexy Surf later that night and a hundred dollars light from losing to The Freak at backgammon, they had been there an hour before Meatballs acknowledged their presence, which had been a vivid reminder of their reduced importance now that they were no longer the top G of flash and flesh.

"Oh, hey, I didn't see you there!" Meatballs had said with feigned surprise, to which The Voice wanted to reply, "Go fuck yourself!" but, Shadow merely nodded like a moron at a man whom was aware of his upper hand, and whom suddenly had no time to waste on Shadow ex-communicado, by going straight for the obvious... "So, you're here looking for a job are you?"

Feeling cornered, all Shadow could do was nod again as they took a sip of their tables drink whilst listening to the cogs of corruption turning within the mind of a phantom lord, whose employment pitch that seemed like jab rather than a job offer.

***REASON FOR LEAVING***: Sweet child of mine

# THE NIGHT MATRIX

## *Mob City, ~ 1998 ~ M.C. Neo*

"Seriously...? Fucking Doorman!?" There was no point trying to argue with The Voice for the last word in a stupefied reality that had them trying to figure out if losing a fight with a drunken patron, could ever hurt more than the shot to their pride when everyone heard Shadow was back to working as a simple, lowly doorman collecting the entry fees for a self serving employer, in a reckless life without a financial plan, or, for that matter, a concrete future goal beyond the fight to survive.

Will tonight be the night someone punches our ticket?" Shadow wondered as they walked to the D.J. booth to tell the M.C. his drug dealer had arrived, but upon trying to get the attention of a pharmaceutical stunt dummy, they were dismissed with a wave of his hand and an insult... "Slob my knob!".

"How about we break that fucking hand off and shove it up your ass!" The Voice said with rising power, which made Shadow pause to consider the blood splattered banner they were about to leave behind upon punching a hole through the empty skull of a sunken eyed slug who...! "Excuse me..."

When a woman's voice behind them made Shadow turn around, they stood gazing into the soul of a brown eyed girl whom was not only the most beautiful creature in the club, but

The Energy radiating from her being was unlike anything they had ever seen, compelling The Voice to claim, "I saw her first!" .

As part of a new troupe of dancers whom had just arrived at The Sexy Surf for a week long rotation, Lace was a gorgeous French girl from Mob City whose youthful appearance not only made her stand out from the rest of the girls in beauty, but watching her perform on stage, where she allowed The Energy to flow freely through her movements had seen Shadow fall instantly in love with a cinnamon girl whom coincidentally wanted to relocate from a big city to a small town life, which found her swiftly moving in with Shadow over at their place with The Freak whom everyone knew was a brat with a tongue sharper than flying daggers and whom wasn't shy about speaking his mind when it came to a living arrangement that, well, let's just say it wasn't exactly just like paradise.

"Tell you're bug eyed Chihuahua she needs to fucking relax!" The Freak said to them after Lace went off like a mini nuke over his comments that she was acting like a neurotic lap dog, which Shadow knew was due to The Energy trapped within such a tiny body …and some other anxiety they could not see.

"Get her to clean bathroom! That will calm her down!" Although The Freak was mostly joking, this only aggravated things for a wild flower with a vibrating bubbly demeanor, whom chose to resent The Freak instead of, well, just fucking relaxing, which led a wandering star to eventually sow the seeds of Fate and Irony by telling Shadow… "You're wasting your fucking life in this hick town! You would do so much better in Mob City!"

"She's half right you know The Voice was compelled to add, "...about the leaving part anyway!" which made Shadow consider a wherever I may roam destiny even more, despite The Freak telling them they were crazy to be running off with a stripper.

"See you in three days!" The Freak had said rolling his eyes, but did not protest further about Shadow's need to explore the world beyond the corporate limits of a small town economy, however, when they told Crippled Crab of their intentions… "Boy, you're like a nomadic moose in heat!" While it was true that Lace had Shadow whipped, they were not simply moving away like some blind man chasing a scent, as Shadow sought to chase the ace of fortune with an ace of spades up their sleeve.

"Are you sure you want to move there?" The Ghost had cautioned when Shadow sought him out for a possible hook up on a chaperone gig, which had been a maybe at best. "Things are… *different,* out in the French Lands!"

Having attended French schools almost against their will, Shadow figured to have at least some hint of what to expect within a different culture that would require them to live and think as seemingly someone else entirely, adding another layer of difficulty, not-to-mention a third personality to an already crowded mental house. When it was time to say goodbye, they were surprised by how easy it was to leave a place that had shown them so much hardship and seemingly held them back, well, except for saying goodbye to their poor mom, which broke their heart to tell a lonely soul that her sons were setting off in search of a better life that would hopefully find them returning one day in a fairytale chapter that would show a parent that their little boy had done something notable if not great with their life.

"What can go wrong!?" The Voice nudged with a hint of sarcasm, as Shadow and Lace drove off in their old sports car of questionable reliability, upon a fantastic voyage that provided a sense of release from the past, upon the eleven hour journey to Mob City, which found them energized with anticipation by the time they arrived and experienced the one thing Mob City was most known for... bad roads and worse traffic.

Racing along upon large highway arteries that were larger than anything they had ever seen or experienced in person, Shadow's mere few years of driving were put to the test as they dodged falling into massive potholes and avoided getting run off the road by impatient drivers cutting them off with last second, bumper to bumper lane changes, which had Shadow on the edge of their seat make precise maneuvers at terminal velocities.

"This is nothing!" Lace had said with passive interest and a surprisingly calm demeanor that left Shadow and The Voice on their own to fret as they fought their way through cross town traffic. "Ok now! No wait! Ok...Now...! Wait!"

By the time they arrived to the location of the exotic club The Ghost had told them to seek out, Shadows hands and forearms were sore from gripping the steering wheel so tightly, as they went to see about the possibility of a chaperone job for them and a dancing gig for Lace, which would establish an income and a lead into the network of a big city exotic scene, however, when upon discovering a low paying bouncer gig in a seedy "extras" strip joint that was staffed by shady dealers and cracked out hookers… "Yeah… No! That's not going to happen!"

There was no way they were going to subject them or Lace to the whorehouse blues that explained why Lace had chosen the slow go eastern stripping scene, as they promptly got back on the freeway and headed for the place they would soon call home, where the thought of taking a hot shower and unwinding after a seven hundred mile drive took precedence over coming up with a contingency plan to salvage a setback that, all things considered, had not been entirely unexpected.

"It's ok, we'll figure it out!" Shadow said with a smile of reassurance, in hopes of hiding a shaken confidence that was made worse by the fucking traffic, where, despite going faster and faster, was seemingly never fast enough to outrun the insanity of a city on overdrive, giving them the impression that the speed limit signs were merely decorations.

By the time they pulled up in front of a plain bungalow where Lace had said she lived with her roommates, Shadow was a basket case of tense nerves whom just wanted to sit there for a moment to allow the world to stop moving, and to regain their composure before going inside to meet their future roommates, whom would hopefully not be freaked out by a large, long haired, tattooed lover boy with boundless ambition. Shadow had a cheerful demeanor when they looked over at Lace sitting the passenger seat in odd silence and staring somberly at her hands resting in her lap, which they found to be a little strange. Shadow was about to ask, "Why the long face?" however, just then, The Voice spied movement in the big window of the bungalow beyond the passenger glass, as two silhouettes suddenly appeared and were watching them,

"There's your roommates!" Shadow said motioning toward the house, compelling Lace to glance at the mystery pair briefly, before quickly returning her gaze to her lap in silence, which prompted The Voice to peer intently at the curious couple looking on, and there, they discerned a middle aged man and woman? At that moment, the obviousness of the truth suddenly hit them square in a third eye that had been blinded by the light of hopes and dreams, upon realizing that Lace's "roommates", were really her... "Those are your parents... aren't they?"

As far as weird goes, being able to hear and speak to voices didn't hold a candle to staying with a bi-polar French girl and her polarized parents, whom had no idea that their daughter was a and closet stripper taking her clothes off to survive on the mean streets of Mob City and beyond, which found them coming up with a last minute bullshit story about an eastern savior, whom had taken it upon himself to guide a wayward voodoo child back home to mommy and daddy, which created a very awkward situation to say the least, especially upon finding out that Lace had a habit of... "Brings home strays... You don't say!"

"Good grief!" The Voice had been exasperated by the reveal, but Shadow had been too tired to care and just wanted that goddamn shower followed by sleep ...for the next two days, in the spare room of Lace's parents house, where they lay motionless in a call back to their top bunk in prison cell, listening to the pulse of a family institution engaging in ultimate arguing championships between a disenchanted sociopathic daughter and her overbearing, neurotic parents. "I see where she gets it from" The Voice said sympathetically, albeit it sadly, as the reality of their situation hit home within a place that was not home.

"Well, this was fucking stupid..." Shadow said of an adventure quickly turned into a nightmare, where, despite the notion they should stay in Mob City to try to capitalize on their presence within a bigger city with more industry to seek out a better life, it was obvious the timing wasn't right. "You know what really sucks..." Shadow said with ninety nine percent certainties, "...The Freak will have been right with his... 'See you in three days' wise crack!"

Thus, on day four, "See ya!" was all they said as Shadow got back in their old sports car and drove straight back to Home Town on strangled funds, which found them rolling into town in the small hours that offered three options to a weary traveler.

"Let's go see what The Freak is doing" Shadow sighed in anticipation of an impending, "I fucking told you so" from their friend and brother, whom, to their surprise... "He moved! There's no one living there!" Shadow said when they arrived at their old place and saw the "for rent" sign in the window.

"Wow... that was fast!" The Voice echoed the sentiment, but Shadow got over it just as quickly since they never figured The Freak to pay for something if he could find it cheaper somewhere else. "I wonder where he went?" they thought as they opted for option two, which found them over at Crippled Crab's place, whom would definitely give them the once bitten twice shy sermon about a horny fool dancing in the purple rain over a pretty woman that left had led them astray.

"What? He moved too? What the fuck?" Shadow thought this time, making them retrace their steps across four days that was beginning to feel much longer. "Talk about shit ha...!

"Don't say it!" The Voice caught Shadow just in time to prevent "those" two words from being spoken.

"Thanks, good save." Shadow's heart was racing from nearly saying the magic words that would evoke the wrath of Fate and Irony, as they got back in their old sports car and sat facing option three... "Looks like this car is our apartment for the night and tomorrow, who knows!" They didn't want to stay where they were so Shadow drove to find a convenient place to park and get some sleep in a car that was designed for performance and not counting sheep, and was going to make for an uncomfortable sleep to say the least, and would be torture over their body.

"Jesus built my hot rod" Shadow uttered as they drove toward The Sexy Surf, where the thought of stopping in for last call drinks to numb their senses suddenly went from a thought to full blown curiosity when they saw a different name on the big tall sign in the parking lot, "The Night Matrix?" Shadow read the words that seemed almost dream like. "Ok, are we still asleep at Lace's parents place?!"

Driven to find out if they had driven through some kind pinch me time portal, Shadow pulled in the parking lot and went inside, where they were greeted by a new doorman they had never seen before, in a club that retained the same layout as The Sexy Surf, but had been repainted with a different theme.

"Well, it's still a strip joint!" The Voice said noting the girl on stage, whom they recognized as Pandora, busy showing her box to the ogling perverts in the front row, as they approached the bar and were greeted by a different bar tender, leaving Shadow at a loss after four days of insanity, but just then, they spotted The Ghost, whom upon noticing them, came over immediately to greet them. When The Ghost revealed that the day after they left he had taken over the club from Meatballs, Shadow could only shake his head at the timing and shrug in defeated weariness over a drink, as they revealed to The Ghost the details of their fateful adventure that compelled their ex-employer and friend to offer his apologies for a dead end job lead in Mob City.

"You know, your timing is spot on...!" The Ghost then said as he glanced toward the D.J. booth, where the obviously intoxicated house M.C. was heard slurring his words on the microphone during Pandora's exit from the stage. "...I just happen to need a new M.C." The Ghost then looked back at them, "You want the job?"

***REASON FOR LEAVING***: Bleed The Freak

# 9

# TOMMOROW'S DREAM

## "AFTER" D.A.R.K.

### *Home Town, ~ 1999 ~ Vampire's Shadow*

"Good evening and welcome everyone to The Night Matrix, the back door to a whole other reality of adventure and pleasures, where our beautiful female agents will assimilate your every desire and leave you begging for blissful release..." They paused for a breath. "...And now, it is show time once again, so please welcome this next gorgeous creature who will leave you incapable of telling the difference between the dream world and the real world..." Another good inhale, "...Let me hear you make some noise for the sexyyy ...Trinity!"

Nearly a month had gone by since Fate and Irony had rewritten a Hindenburg love story about a hard luck woman and a love hungry man, which had not only taught them a lesson about falling for a pretty face, but now found them more reserved around the wanton women within their nightly Matrix, where they used The Energy during every shift to excite the masses and make people feel like they belonged in a world of illusions.

"Is it weird the sight of a naked woman doesn't excite us the same as it used to?" Shadow wondered as they glanced at the naked dancers in their change room off to the right of the D.J. booth, which only they could see to queue the girls for their stage acts. "That's not what you were saying last night with two of them in our bed!" The Voice countered with enthusiasm.

## Professional Shadow

Shadow quickly looked the other way as they smiled at the benefits of living next door to a dozen or so strippers, whom had zero inhibitions about their wants and needs. "Yeah, he really helped us out there!" They acknowledged The Ghost for granting them a room upstairs above club, right across the hall from the dancer's quarters. At that point, it occurred to Shadow that while their attempt to find a new life elsewhere had failed because of Fate and Irony, Fate and Irony appeared to be responsible for their wins and successes too.

"Are they sadistic or just undecided?" Shadow struggled to find peace with the way things turned out, which continually pulled upon their instincts as though another chapter in their life was waiting just around the corner, however, without an end in sight to the only job that was remotely worth the effort for a dropout ex-con trying to survive in a world of certified careers, it seemed like The Night Matrix would continue to be their pod of blissful ignorance in a clubbed to death future.

Clearing their mind of a post-mortal ejaculation, Shadow grabbed the microphone to conclude the stage act in progress, before putting on some filler music and going to shake a leg for a drink refill, where a busy house found them having to push their way through the drinkers and dreamers to the back of the bar, where they waited in the staff only area for the bartender to make them a paralyzer and…!

At that moment, the pull on their instincts grew ever more pronounced causing Shadow to straighten and pause when The Energy of a familiar presence was suddenly felt nearby, which revealed the source long before they turned around to look upon a vampire, a friend ...and a brother.

"So you don't fucking call me!?" The Freak said in a failed attempt at tears in heaven that made them laugh both inside and out. Standing there like a count, The Freak looked wilder than ever as The Energy radiated from his being, which augmented an immortal persona that was both savage, yet, elegant in appearance and movement.

"We haven't reached out to anyone since we got back." Shadow said of their self-imposed exile, with the exception of visiting Mom of course.

"How is she?" The Freak asked without words.

"She's better than us!" Shadow replied with the obvious as they grasped each other by the forearm in a reunion of Fate, Irony and The Energy that was felt by everyone standing nearby. "What brings you here? Is someone bleeding?" Shadow joked about the presence of a vampire within a human meat market, whose distaste for sinful humans and their vices meant that The Freak wasn't there to watch the show or mingle with the mortals.

"I knew you were here" The Freak said deflecting a question, "You should come see me at the house here when you're done tonight. There's something I want to talk to you two about."

"...Here?" Shadow frowned at the word, unable to break down the walls of confusion to see the obvious. Obviously, after they had run off to Mob City with "the bug eyed Chihuahua", The Freak had moved out of the shitty apartment they had been living in, but what really baked their noodle was when their friend and brother revealed that he had rented the shanty shithole right behind the club, where the dancers had once stayed in squalor during their rotations. Stunned, Shadow couldn't believe that one, their friend had been so close the entire time and they never knew it and two... "Why the fuck would you do business with a lowlife like Meatball's idiot brother Dimwit?!"

In response to a wordless question, The Freak merely stated the obvious through a simple shrug of desperate times called for desperate measures, "Because it was fucking cheap!" leading Shadow to agree to a friend's request, "Yeah... Sure. We'll go see you after our shift tonight!"

For the rest of the night, curiosity lay upon their mind and thoughts as Shadow tried to imagine what The Freak wanted to speak to them about, to which The Voice had a few theories... "He either wants to give *us* a tattoo, or, he's going to fucking murder *you* for bailing on him!"

"Maybe" Anything was possible, but Shadow sensed it was something else when they stepped out into the crisp winter night after closing time, where they allowed the cold stillness to purge the mass appeal madness of sex and candy from their thoughts, before walking around behind the club to the derelict dwelling right there on the corner, forever rooted in the eternal shade of Home Town High School across the street with its centuries old gothic stone walls and tall gargoyle peaks, which seemed to fit perfectly with a certain vampire's nocturnal personality, leading Shadow to wonder if it had been Fate or Irony that compelled The Freak to move into a shithole that was in such a dilapidated state that it was apparent even in darkness, however, upon considering the ultra prime location, which saw an endless supply of coming of age students as prime fodder for a potential tattoo business that…

"Oh…!" The Voice suddenly figured out the reason behind a vampire's earlier invitation, as Shadow carefully climbed up the rickety steps leading into an enclosed veranda, which spanned across the entire front part of the house facing the school, where they couldn't help but notice the crude carpentry work that had gone into a poorly built add-on to a weathered domicile that…!

"Holy shit! Looks better on the outside" The Voice said when they stepped into a place that echoed the morbid tales of struggle and strife from the previous tenants before the strippers had a go at the old shack, which was devoid of furniture leaving nothing to obstruct their view of severely tattered carpets and grotesquely outdated wallpaper peeling off walls that bore holes in many places, leading them to wonder, "Is this place even fit for human occupation?"

At that moment, it became morbidly obvious that Dimwit the slumlord had cared more about collecting the rent than performing basic maintenance to a place that by all means looked like it should have been condemned, but before Shadow could give a shithole another thought, The Freak called out to them from an adjacent room just off the foyer, whereupon entering, the sight of a broken tile floor and more cracked walls made them cringe as they found their friend sitting upon a tiny stool in the corner of the room, where he was busy tattooing the beginnings of a large back tattoo upon some meek looking mortal sitting uncomfortably upon a broken chair, whom winced in pain from the million bloody kisses being applied to his skin via The Freak's rattling tattoo machine.

"How are you?" The Freak inquired without taking his eyes off his task, to which Shadow, still absorbing a pitiful sight could only shrug, while The Voice, not feeling guilt answered for them, "Better than this dump!" At that moment, The Freak pulled away from his paying prey and took a deep snarling breath, which bore his dentist implanted fangs. Steadying himself, The Freak calmly dipped the needles of his tattoo gun into a tiny cap of ink that was stuck to a piece of paper towel on his lap, taking his time to thoroughly coat the pins of pain as he carefully considered his words, before finally looking up at Shadow whom could see the intensity in the eyes of someone digging deep to muster the weakness to ask for....

"It would be so fucking awesome if you two helped me to rebuild D.A.R.K. Tattoos!" The Freak said with hope and imagination, using The Energy to plant the seeds of a dream within their thoughts that suddenly created a mental image of a future bathed within the ecstasy of gold, which appeared to hint to a purpose as yet unseen that...! "Don't over think it!.." The Freak said mentally. "Just say Ozzy and you'll do it!"

This time, it had been Shadow's turn to take a deep breath and bare their teeth to a massive undertaking that threatened to test not only their will to help a friend and brother build his business but also their skills at renovation when it came to the matter of turning a shithole shanty into a stellar tattoo studio that, quite frankly, was going to take a lot of improvisation, however, upon seeing the look on The Freak's face whom was well aware of the obvious, a sudden surge of The Energy was felt within both of them, compelling Shadow to take up the challenge, but not before making something perfectly clear.

"If we do this, there can be no fucking bullshit of not paying bills and no half-assed effort! We do this we go all the way and become bigger than everyone else! We become more human than human!"

And so, Shadow began going over to The Freak's place every night after their shift at The Night Matrix, where they were guilty of breaking virtually every building code Home Town had a law for, as major alterations were performed to Dimwit's rental property without permission in the form of large holes cut out of the exterior walls of the living room in a feat of "pretty sure that will hold" engineering that, when finished had absorbed the long enclosed veranda wrapping around the front of the house into the living room to create a wide open reception foyer capable of accommodating more paying victims.

"Do you think he'll notice?" Shadow asked jokingly about Dimwit's eventual reaction to the third world renovations taking place within a rental residence.

"Fuck him..." The Freak replied defiantly and without any hesitations, "If he complains, I'll knock him the fuck out!"

Inspired by "I've no more fucks to give", they proceeded to knock down walls within Dimwit's derelict domicile and within them as Shadow summoned all of their skills and knowledge in the art of interior redesign, until finally, the foundations of an empire had been built around a vampire whom placed the finishing touches upon a dream with a gothic theme by using his mastery of the arts to airbrush the walls in gothic faux stone, which gave the place an authentic castle ambiance that would grant an experience beyond the tattoo for all whom entered a brand new studio with a style all its own, especially after The Freak parked a coffin the foyer and hung medieval weapons up on the walls that compelled Shadow to ask, "Where the fuck did you get all these!? They must be worth a fortune!"

The Freak smiled, "The guys at the machine shop are making them for me out of metal scraps for fifty bucks a pop!"

At that moment, they saw the true value of chasing dreams however, there was one last detail to cover, "…So, what are you calling this thing?"

At first, The Freak wanted to keep the name, "D.A.R.K. Tattoos", but it just didn't seem to fit with the sign of the times beckoning them to leave the past and grow beyond what Fate and Irony seemingly intended, and it was here that The Freak simply repeated the obvious, in a moment of forward thinking that inadvertently placed a studio first in the phone directory…

"After" D.A.R.K. Tattoos & Body Piercings"


***REASON FOR LEAVING***: Escaped the Matrix

## Professional Shadow

# DEVIL'S RIGHT HAND …INK?

"If a vampire is casting a 'Shadow' …he is not alone!"

…Rob?

## *Home Town, ~ 2001 ~ Professional Shadow*

"You can knock it off with the cryptic shit!" Shadow said with annoyance whilst they descended into the unfinished basement of a vampire's shanty castle, where large cob webs reaching down from the ceiling to the dirt floor always inspired the thought...

"Where's the creature that made all those?"

An eerie image suddenly triggered the memory of growing up in run down homes with impoverished parents barely surviving their struggles and strife, which sent a chill running through their body, making Shadow forget why they had gone down there to begin with.

"For fake sakes…" When Shadow turned to go back upstairs, he bumped their forehead upon a low support beam stretching across the unfinished basement ceiling, which was all that was preventing the old shack with a facelift from falling in on itself, causing Shadow to stumble back and trip over some junk behind them, sending their ass to the dirt floor, where The Voice suddenly noticed the glint of something metallic embedded in the earth... "What's that?"

When Shadow reached over with curiosity and dug out the mysterious item, they discovered that it was a metal keychain, upon which was stamped the words "Certified Crazy Person", which compelled Shadow pause upon the trinket to consider a deeper meaning within a fanciful find...

"Certified…" For them, the word inspired the theory that a diploma or an academic certificate was supposed to be the key to unlocking the doorway to one's future success, but since they had neither the certificate, nor the success, the tarnished trinket in their hand suddenly became their certificate of achievement …of sorts, in a twisted tribute to twenty five years of crazy living, which had often found them ready to break stuff in defeat and despair, whilst waiting for Fate and Irony to throw them a bone.

"Given the life that we've lived, if there was ever a course on how to be crazy, we would have passed that test with flying colors!" The Voice acknowledged, as Shadow got back to their feet and then stood there frowning upon realizing that he still could not remember why the fuck they had ventured down there, but, just then, The Voice suddenly offered a deal… "Give me a name and I'll tell you why we're down here!"

At that moment, Shadow rolled their eyes to the repeating verse, "Not this shit again…!" he shot back to a split personality attempting to capitalize on a momentary lapse of reason. "You're just not going to quit with that, are you?" Upon stating the obvious, it was a question to which Shadow already knew the answer, but did not want to entertain, however, the will to escape a creep show basement led to the conjuring of a name off the top of their brain… "Alright, alright…! How about …Rob?"

Hoping to pacify the attitude within, Shadow waited for what seemed like an eternity before The Voice, or rather, "Rob", gave up the answer, "The water valve" which made Shadow slap their forehead upon remembering they were fixing the leaking toilet upstairs, but only aggravated the soreness from bumping their head a few moments earlier, "Owe!"

Back upstairs, they showed The Freak their new metal trinket in a moment of levity that was short lived when their friend and brother looked at them with a serious look and said, "What are you going to name that thing?"

Confused, Shadow frowned whilst wondering, "How the fuck did he know that I just named my alter ego?" however, when The Freak pointed to their neck and said, "I think you should call it

## Professional Shadow

Ed, you're second head!" Shadow reached up to feel a large lump on the left side of their neck and quickly went to the mirror to inspect the presence of a worrisome growth, which spawned a million questions as to why it was there, leading to a visit to a clinic, where they were informed that it was a benign fatty tumor called a Lypoma, which would eventually need to be surgically removed in a less than thrilling chop suey procedure involving a local anesthetic and a fucking scalpel, which didn't seem like a too big of a deal until they were told that they would be awake for the entire process?

That night, they felt queasy from the uncomfortable mass that had strangely only begun to bother them after noticing it, in a weird mind over tumor that made it difficult to be cheerful on the microphone at a job that had begun losing all its appeal for someone feeling like they were wasting their life instead of pursuing a greater purpose.

"You need to be self employed!" The Freak told them that night in the studio, which never ceased to amaze Shadow how their friend and brother just seemed to know what to say as though reading thoughts, however, an obvious need still did not reveal a not-so-obvious deed, until The Freak then suddenly told them, "I want you two to work for me as the manager of the studio, then the franchise when we expand, but, I need to pay you as a business, like an artist renting a chair!"

For some reason, Shadow had always imagined starting a business that would create and sell a product, but since they had no business and no product except for The Energy… so that's what they went with.

"How do we market "The Energy" of a taxed to death employee, without being one?" Shadow hung the hint of success in the air for a second, "…We become a personal consultant?"

Upon saying it, the thought of a large consulting firm with an army of agents advising multibillion dollar corporate clients flashed within their thoughts, which firmly planted a mountain between a dropout ex-con and a successful white collar career that was seemingly and forever unattainable for a king nothing with nothing for resources… so, they went with that too.

"In prison, we were a "Shadow" of society existing with nothing except The Energy, which we discovered and now use to defeat an impossible game…" Rob tossed and flipped the hint of an idea around like pizza dough, "…while out here the game of survival has got us learning and working jobs without diplomas or certification in any profession, which pretty much makes us a …professional shadow?"

"A Professional Shadow…" Shadow repeated the fateful title with an obvious, albeit ironic self reference, however, the obvious that wasn't still eluded them, "So, a Professional Shadow is… someone with the ability to envision or imagine any "legal" or "truthful" idea or dream of a client no matter how crazy, to which we apply a 99 and 1% approach based upon the theory that we believe in someone or something with ninety nine percent certainty, however, one percent of us will always remain objective to everyone and everything?"

"That's me!" The Voice acknowledged ownership of an insane notion, which threatened to keep things brutally honest and compelled them to go for it even more, however, upon making the choice, they were immediately faced with the first challenge of any business... "We need a name!"

It had to be something that would mirror the services they provided, whilst reflecting personality, their environment and... their client? When they looked at The Freak with his vampire persona and naturally devilish appearance, something compelled the universe to open up and spit out an answer so crazy, it was perfect...

"Devil's Right Hand ...Ink?" The words had rolled off their tongue with such ease that a moment of Fate and Irony that no one else in the world would ever experience, had felt too natural to deny as they registered a crazy name for an unlikely business, which suddenly found them self-employed as a "Professional Shadow" serving a vampire within a spill the blood industry, as the details Guy for a best friend whose outlook, thoughts and movements they cloned within a scripted act that wowed and amazed the spellbound mortals.

"If you can't be number one, you want to be the Guy standing next to him!" Crippled Crab had said when he, along with the rest of the Brotherhood in Rage crew learned of their success, which garnered praise from some, while others ate their words when a steady stream of curious clients coming through the front door echoed prosperity that ushered in the next phase of an "in your face" promotional plan, which saw a giant business card billboard placed atop of the long enclosed veranda facing the school across the street, where hundreds of students looking out of the classroom windows suddenly found themselves staring at a hint of forbidden fruits that would become rooted in their psyche, which at first beckoned only the most brave or fool hardy of younglings to cross the street in hopes of catching a glimpse of a real life vampire, however, within a few weeks a trickle of teenagers had morphed into hoards of young humans dotting the property at lunch hour, prompting Shadow to hire Dingus, the homeless teenage dirt bag they had discovered sleeping under the front veranda, whom they fed and gave a place to sleep in the coffin out in the foyer, in exchange for cleaning the studio and being a liaison to a younger generation of "mini-sips" as The Freak called them, whom, despite being too young to get pierced or tattooed without parental consent, simply their presence outside the studio made the place appear slammed every day, in another marketing ploy that soon attracted the attention of legal aged people driving by with more than lunch money in their pockets, translating into greater profits for The Freak, whom became so busy that his "Professional Shadow" had to find another tattoo artist to work in a vampire's castle, which at first had seemed like wishing upon a lucky star, until they ran into Skinny Jesus at The Night Matrix, where they still retained a part time gig doing the M.C. thing.

It had been years since they last seen Skinny Jesus whom still retained the same mundane personality and, quite possibly, was still wearing the same clothes? Nonetheless, his tattooing ability just happened to fit perfectly with their nocturnal theme, in a moment of Fate and Irony that saw Skinny Jesus become the full time daylight artist in the studio, which permitted The Freak to offer his tattooing talents by appointment only …after dark of course, and while this arrangement workout fine for a time, things soon got even busier compelling a Professional Shadow to recruit another artist, whom also conveniently showed up at the Matrix, leading to Slick Steel getting hired, who was an up and coming tattooist that specialized in the cartoon style artwork, and whom completed the foundation upon which The Freak could now grow the reputation of the studio, as the most revered tattoo shop in Home Town, and from there, well… there were no limits.

***REASON FOR LEAVING:*** The Freak won the wrong fight.

**10**

# *IRONMAN*

## PURGATORY PACKERS

### *Manure Town, ~ 2002 ~ Gut Stacker*

When the mortals began coming in from far and wide to get inked by a vampire and his brood of acolytes, and it was here that things got so busy that they tepidly made the decision to leave the M.C. gig for good and took up residence upstairs above the studio, from where they began running with the devil in a "two's up" scenario, which Shadow took a step further by writing a script of premeditated scenes they would act out in front of the unsuspecting clients with the purpose of creating an impression of telepathy between a vampire and his "Shadow", which proved to be the added touch to immortalize an experience beyond the ink and found everyone coming back for more and saw business booming for two friends in tune with The Energy, whom were defying the odds and the doubts of so called friends, namely those from a certain so called "Brotherhood", whom suddenly began kissing their asses, but The Freak and his Professional Shadow were just getting started.

After The Freak won eleven out of the fourteen tattoo art categories in Home Town's first ever tattoo expo, the stage was set for a hotter than hell tattoo studio to grow into the franchise The Freak had always dreamed of, which saw them open three more studios in quick succession, with one in Stink-Ville a few hours to the south west, one in Fed City two hours due west and one in Dynamite Harbor two hours due east, which invariably led to the hiring of more artists and body piercers until they were known as the "After" D.A.R.K. family, which even saw The Freak create his own body jewelry manufacturing line to supply all the tattoo studios that had begun to attract the attention of outside investors, as everything came together in preparation of the ultimate goal of opening a studio in every city right across MY-BIG-HOUSE, where it seemed like destiny, however…

Blinded by the light of fame and fortune, Shadow had become so immersed with the business that they had failed to notice how much their friend and brother was struggling under all the pressures of running a successful business, which The Freak had kept hidden inside like a tough guy, leading to the genie in a bottle effect that found him numbing The Energy surging within him to the point of overload, with prescription painkillers that he had been quietly getting from The Squid, whom had suddenly reappeared looking noticeably thinner and much whiter than usual, and from there, everything began to slowly fall apart.

While at first it seemed that The Freak had a handle on the wicker man of indulgence, when The Squid began showing up three times a week and things began going unpaid, like Shadow for instance, it didn't take a medical degree to know that their friend and brother had come down with the sickness of a hardcore pill addiction, which, having learned the consequences of drugs and addiction firsthand, Shadow knew their words of reason went mostly unheard when upon trying to reason with a best friend and business partner who was becoming ever distant thanks to the numbing effects of the synthetic troches he was eating.

"You're gonna fucking lose everything!" Shadow had told The Freak one night whilst standing in the jewelry making room, where hard words led to a shoving match between a vampire and his reflection, who bounced back with a flying fist that was aimed at waking a best friend from an illusion, but was pulled back at the last second by a one percent instinct… "Not him!" …which missed its intended mark in Death Valley and landed harmlessly above The Freak's left eye, who for a split second couldn't believe the martial arts student had struck the master, before initiating the foreclosure of a dream that sent the twin towers of Fate and Irony crashing down at freefall speed, leaving Shadow with a nasty black eye thanks to a heavy fist adorned with long finger rings that had failed to cut deeper than words when their best friend suddenly told them, "I don't want to feel guilty anymore doing my shit …so you need to leave."

After being served their first ever loss in a fight, Shadow sat at Crippled Crab's place looking like a homeless raccoon, contemplating a winless life that had just been thrust back into uncertainty, where a hard lesson in self defense and self preservation failed to soften the blow of losing a friend, a brother… "And our only fucking client!"

"Talk about searching with my good eye closed!" Shadow thought of their swollen right eye, which made looking for today a difficult prospect considering that they didn't seem to have any prospects left in a small town that had fallen prey to an epidemic of pharmaceuticals, which suddenly led them to look to the horizon for salvation, only, where to go?

"Where are you going to go?" Crippled Crab had asked the ultimate question, to which they did not have an answer that could provide a final destination within a life story of burnt bridges, however, when Tombstone happened to drop by to visit his best friend Crippled Crab, a faint glimmer hope was revealed when he mentioned some bad man living out west upon a distant prairie, whom just might be able to offer them a new lease on life ...if they could make it there.

"The Bad Man... Where have we heard that before?" Shadow wondered about a familiar name they could not place, to which a one percent instinct merely summarized, "We've met a lot of bad men!"

With a newfound direction in mind all that remained was to make the journey, which invariably brought back the memories of two previous long distance attempts at starting over, which made the notion of another leap across MY-BIG-HOUSE feel like a dangerous affair for someone about to once again put themselves and the mercy of Fate and Irony out on the open road, where the only thing they would be able to count on was them and nothing, after saying goodbye to romance one more time to a place that no longer felt like home, to which the only hard part about leaving again was saying adieu to dear old Mom, whom only wanted her sons to be happy as they set off into the sunset toward a without me future, all the while praying their old enduring sports car would make the four days trip across MY-BIG-HOUSE, where, the idea had been to stay a step ahead of Fate and Irony in hopes of avoiding catastrophe, but...

# Professional Shadow

"Well, praying was useless!" Shadow said after Fate and Irony had caught up to them in their sleep and killed an old whip beyond their ability to repair in the middle of nowhere, less than half way into the journey, which had suddenly placed them on foot to make a very long trek that didn't take long to make Shadow realize exactly how big MY-"BIG"-HOUSE really was, as they walked along endless, deserted woodland highways that became the final resting place for personal effects deemed too heavy to be carried, which had seen them liquidated via the roadside ditch in a literal trail of tears over losing everything they had in a highway man story of survival and hitched rides.

"You were supposed to be watching out for Fate and Irony!" Shadow muttered with disdain, as they stood on the side of the road dressed in a dark hood and their long black leather trench coat shielding them from the wind of passing vehicles.

"What… they snuck up on me!" Rob defended as cars zoomed past them, leading Shadow to imagine what must be going through a motorist's mind upon seeing a dark and mysterious figure in the hazy distance, which at first Shadow feared might make them appear too fearsome to be picked up, but to their surprise, it actually help stoke the curiosity of motorists, whom stopped to ask… "Where's the Harley?" …before giving them a lift that got them a few steps closer to Bastard Hamlet, a tiny tumbleweed town they reached four days later, by which point there was only one set of footprints in the sand, as Rob carried Shadow those last sore steps to a small diner, where they had been given instructions to meet The Bad Man and their potential savior.

"He chose a wise place to meet in case we don't make the cut!" Shadow thought about a neutral setting for a vetting, as they entered the tiny western eatery and suddenly felt like they had stepped back somewhere in time, when they saw a dining room filled with bonnets and top hats, whom suddenly stopped eating to stare and offer a stiff upper lip at the trench coat wearing drifter with the black bandana and sunglasses.

"This is weird!" Rob said on the inside as their attention upon the big burly man with the hard scowl seated alone at the table right in the center of the dining room like a circle surrounded by squares. "Double that!" Shadow whispered in the back of their mind as they took a seat across from the meanest looking S.O.B. they had ever seen, whose leathery facial features and thick bone spurred knuckles beheld the scars of combat, which bespoke of an individual whom had survived a hard fought existence and whom showed no emotion behind an iron gaze that was vaguely familiar?

"Welcome to the Desert Plains!" The big man said in a gruff voice that perfectly matched his rough appearance, as Shadow sat down across from someone whom looked like he could break the tiny table between them. Although they had a million questions, Shadow when straight for the one burning upon everyone's mind... "Have we met before?"

After a three thousand mile journey with over half of it travelled upon blistered heels, they were too exhausted to square dance around the obvious, but when The Bad Man asked if they had ever been to The Abyss Penitentiary and had known a certain lifer named Homestead, all of a sudden, a decades old question had been finally answered... "You're 'that' Bad Man?!"

Unbeknownst to Shadow at the time, Homestead had reached out to The Bad Man upon seeing someone with vaguely similar traits whom was possibly related, to which The Bad Man, upon learning that Shadow was doing time for a solid bit had given his blessing that a possible relative be looked after. "That's fucking crazy!" Shadow admitted, "They never told us that we had a guardian angel!" At that moment, The Bad Man merely chuckled and corrected them as they rose from the table, "Oh, No! I'm not one of those ...not officially anyway!"

After a hot shower and a solid meal followed by two days of comatose sleep, Shadow awoke to a fresh start that not only beheld the opportunity to move on from a dead and buried history, but it also gave them the rare chance to become someone else entirely, when The Bad Man asked, "So, what do you call yourself?"

At that moment, a life laid to rest flashed before their eyes creating a falling away from me moment that suddenly saw Shadow trade places with an alter ego, permitting Rob to come forth and take over "the wheel" of their body, as well as this story, while Shadow regressed within to become one with The Energy.

"So this is what it's like! I can see for miles!" Rob said with amazement, as he gazed with new eyes upon the endless rolling hills of a flat elevated landscape, where a person could watch their dog run away for three days, and where they were poised to begin a new journey as a new man, so to speak, with Rob now existing as the ninety-nine percent, and Shadow the one percent instinct upon a gypsy road travelled too many times. From that point on, it was Shadow's job to watch out for Fate and Irony, while Rob focused on getting it right in a last minute life, beginning with the reason they had travelled three thousand miles in the first place... "So, what is there for jobs in this sleeping village?"

"Ha! Ha! Ha!" When The Bad Man laughed wholeheartedly, Rob had been confused by their cousin's response to an honest question, but soon realized that the chase is better than the catch in a dusty outcrop of civilization, where The Bad Man explained, "There's only two things to do in Bastard Hamlet and that's hunting and fucking!"

Frowning, Rob failed to catch the obvious, and instead tried to imagine what type of game was hunted upon a baron prairie expanse, leading him to ask, "What do you hunt?" At that moment however, Shadow rolled their third eye to the inevitable punch line, as The Bad Man puffed his chest and stated proudly, "Something to fuck!" Although Rob smiled at their so called cousin's humor, a sudden twitch of anxiety at the thought of being stuck in a place that had zero job opportunities suddenly took root within the pit of their stomach, however, just when it seemed like they had wasted their time...

"Don't worry about it! I'll get you a spot on my night shift maintenance crew at the packing plant in the next town!" The Bad Man told them, which had been a relief at first, until Shadow echoed from within with two words that made them consider going back home... "Packing plant?"

"Ugh! What the fuck is that smell?" Rob asked in disgust as they drove along the hazy highway toward the place that was to become their source of income.

"That, my cousin… is the smell of profit!" The Bad Man boasted with a wide shit eating grin, which went unshared in the midst of a powerful stench of cattle feces, as they arrived at the packing plant, aka, a fucking slaughterhouse, which was a massive fenced compound that resembled a correctional facility on the outside, but in the inside, the place was a factory of death, churning out around the clock profits from the slaughter of thousands of head of beef cattle day and night, in a billion dollar babies protein industry feeding a savage world that counted for nothing to Rob, whose lack of certificates and high school diploma meant they were unable to join The Bad Man's maintenance crew, leaving only the freight department as a consolation prize.

"It's that or the beef chuck line in processing, where you'd be working standing up in one spot dressed like a clown all night next to a thousand foreigners with knives!" The Bad Man had warned after pulling a few strings to get them a "cushy" position within the freight department just off the kill chain?

***REASON FOR LEAVING***: A jailbreak from my own prison

## BROKEBACK WELL SERVICING

### *Manure Town, ~ 2003 ~ Roughneck*

Having just become just another cog in a suicide machine, Rob felt like a stranger in a strange land as they were led through the bowels of Purgatory, where they witnessed all the steps that thoroughly dissected a once living creature in the name of profit, in a scene that had been disturbing enough to imagine without seeing it in the gory flesh. Upon arriving to their post upon a tiny steam filled loading dock that was sandwiched between a blast freezer leaking ammonia and a scorching hot kill floor, there it became their job to stack endless boxes of cow innards all night long, whilst working next to a room painted psychopathy red by bloody guts. At that moment, Rob felt like they had just begun doing time all over again, which proved too much for Shadow to accept after having experienced purpose as a Professional Shadow, causing him to let go of reality and drift away as a supernaut of insanity, leaving Rob suddenly all alone to live and work without a one percent instinct in a place where even Fate and Irony did not wish to be.

"The things I do for money!" Rob told himself over and over, night after night, whilst dropping the beef tripe boxes taken from a conveyor belt onto a nearby pallet destined for cold storage, all the while dressed up in a hard hat, safety glasses, rubber gloves, rubber boots, and yellow rain pants, which made him feel like a goddamn clown in some merciless circus of blood and guts, waiting for a sign from the universe that would signal an escape from a waking nightmare of skinless cattle heads with eyeballs hanging out, which haunted his thoughts beyond a massive shop of horrors, leading to a taste for alcohol after work at home or at The Black Eye Saloon on weekends.

As the only watering hole in Bastard Hamlet, The Black Eye Saloon was where The Bad Man could be found putting away multiple rounds of one scotch, one bourbon, one beer, before knocking out some random rigger or dumbass cowpoke crazy or stupid enough to twist with a born fighter whom would first threaten his victims… "My cousin Rob here could knock your head clean off your fucking shoulders!" *BAM!* …before hitting the fool himself, since the dumbass was stupid enough to stand there listening instead of fighting, leaving Rob to sit there like a funeral bell to bloody barroom brawls within a faraway place that, unlike Home Town with its life to lifeless economy, the brown fields of a beef industry and the black sands of an oil industry guaranteed everyone had cash to burn.

Every time he heard the words "oil rigs", Rob had dared to imagine working upon the large heavy metal structures, drilling for the black blood of the land for which companies were said to be starving for workers and willing to pay top dollar to anyone with a pulse and a driver's license, whom was hardy or simply crazy enough to go work heavy labor in a high hazard environment of toxicity, which, in the span of one hundred years had transformed a once natural landscape into a petrochemical wasteland fueling humanity's insatiable need to get it on credit, all the while altering the future for the next generation that was certain to inherit…

"Oblivion…" It was Shadow's first word in over a year, which invoked a surprised, reflex reaction from Rob.

"Well, if it isn't the quitter!" Rob said aloud whilst sitting at the table with The Bad Man, whom immediately began looking around for a victim… "What? Who? Where…?" but, they merely waived him off, "Just thinking out loud. We're going for a leak!" In the washroom, they stood away from the disgusting urinal, where Rob read the writing on the wall for a good time, while Shadow hailed the coming of a very different future…

"It's time to seek out a purpose beyond the shitty low wage beef job… So, we're going to go work in the oilfields!" Shadow had said it with such conviction that Rob was inclined to believe they had it all figured out, "Oh yeah, so, what's the plan?"

"I don't know"

At first Rob was confused, "How the fuck is not knowing where were going and what were gonna do make any sense?" Moving to the sink to wash their hands, Rob gazed at their reflection in the dirty mirror, "Did Fate and Irony put you up to this?"

"No, it was Karen." Shadow replied casually like it was no big deal, which left Rob even more confused, "Who the fuck is Karen?"

Before a one percent instinct could reply, someone entered the washroom leading Rob to be silent and passive as Shadow whispered, "It's a long story. Just be ready for change when it happens!" There was no arguing they could do better than a shitty low wage job that had taken a year to save a few thousand dollars beyond the cost of The Bad Man's jalopy car, which Rob had bought and installed an a multi thousand watt sound system just to have ear shattering tunes playing on their way to a job within the programmed security of a shitty, yet, steady employment that Rob was hesitant to leave, however, when the beef industry was suddenly struck with some crazy cow disease that made a once steady job become unpredictable, it became vividly apparent that Fate and Irony had returned to rewrite their story…

"Ok then…" Rob agreed upon find the courage to leave Hell's half acre of death. "…Let's get the fuck out of here!"

Upon using their hard earned meager savings, Rob enrolled them into the necessary safety classes that were a prerequisite to gain entry into an industry of immediately dangerous to life realities, which would test both their wits and The Energy in ways they never before experienced, but would hopefully lead to a better state of survival, not-to-mention large paychecks for a junior high dropout looking to get on their feet quickly, so they could find another place to live away from The Bad Man and his bad habits once thought buried and forgotten, which had resurfaced to reveal why their cousin had chosen exile in Bastard Hamlet to begin with.

"Yeah, living there is becoming a pain in the neck!" Rob acknowledged about someone they respected, but could never fully trust in light of a nostril for narcotics.

## Professional Shadow

"Never mind him…" Shadow advised, "We've got a bigger neck problem to worry about before we go to work busting our ass in the oilfields!"

Sitting in the paid to pass first aid class, the waking memory of being brutally mutilated by some country quack, whom had hacked out a golf ball sized tumor from their neck, had left Rob looking worse that the C.P.R. stunt dummy they were practicing on, which had left behind a nasty scar that would need to be tattooed to remotely hide.

"That fucking sucked!" Rob admitted as they were given the last certificate to become another oilfield greenhorn, ready to go to war with Fate and Irony within a bleed for me industry, where a military management hierarchy acting like generals without the integrity, ensured that no one sang a happy earth song for long.

After getting hired with a resume bearing zero qualifications beyond a driver's license and the ability to breath, the desperate oilfield servicing company made them sit through a miniseries of shift the blame videos, followed by the signing of liability release forms aimed at covering a corporations ass, before expediently being put in the line of fire upon their first ever service rig as a roughneck, where a test of physical and mental endurance posed the ultimate question about whether or not their skin would be thick enough to survive an asshole rig pig crew bent upon breaking another greenhorn newbie, which created a bad vibe right from the start upon meeting their boss, Little Pushy.

Known as the rig manager, but described in the field as the "tool push", it didn't take long to discover why so many new hires did not last in the oil industry as Little Pushy made them work at a frantic pace risking injury, all the while barking orders and insults that crossed a thin red line more than once, leading Shadow to envision slapping the hat off someone with a clear inferiority complex...

"He's just a full of shit cokehead!" Shadow had deduced upon learning that Little Pushy liked snorting lines of coke off his desk in the rig shack when the oil consultant wasn't around, before marching out onto the oil lease to begin acting like ...an asshole. "C'mon you fucking idiot! Hurry up and lift those joints you pussy!"

Combined with good eating, the act of manually lifting the end of heavy pipe sections into the rig elevators all day long over seemingly endless work rotations had seen them regain the size and muscle mass of Shadow's previous prison workouts, resulting in regained strength and the ability to beat up their coworkers...

*REASON FOR LEAVING*: Little Pushy... pushed too far

# CRASH COURSE PIPELINE

## *Manure Town, ~ 2005 ~ Whipping Boy*

"These fucking clowns have no idea what we've been through …or what we can do to them!" Shadow plotted from back of their mind, as Rob continued to rise to the challenge of a career filled with adversity, all the while abiding by the unspoken rule of "what happens on the rig stays on the rig", meaning the job and all the bullshit involved with it, should never follow them to the dinner table, where sadly, Little Pushy dared to believe the rules did not apply to him.

Even off the rig, Little Pushy was a miserable prick to deal with, which often led Rob to quickly eat their meal and spend most of their time in the hotel room doing fitness training, when not writing down memories in a new pass time that provided a mental escape to being locked into a labor grind that was slowly taking a toll upon their body, however, on one particular evening, for reasons only Fate and Irony could conceive, Rob had decided to linger at the table after dinner, where they watched the guys get stoned and drunk within their hypocritical zombie ritual, which flew in the face of an industry drug testing everyone upon entry. It was about two minutes to midnight when they had seen enough and figured upon retiring to bed, however, when Rob got up to leave, Little Pushy decided to take one final fatal jab at destiny…

"Where are *you* going? Ha! Ha! Look at the lightweight! Run along now you fucking pussy!"

"Little Pushy is a fucking idiot, so never mind him!" Shadow had dismissed, however, when Little Pushy added, "You fucking stupid piece of shit!" Shadow suddenly changed their stance on a previous suggestion… "No more mister nice Guy… Go!"

In one motion, Rob placed their right foot upon the chair they had just risen from and used it as a launch pad to vault over the table at Little Pushy, whom was seated directly in front of them and whom fell over backwards in his chair in stunned surprise, when some kind of monster landed upon his chest and rode him bronco style to the floor whilst feeding him fists of fury, which put a rig manager to sleep along with a rigging career that had seen the largest paychecks they had ever earned, but failed to cover a tab of honor and respect.

"Feels good to stand on someone's throat and piss in their eyeballs, doesn't it?" The Bad Man had said with disturbing enthusiasm upon hearing Rob's tale of suffering overdue, as they sat over at The Black Eye Saloon where, flowing drinks paid for by a bank account padded with oil dollars had found them treading the blackened waters of a career choice that was seemingly always going to be an enduring fight.

"The little prick deserved it" Rob confirmed in an attempt to appear hard as a rock to someone with a "if you want blood, you got it!" outlook, which had been a vivid reminder of The Freak and his theories about violence whenever dollars could not solve a problem. On the surface, Rob was just cool surfin, but on the inside, he was at war with Satan, aka, Shadow, his one percent instinct warning of hardships within a life story guided by Fate and Irony... "If we haven't noticed by now, it's always give and take with those two, so we need to be the gambler and play the game until we get a grip on our purpose!" However, Rob didn't like the idea they were not in control of their life...

"Fuck that shit! Those two need to take a cosmic chill pill and back the fuck off our...?"

"Hey! Rob!" The Bad Man had tapped their shoulder to pull them from deep thoughts long enough to notice the fair looking girl whom had approached their table, whom they recognized as Caffeine, the bubbly socialite they had seen at the bar on Friday nights known for drinking copious amounts of coffee and hosting marijuana socials at her place. While they had never been attracted to her before, on this night they were sloshed and decided to go "hunting", leading Rob to follow Caffeine home after the bar for "coffee" at two AM, which was code for oral sex within a meaningful overnight relationship that turned into multiple returns, leading to a lingering presence over at her place in a who cares wins scenario that conveniently served up another place to be outside of The Bad Man's place, whose drug habits were becoming steadily worse in rerun scene they had watched too many times.

Standing at Caffeine's backdoor one groggy morning, gazing out to the back yard upon an old broken down sports car that was an identical match to the make and model they once owned, but had died whilst crossing MY-BIG-HOUSE, Rob was undecided if they were crazy or high to entertain a long term relationship with Caffeine... "You think she's a keeper?" Rob asked a one percent instinct, daring to wonder if a white picket fence reality could ever be in the cards for them, however...

"Our purpose will be revealed to us in time, but, until then, its best we travel light!" Shadow replied. Deep down, Rob knew this to be true and hated Fate and Irony for their crazy unpredictable life...! "Who are you talking to?"

It was Caffeine standing there in her birthday suit.

"I'm making a coffee and going back to bed! You should join me!" If there was ever one thing certain in their life, it's how uncertain it could be as they stealthily made Caffeine's place their permanent residence and became a social plug for a socialite and all her girlfriends, whom were the Bastard Hamlet gossip club that ritually gathered at Caffeine's place to turkey babble about all the latest happenings in a place where nothing ever changed, all the while drinking six pots of coffee and getting high on the shitty weed she was getting from her loser brother Flaky, whom was deathly skinny and kind of aloof, however, having grown up locally, was seemingly well informed about the semi local jobs scene.

"Just about every company out here is servicing the oil industry in some capacity, meaning there's more than just rigging jobs out there that pay just as good with less back breaking effort..." Flaky had said one day whilst resupplying his sister with his rag weed marijuana. "...like this blasting company I know about in Manure City. You'll get hired right away!"

Shadow had sensed something was off about The Energy in Flaky, but upon hearing the word "blasting", the thought of blowing stuff up had peaked their interest, so the next day Rob drove to the company Flaky had mentioned, only to discover that it was "sandblasting" outfit using high pressure air and sand to clean up large oil filed structures, which revealed a tedious and messy job they were not interested in doing, but also revealed Flaky to be the joker type whom liked to play head games.

"Why that little prick!" Rob said with contempt as they spun their old jalopy car around to leave, but just then, a sign in front of a building across the street suddenly caught Shadow's ethereal eye... *Hiring! Pipeline Laborers* ...so they went in there to apply with resume in hand in a last minute shit toss at the wall of fortunes, which got Rob hired by pipeline construction company?

"Take that Fate and Irony!" Rob said about their luck, when they were got hired on the spot and were handed the keys to a brand new pickup truck, which had been leased for a large pipeline project for which they had just been made the logistics Guy, which not only suddenly found them riding in style, but also impressed Caffeine when they got home to show off their new ride in which she suggested..."Let's go parking!"

Needless to say, Rob had a smile on their face the next morning when they reported for duty like a boss, where they met their co-workers in a flash of new faces that revealed large gaps within a labor pool of competent laborers, and explained why Rob had been given the logistics driver position over the others. There, within the mid stream sector of the oil industry, they filled a job role at a pipeline construction company that had been tasked with building a spider web of pipelines across hectares of farmland that would carry the hydrocarbons fueling society, which had been an eye opening experience leading them to realize how much stuff was actually buried beneath everyone's feet.

"This is good gig…" Shadow admitted over a month later, as they sat in the nice new rental pickup truck on their work break, reading their horoscope that predicted they would find work in a different field? "…It's just too bad this isn't what we're meant to do."

"The fuck you mean!? This job is cake!" Rob said in defiance as they got out of the truck to go use the disgusting portable outhouse, next to the safety shack in the materials lay down yard. "I think you're just overreacting! This job is too legit to quit! So, you just tell Fate and Irony to relax and not get their panties in a twist because, *we*, are not going anywhere!"

"As you wish…" Shadow said with resignation, just as Rob dropped their pants and hovered over the gross opening, "Sadly however… it's not *our* choice to make!"

At that moment the sound of a vehicle door slamming shut was heard nearby that commanded their attention, *SLAM!* followed by the revving of a familiar diesel engine, *VROOM!* which suddenly inspired a sour look upon Rob's face that had nothing to do with the smell of an outhouse. Frantically pulling up their pants, Rob opened the door just in time to watch as their nice, brand new rental pickup truck drove off without them!

***REASON FOR LEAVING***: High speed dirt.

# 11

# *ELECTRIC FUNERAL*

# DEAD-ZONE LANDSCAPING

## *Manure Town, ~ 2005 ~ Stunt Dummy*

"Well now… that's getting caught with your pants down!"

Shadow's stab at the obvious had only scratched the surface of a crazy scene that none could have foreseen, when one of the trench laborers got drunk at work and stumbled out from behind the job shack, only to find a brand new pickup truck just sitting there ready to go for a joyride, which had seen a fool drive recklessly along the pipeline right of way that ended when an idiot drove their new truck into the pipeline trench, causing damage to both the truck and the pipeline leading to a site wide safety stand down that carried other consequences beyond a "some heads are gonna roll" incident, as a pipeline construction company with a poor safety record was suddenly blacklisted by the oil client and subsequently punted from the project, leading to everyone including Rob being swiftly laid off in a double whammy of Fate and Irony, leaving them unemployed again and back to driving a jalopy car.

"…For fuck sakes!" Rob said with anger and frustration, over a series of unfortunate events that had been seemingly orchestrated by two cosmic entities with a fetish for screwing with their life and career. Although they felt trapped by the anxious mortal feelings gripping them, Shadow somehow remained optimistic…

"Just relax, our purpose will be revealed soon, I can feel it!"

Having heard that before, the thought of purpose in a scattered life was taken with a grain of salt by someone determined to prevent life from going back to the hardships of the past, but, since destiny was taking forever to reveal an elusive purpose upon a blind path, there seemed to be no other choice than to seek out another job that would at least provide a slim chance to survive long enough to see something happen.

"Fuck Fate and Irony...!" Rob said with renewed defiance, "We're getting another job!"

"You just have to rock the boat, don't you?" Shadow said with futility, when the engine in their jalopy car suddenly died the following week and was beyond their means to repair on a rationed budget, which suddenly created a tough reality for someone living in a remote tumble weed settlement that beheld no industry except for a potato mill and a sheet metal shop that Caffeine worked for, which wasn't hiring, leaving only curse words to express an opinion about the galactic fisting they were taking from the universe, "Fack!"

"I'm done talking to you. Just don't kill us!" Shadow said with exasperation, before going back to the silent lucidity of eternity, leaving Rob to stress out solo as they walked to the gas station near the highway for a pack of cigarettes, which gave them time to think away from Caffeine whom was being extra skittish that day thanks to all the coffee she was drinking with her girlfriends.

"I don't remember seeing that place there before" Rob noted as they strolled past a small warehouse that neither of them could ever recall seeing since their arrival in Bastard Hamlet, which made Rob pause in their tracks to peer at a tiny nondescript sign in the window, which revealed the place to be a landscaping company. "Hmm…?"

All of a sudden, Rob spawned an idea and went inside to get hired before Shadow could even say, "Here I go again!" where they spoke to the nice business owner, whom surprisingly, knew who they were thanks to the reputation The Bad Man, a perceived cousin whom the entire hamlet was afraid of.

"Stick that in your pipe and smoke it Fate and Irony!" Rob said with renewed cockiness after scoring a job as a mower rig operator, tasked with cutting the tall grass and vegetation along the highway roadside, which was met with silence from a one percent instinct, "What? You got nothing to say?"

Hoping that a last minute low paying job grab would at least offer spending cash, Rob tried to look to a future beyond a paycheck to perhaps going back to school to study for a real career, as they reported for duty the next morning with their best fake smile when the nice business owner introduced them to Beanstalk, a tall, lanky fellow whom was to be their supervisor out in the field.

At first greetings, Beanstalk had seemed like a nice guy whilst standing in the presence of the company owner however, once they were alone out on the side of the road next to the equipment, a smile was quickly replaced with a scowl of impatience, which made Rob suddenly look at Beanstalk like he had three heads and ask him… "Is there a problem?"

"Look at me weird all you want…" Beanstalk spat with a sudden arrogance, "Out here, I run the show! So, if you don't like, it you can quit now!"

Clearly not one to beat around the bush, for a split second there, Rob thought they could hear Fate and Irony laughing at them, after revealing their supervisor to be a two-faced human, however, upon double checking with a one percent instinct to see if they should knockout Beanstalk right then and there, a no-reply from a suicide messiah led Rob to grit their teeth and face the challenge ahead of them, hoping that it was the right move.

Aside from a slightly technical pre-trip inspection of the farm style tractor and the attached pull-behind mower unit, the rest of the job was child's play for someone of their skill and ability, which found them easily master the controls and the handling of a mechanical machine that crawled along at a snail's pace on the of side of an endless highway to hell all day long, mercifully secluded from their fucking dickhead supervisor except for the two way radio through which, Beanstalk used to communicate his commands and insults, from his own tractor rig on the other side of the roadway.

"I am the highway" Rob sang on the bright side of a boring job, which found them rumbling and bouncing within a tractor rig that was surprisingly equipped with an impressive stereo system, upon which they played heavy fucking metal really loud to drown out the mower noises and Beanstalk, whom continually threaded the needle of disrespect with his taunts, jeers and all around idiot comments...

*CHIRP!* *CHIRP!*

"What the hell are you doing over there!?" Beanstalk barked over the two-way radio about their lagging pace. "What's the matter? Are you just a little chicken shit pussy? Go faster! Or today, will be your last day!"

"We just gotta ignore Beanstalk and focus on the music!" Rob thought with slow and controlled breathing, allow their mind to escape the confines of the tractor cabin the same way their imagination could not be contained by a prison cell, which enabled them to journey back across the eras and memories that had seen good times, bad times and the ugly side of life, when Fate and Irony had taken a dump their cereal bowl of harmony, and interrupted their illusions of prosper...!

*CHIRP!* *CHIRP!* "C'mon dipshit! Go faster!" At that moment, rage began surging through their veins as Rob cursed Beanstalk out loud in the tractor cabin, "Who the fuck, does this asshole think he is!?" while maneuvering around power poles and their anchor wires, which added a layer of difficulty to a normally mindless task as the weight of anger found them pressing harder upon the accelerator, sending them rumbling over the rough terrain, making last second swerves around dangerous obstacles in one close call after another, all the while guided by a singular burning thought... "Die motherfucker die!" Rob seethed. "Beanstalk can go fuck himself, along with Fate and Iron...!"

Like every other time they came upon an anchor wire, Rob had veered sharply to the left just before reaching the steel cable rising up from the ground to the brittle wooden power poles, and then cut back hard to the right in a flowing zigzag movement that enabled the articulating mower unit to slither around stationary objects, however, given their increased speed, Rob had failed to notice an old anchor base jutting up from the earth, which had been obscured by the tall grass until the mower body suddenly hit the unyielding steel stub with a loud... *CLANG!* ...that suddenly caused the mower to hop violently to the right, where it landed upon the new anchor wire rising up to the power pole it was fastened to, and at that moment, Shadow finally spoke up from within their house of doom... "Oh, shit!"

In a chain of events that happened too fast for Rob to react, when the powerful mower blades made contact with the anchor wire, the steel cable was not only severed, but it also became ensnared within the spinning blades, which began reeling in the cable that produced a violently tug being applied to the top of the old power pole, effectively snapping it like a dry twig and sending the broken pole top carrying three live high voltage wires that crashed down upon their mower rig, which was now held fast by the anchor wire tangled in the mower blades.

*BOOM!* *CRASH!* *ZAP!* When the power lines made contact with the metal cab of the tractor, the sudden explosion of lightning outside the glass to their right caused the window to shatter, prompting Rob to immediately shut their eyes and instinctively curl into a fetal position within their seat, which protected them from the flying glass, but did little to lessen the concussion from a blast that hit them with such force, everything suddenly went dark, and when Rob came to, he was standing total darkness next to …Shadow? "Where are we?" Rob asked whilst looking around the emptiness, but Shadow did not reply as first as a faint glow suddenly appeared the distance, which appeared to merely linger in one place before suddenly beginning to get closer, moving ever faster as it drew near until the flicking light stopped before them, revealing it to be a burning candle resting atop an ancient desk of dry splintered wood, at which sat a mysterious figure shrouded by a brown cloak whom appeared to be looking over some old parchment papers that were unfurled upon the desk, and it was here that Shadow shared the obvious answer to his reflection's question. "We're in deep shit …that's where we are!"

For a moment that felt like a hundred lifetimes, they stood there in silence watching the cloaked presence, which seemed to be oblivious to their presence, until Rob opened his big mouth that is, "So, which one are you …Fate, or, Irony?" At that moment, Shadow bowed his head in defeat as the ethereal character turned its head toward them, revealing that it did not have a face.

"I'm Karma, but you can call me Karen…" the faceless figure replied in a cold tone that cut to the bone, "…And your asses are not talking your way out of this one!"

**REASON FOR LEAVING:** Ride the lightning

# MARATHON MODULAR HOMES

## *Crater City, ~ 2006 ~ Skinny Plumber*

When Rob blinked, they were back in a full fetal position inside their tractor rig, which was still trying to crawl its way forward, but held fast by the anchor wire entangled within the jammed mower blades!

Thinking quickly, Rob used their booted to kick the emergency kill switch that shut off the tractor engine and cut power to the mower, bringing everything to an eerie standstill that only amplified the sound of the electricity surging through the metal cabin around them.

"What do we do now!?" Rob asked in borderline panic to their dire situation, leaving Shadow to identify their only option, "…The two-way radio!"

Grasping the radio from its perch, Rob begrudgingly called out to Beanstalk, whom at first continued with his slander, unaware of the situation, "What's the matter pussy, can't figure out the accelerator pedal?!" which caused blood to boil once more as Rob calmly advised… "You should turn the fuck around and look …asshole!" To little surprise, when Beanstalk saw the accident he went into panic mode, "Holy shit! Don't fucking move!" to which Rob simply rolled their eyes to the obvious.

"We don't die here" Shadow reassured, as they sat waiting for the power company to arrive and free them from their electrified tomb, where they had time to reflect upon their encounter with Karma Karen, whom had not only revealed that Fate and Irony were pissed off at them for wasting time at dead end jobs, but, the time had come to begin pursuing a greater purpose.

"Uh, what exactly is our purpose again?" Rob asked with a hint of regret for not paying attention in a life and death situation, just as the power company finally showed up on the scene. "We're supposed to use The Energy to help others find it within themselves…" Shadow replied with a level of clarity that was remotely comforting in their moment of tragedy. "…however, before any of that, there's something we need to do once we get out of this mess!"

In all the commotion, passersby had stopped to witness the accident resulting in a sizable crowd gathered on the side of the road, where Beanstalk stood amongst the onlookers pointing and laughing as Rob sat trapped within a deadly predicament, until they were set free that is, when they marched straight over to their supervisor whom was still running his mouth when Rob got within two paces from the tall prick, at which time a one percent instinct took over that saw Shadow jump up to look an asshole dead in the eyes before exploding with an electrifying, hard right fist, which stuck Death Valley upon Beanstalk's face in a lightning crashes move that sent a now former supervisor to the pavement with blood leaking from his face!

"Fuck you! We quit!"

"You knocked out *another* supervisor? Oh, Rob!" Caffeine said with exasperation after they came home and told her the news about a near death experience. On that day, the notion of living out the rest of their life at shitty dead end jobs and go nowhere careers had died in a blinding flash, and been resurrected as a sworn vow to quit, or walk away from, anything or anyone that got in the way of one day sharing The Energy with the world, no matter what it took… "Hey…" …so they could live the life they were always meant to… "Hey…!" …and finally be free from a labor reality come hell or higher water and…!?

"Hey, Rob!" Caffeine had been trying to get their attention, which pulled them from a waking rant. "So… what are you going to do now?" The motive behind an innocent question was unmistakable, which instantly placed Shadow on their guard as Rob replied with an answer that deflected away from true intentions, "Not sure…"

Truthfully, their immediate plan had been to take the coming winter off and use the rest of their oilfield savings to fix the sports car in the back yard, which Rob had pickup off your Caffeine's landlord for next to nothing in its dilapidated state, and use it to go get a *job* in the spring. The very thought of going back to work at some shitty, hourly employment left a sour taste in their mouth, especially after what they had just experienced, which immediately placed them in state of unease upon sensing that Fate and Irony were already plotting their next clash with reality, they already wanted no part of, but quickly forgot about when Caffeine suddenly said with enthusiasm, "Perfect! Can I ask you to do something for me then?"

When Caffeine described how she was losing money selling weed to her friends for less than what she was paying to her brother, their first thought was, "So… you suck at math!" however, when she asked them to take over her small time black market marijuana business, Shadow replayed the cocaine blues that sent them to prison, prompting Rob to refuse the invitation outright. "No thanks!"

"Aw, please! I suck at selling weed!" Caffeine accurately pointed out with her most innocent face and an arched back pose, which had no effect upon a decision they believed was final, however, when Caffeine bit her finger nail whilst looking at Rob's crotch… "I'm great at sucking something else!"

With nothing but time and pleasure to kill over the harsh western winter, the first order of business had been to cut out Caffeine's brother Flaky from the equation, which found them resorting to an option they knew could yield consequences when

Rob tapped The Bad Man to hook them up with a cheaper and better product from his contacts in Bovine City, a few hours north of Bastard Hamlet, which saw their cousin doing the pickups for a fee, after which they portioned out the quantities before handing it off to Caffeine, whom sold the sweet leaf to her girlfriends just like before, only now any deals had to go through Rob, whom was immune to the "but we know each other" con lines, in a same shit different day reality that now found Caffeine turning profit, while they made a cut for essentially doing nothing, which was just fine as Rob turned their focus to the back yard and to the undertaking of a rebuild project to transform a derelict old sports car into a new abortion of hopes and dreams that hopefully, would one day be their ticket out of Bastard Hamlet, with, or without, Caffeine.

Across the frozen months, Rob went from Caffeine's warm bed to the cold, snowy back yard, where they weathered the elements to painstakingly restore an old classic to its former glory, taking care to address every little detail within a hobby stress release and meditation, until springtime finally arrived and a once doomed automobile destined for the scrap heap had become to a thing of beauty once more.

"Wow!" was the common word used by everyone to praise their efforts driven by The Energy, not-to-mention the ability to create something out of nothing using meager resources and a shit ton of ingenuity, which had all been proven true the moment Rob turned the ignition key and the engine roared to life in a proud Mary moment of smiles and cheers over having beaten the odds, which was suddenly interrupted by Caffeine yelling out to them from the house, where they walked in to announce with

## Professional Shadow

excitement, "It's alive!" only for Caffeine to make their cheer disappear, "Uh... I think we should split up!"

According to her, Caffeine no longer wanted the be around the weed business, which had grown exponentially since hiring The Bad Man to feed the supply, however, the fact that she had gone straight to the part of break up instead of simply requesting Rob give up the flower business, it was easy for Shadow to spot the obvious that wasn't... "She's got eyes for someone else!"

While they had actually grown fond of Caffeine's bubbly company, when Shadow reminded Rob of their vow to not waste time on dead end destinies, who simply said, "Ok..." and packed up a renewed hot-rod with no love lost, and headed up around the bend to The Bad Man's place, where they moved back in the basement.  and then relinquished all interests to a black market contraband business, which had stained their sense of morality by forcing at times to forget they had any, whilst surrounded by people with no ambition to make anything of their lives except to get high and dream about a future they could not see and would never make happen.

"The fairytale is over" Shadow said in eulogy as they tried to envision an escape from a soul sucking place, by looking at a map of MY-BIG-HOUSE and attempting to use The Energy to teleport their mind to places they knew nothing about, in hopes that something might reach out from the unknown and grab their interest. Alas, when nothing was all they encountered, all they could do was sit at the edge of tomorrow and wait for the universe to give them a sign that would give them direction in a new subchapter that...! *BUZZ* *BUZZ*

## Professional Shadow

"Hey..." It was Caffeine calling, which nearly put a smile on Rob's face in the hopes that she was looking for a bootie call, however, when she asked if they could fix up her friends from out of town with drugs, the weight of an inescapable rap game found them stone faced and somber, as they reluctantly agreed to help a hypocrite, which led to a ball and biscuit favor for Gum Rot, an electrocution survivor with exploded teeth, and for Longshanks, a smooth operator whom was capable of using The Energy to make the mortals fall to pieces, which Shadow had easily seen through and warned Rob to..."Don't believe the hype!"

At first glance, it all seemed like another meet and greet that would not lead anywhere, but when it was revealed that Gum Rot and Longshanks worked at a company that constructed modular homes and they could get Rob a job there, a disdain for drug addicts was ignored when Gum Rot and Longshanks said almost jokingly that they could give them a tiny spot on the floor at their place in Crater City, which was about two hours south of Bastard Hamlet, where they ended up that very night after packing up the old sports car and driving away from a place they hoped to never see again.

"You think this was a bad move?" Rob asked with ninety nine percent apprehensions, upon walking into a flophouse filled with wayward runaways and homeless transients. "Of course..." Shadow replied without hesitation to an unexpectedly difficult situation, which had just revealed that their hosts had not been kidding about a "tiny spot on the floor", as Rob dropped their travel bag full of clothing into a free corner within a living room populated by the hapless and the hopeless, using it as an ass mattress to sleep upright between the walls of Fate and Irony until the next morning, when they awoke sore and weary from a seated slumber, only to discover Gum Rot and Longshanks still up doing drugs with less than an hour to go before they had to report for work.

Needless to say, Rob did not use the reference of junkies, nor did they reveal any association to the sons of plunder in the on-the-spot interview at the modular home company, where an available position within the plumbing department that was always desperate to find someone retaining manual dexterity and the ability to read a measuring tape, which seemed like a job that was right up their alley as Rob was hired on the spot and swiftly placed upon the largest assembly line they had ever seen. There, they were introduced to Lard Ass, the plumbing supervisor whom complimented them for the first three days working together, "You've got a bright future here!"

"More like famous last words!" Shadow said with disdain when Lard-Ass, the certified lazy plumber disappeared to hide in his office and left a new hire alone to do the job of two people, in a death march of endurance that found them literally having to run up and down a very long production line to reach their moving work stations, where they measured all the piping pieces to fit an ever changing floor plan thanks to a flooring crew that didn't give two shits about accuracy, before running all the way back to a saw to cut said pieces and then run all the way back again in a relay race of labored futility...

***REASON FOR LEAVING***:Run rabbit run

# SAINTS & SINNE'S FABRICATION

## *Crater City, ~ 2005 ~ General Apostle*

"This is fucking stupid!" Rob grumbled as they limped upon blistered heels at the edge of exhaustion from a lack rest within a realm of chaos filled with wayward addicts whose sole purpose was to party all night to the doping persuasions of Gum Rot and Longshanks, whom were aware that Rob was wise to their games that led to an atmosphere of reduced chivalry toward the only one whom was sober and irrelevant, like an elephant in a room filled with the fallen whom had sold their souls for that next hit.

"We can't do this much longer" Rob warned as they grabbed a handful of earplugs from work in anticipation of the open house party taking place that night back at the crack shack, where even more addicts would be showing up to participate in a toxic trace of empty belonging that found them sitting in their tiny corner that night trying not to pass out in the presence of twenty something other humans getting wasted.

Simply being in a place surrounded by human black holes was a drain upon The Energy to the point that seemed like it would flameout, however, just as Rob was about to exit stage left from reality, Shadow suddenly sensed The Energy of salvation enter the scene in the form of two late arrivals to the party, whom suddenly offered the unwitting opportunity for Rob to score a mercifully quieter sofa in a cleaner environment over at Twig and The Douche's place, where they got a decent night's sleep after convincing a pair of early twenties posers with no driver's license that, having someone to chauffeur them around in a cool sports car was better that having to walk everywhere, in a hustle of egos that provided an escape from a shithole they would never return to.

"Not where I thought we would be at our age!" Rob admitted upon contemplating the last 14 years of crazy, which found them with no home, no credit, no savings, no education, and a criminal record forever haunting their steps like an invisible specter of limitations. "Yeah… It's going to be a rough go, but our time will come!" Shadow reassured as Rob sat upon a sofa of saving grace, where they got to know their hosts, Twig, the scrawny and timid one of the donkey duo whom they had easily swayed to provide them with a place to crash, while The Douche, as the big and bulky brute with an openly ignorant attitude to match his large body size, had been the tougher nut to crack, necessitating the purchase of drugs from Longshanks to seal the deal and appease a phony "I'm the man" ego that was more annoying than our typing errors in a future biography.

In a bid to keep things positive, Rob shied away from arguing with a procrastinator born of a condescending ego, all the while trying to outrun the "I quit clock", at a job that was a physically and morally draining marathon of madness for a paycheck rivaling a government social assistance payment. Although the goal had been to earn enough so they could quickly find another place to live, lacing up steel toed boots that now felt like they were made of concrete, the inevitable was already written drove to work under ominously familiar grey skies, which never fail to set up a suspenseful twist within a hard fought story of destiny and survival that Rob wished would simply end.

"Careful what you wish for!" Shadow said when Rob could go no further at a job that had seen an 8 mile shift before lunch break, when they told Lard Ass the lazy plumbing supervisor hiding in his office… "Better lose weight cupcake! *You*… have a job to do!" …before leaving for good in yet, another "I quit" finale that, despite granting an instant feeling of relief from having to endure a slave routine of solo suffering, the sudden return of anxiety over the loss of a much needed income had seen the return of the same old question…

"What are we going to do now?" Rob wondered as they glanced through the jobs obituary in the local Crater City newspaper, whilst sitting in their trusty old sports car at a coffee shop they drove to each morning to maintain the appearance of still being employed, and to avoid giving The Douche the advantage over their difficulty situation, whom would surely seize upon a rock bottom opportunity to worsen a period of vulnerability.

"What they don't know won't hurt us…" Rob had resolved in their quest to find employment elsewhere, "…As long as we have wheels to drive our sorry ass around, we'll be useful to our hosts, and will find another…?!

When Rob placed the car in drive and it didn't move, a sudden rush of worry washed through them upon remembering how the occasional hesitations emanating from the car's transmission, had inspired to the notion that a future problem might catch up to them one day.

"I guess today is the day" Shadow said about their luck and how shitty it seemed to be, which they both knew was the result of Fate and Irony playing tug of war with The Energy, leaving behind a mechanical problem beyond repair with available resources, which suddenly removed the one bargaining chip to warrant their presence upon a precarious sofa, where they were instantly at odds with their hosts, namely The Douche, whom jumped all over the chance to impose his will of arrogance upon another's misfortune.

"Looks like you're useless to us now" The Douche gloated at having the upper hand over Rob's reality, which had set in motion an unspoken deadline to their presence, within a tense living arrangement that eventually reached a breaking point that weekend, during the open house party hosted by Twig and The Douche, where the addition of alcohol removed a veil of chivalry and civility, leading to a heated argument about integrity …and a fucking driver's license, in front of a drinking and snickering crowd that prompted The Douche to demand that they leave when the party was over...

"…Because he's really just a pussy who can't physically throw us out!" A futile confirmation by Shadow did nothing to change the fact that they were going to be looking for some park bench to sleep on that night, as Rob smoked a cigarette outside to calm down before going back in to collecting their meager belongings, which had brought about a sinking feeling of vertigo in a hopeless moment of…?

"Excuse me, can I have a light?" A fair looking woman holding a liquor bottle had walked up and asked them for a light for her cigarette, to which Rob accommodated with a perturbed look on their face that compelled the mystery girl to inquire... "Are you two ok?" ...which totally caught Rob off guard in a sabbra cadabra moment that even failed to prepare Shadow for what they heard next, "You know, it's *His* will that none should suffer alone" the woman said with a wink before turning to saunter back into the house, where she gave them a quick glance before entering.

"Well, how many invitations do we need?" Shadow asked with exasperation, which found Rob going back inside to seek out this mysterious maiden, whom offered up an unexpected miracle when Sabbra told them that they could stay at her place until they got on their feet? "Just a minute, we'll go get our things" Rob said with a one finger gesture, before going to grab their travel bag of clothing and scant worldly possessions, only to return and find The Douche attempting to push up on their drunken salvation, which immediately set in motion a scene of redemption versus retribution as Rob switched their travel bag from their right hand to their left and calmly approached a princess and a prey.

"I'm ready, let's go!" Rob said to Sabbra standing in front of them, which naturally evoked an offensive reaction from The Douche standing off to their left...

"Hey! Fuck you!" The Douche said in drunken protest as he predictably attempted to shove them away using his right arm, which Rob deftly avoided by suddenly leaning back out of the way causing The Douche to miss his mark and place him into an off balance, forward lean that left him wide open to receive a right hook haymaker coming up from under his outstretched right arm, which caught a dumbass in Death Valley between nose and cheek bone, in a get back counter strike powered by The Energy that jolted the room into stunned silence, as a bully's face began raining blood as he crumpled to the floor unconscious.

"Well, have a good night everyone …and you're welcome!" Rob said with a smile as they took Sabbra by the hand and left a lame duck party to escort her home like a rolling stone, whom could not believe a last second stroke of luck at having dodged the proverbial bullet of banishment.

"Did this just happen?!" Rob thought with disbelief and a measure of satisfaction, as they arrived at a large Victorian style home that even compelled Shadow exclaim… "Fucking score!" …upon seeing the large majestic dwelling that Sabbra said she lived in all by herself. Indeed, Rob felt like they had won some galactic lottery upon entering the grand residence, only to realize that a magnificent manor had been butchered into multiple living units for profit, and that Sabbra lived all the way up in the oddly tiny attic loft, which was no bigger than a fucking bird cage? "Ok, what!?" Rob questioned as they stood at the entrance of Sabbra's tiny bachelorette suite, where she immediately bolted to the bathroom to clean up her act, whilst yelling over her shoulder… "Make yourself at home!" …before slamming to the door shut, effectively leaving them still standing at the entrance.

"She's probably taking a dump!" Shadow figured while Rob took in the claustrophobia of a tiny apartment that could be viewed with just one glance from where they stood at the entrance, revealing a woman's place heavily decorated with religious pictures, statues …and religious trinkets?

"What in the holy Hell…?" Shadow echoed Rob's curiosity, whom stood in open mouth awe at the sheer amount of religious crap and faux artifacts plastered all throughout the place, which had suddenly revealed a keep the faith obsession bordering upon possession, compelling them to look back out the still open entrance door behind them, where Fate and Irony stood blocking their path. "Fuck… nowhere to run!"

At that moment, the bathroom door suddenly swung open and Sabbra reappeared in the doorway wearing nothing but her birthday suit singing… "I'm ready!" …which made Rob wonder if they were "ready" to take one for the team. "Amen?"

After a weird weekend of sex and sweaty sermons about being a holy daddy's favorite apostle, Rob had no more doubts about having fallen into the clutches of a sociopathic holy roller with a dissociative disorder, whom was on some divine mission to spread the good word by apparently spreading her legs and kissing little popes? "Whoa! Whoa! Wait a minute…" Rob couldn't believe their ears. "Are you saying that God is your Daddy?!"

When Sabbra nodded with enthusiasm and replied, "Daddy is in the room with us right now!" the thought of being in some spiritual spit roast suddenly found them feeling uneasy about being hooked up with a crazy broad with an affinity for anal absolutions, whom believed that everything she ever wanted in life was simply going to fall from the sky?

"Don't you mean that you're hard work at your job and the money you save will buy you these things?" Rob attempted to paint logic to Sabbra's otherworldly statements, but when she remained defiant in her faith that it would all come from her Big Bang Daddy in the clouds, Shadow thought, "That's it, we're sleeping with a weapon from now on!" while Rob suddenly wondered, "What *do* you do for money, honey?"

They breathed a sigh of relief when Sabbra did not say "nun", or "prostitute", or both, but instead revealed that she was a welder's assistant in a steel fabrication shop, where, despite picturing her in a straight jacket, Rob had been somewhat impressed by the thought of a woman doing a tedious job within a predominately male chauvinist industry, which suddenly seemed like a job they could do… "Are they hiring?"

On the inside, Shadow thought for certain the idea would be shot down in flames, however, when Sabbra told them that she could get them hired at her place of work, Rob actually thought they might be able to overlook her Holy Father fetishes, until… "Yes! I can get you hired!" Sabbra said with enthusiasm, but then added a strange stipulation, "But, you can't say we're sleeping together!" compelling Shadow to wonder with one percent curiosity, "Now why would she feel the need to say that?"

***REASON FOR LEAVING****: Divine intervention*

# 12

# *LORD OF THIS WORLD*

# DREAMS, REALITY, HEART

## *Crater City, ~ 2006 ~ Visionary*

In an era when the advent of social media beckoned everyone to plaster their faces all over the internet and expose their personal lives like an open book, a distracted world could not see the folly of worshipping prophets of profit whom preached about salvation through "send me your money" sermons, all the while refraining from pointing a bought and paid for finger at the holy wars financed by genocide junkies profiting from death and killing in the name of the almighty dollar.

"It's all shit…" Rob dismissed with an Atheist's point of view, whilst secretly praying for an escape from a faithfully futile situation, "But, if there is a God up there somewhere, we could really use a fucking miracle right about now!" When a moment passed and nothing happened, the arms of sorrow embraced them with visions from the dark side for believing that anything except for The Energy inside them had the power to initiate change in their life.

"Don't bother…" Shadow corrected as the only one how knows, "…Mr. 'Fire-in-the-sky' never answers. Its Fate and Irony we have to bribe!" Speaking of bribes, when Rob finally did their taxes for years gone by, they realized that a system of taxation was like a casino, handing out less than it takes in without caring about individual heritage, or, even a name, so long as an Adamu could be linked to the sinful number that enslaves everyone at birth to an economic straw person, governed by laws that are not taught in public schools. "Congratulations, we are worth a whole twenty eight hundred bucks!" Shadow mentally pat them on the back, as Rob opened the strangely large brown envelope that also arrived in the mail at Sabbra's place, after revealing their exact location to a government system...

*NOTICE OF DISSOLUTION*

Their eyes grew wide upon reading a corporate death certificate stating that a once fulfilling career as a Professional "Shadow" through their "Devil's Right Hand Inc" consulting firm, had been dissolved due to non-activity, thus driving the final nail in the crucifixion of a dream that never fulfilled its destiny, leaving Rob to stare blankly at a black and white memory that doubled as a bullet with butterfly wings within a life that seemingly was never going to play nice. At that moment, not even a few thousand dollars tax return could stop them from feeling small on the grand stage of life, leading Rob to bow their head in shame and mourning…

"My body is a cage" Rob sighed before leaning back in the chair and glancing up at the wall, where their gaze fell upon the obscenely large cross that Sabbra had hung up to worship the death of a rumored healer and protester, whose sacrificial suicide had gotten him served once upon the cross for defying a totalitarian rule that would go to any lengths to kill The Energy within someone supposedly resurrected three days later?

"To live is to die" Shadow echoed from within a mortal prison, which suddenly inspired Rob with the notion that, for Devil's Right Hand Inc to live on, it had to die and pass on before it could ever ascend to something greater as…? Rob paused to look at their now defunct business title, where they killed off the words of a forgotten past one at a time, while retaining the first letter of each word to find a new meaning for… "D… R… H… Inc…"

Distracted by the weight of destiny and a freak show religious reality, Rob could not muster the black magic to see past the crazy they were caught up in, so Shadow found a way… "Dreams… Reality… and Heart…" The words lingered in the air like a holy trinity waiting for Fate and Irony's blessing to become the slogan of their devotion, "…If you, want your 'Dreams' to become a 'Reality', you need to have …Heart?"

Unsure if an ode to courage, strength and wisdom was a great quote, it was nonetheless a reminder to never quit chasing dreams with all their heart regardless of people, places, or fucking jobs, which had been uplifting enough to motivate them to share their revelation with Sabbra, whose affinity for all things spiritual healing seemed to make her the perfect candidate to test out a slogan for a possible future foundation of personal motivation that might one day become Dreams-Reality-Heart…?

"No! Only Daddy can tell me what I need!" When Sabbra resolutely cast aside their rebirth of a dream, Rob was floored through the seven gates of Hell by a religious hypocrite with a psychotic devotion to a biblical soap opera, which had just reached its finale with Shadow whom thought they might throw up at the next mention of a divine daddy. "Ok, time to bail out of this cuckoo's nest!" Shadow stated with urgency, but again, the question arose... "Where are we going to go?" Drowning in a pool of uncertainty, Rob knew they just couldn't simply go stand on the side of the road with their thumb out and hope for Fate and Irony to...!

*BUZZ!* *BUZZ!* *...BUZZ!*

"Hell!" When Rob answered their cell phone, they had not been expecting to hear the voice of an old acquaintance after years without any contact, however, when The Goblin spoke; his words knocked Shadow clear out of their mind once more upon learning that... "Crippled Crab is dead!"

At that moment, Sabbra and her bad religion, along with the rest of the solar system suddenly ceased to exist, and was replaced with the singularity's sorrow as they mustered The Energy, to ask a singular question, "...How?" Nothing could have prepared them for what The Goblin described next, which involved a crime scene straight out of a murder movie when they learn that Crippled Crab had murdered his longtime girlfriend Paula, after she revealed that she was leaving a broke and broken man, whom took out his twenty five caliber handgun and shot his soon-to-be ex-girlfriend in the head whilst she slept, before turning the gun upon himself and taking his own life?

"Wow..." It was all Rob had time to say before Shadow choked off an airway with the grief of losing a, "...A true friend in my darkest hour..." Sadly however, given the heinous act committed by Crippled Crab when he punched two tickets to the afterlife, a man once considered a friend and brother could no longer be remembered as anything more than a coward ...and a murderer. "When did it happen?" Rob asked from a near catatonic state, as if a timeline would change anything.

"Two weeks ago" The Goblin answered with a cold finality that had already moved on from a road kill morning. "I would have called you sooner, but you're a hard person to track down!" A flash forward of events filled their mind as Rob admitted, "Yeah... sometimes we have trouble finding ourselves" but just then, Shadow suddenly remembered that Crippled Crab had been close friends with Tombstone, compelling the question, "How's Tombstone taking it?"

The Goblin took a deep breath, which somehow sucked all the air out of the room through the phone, "Like shit! He couldn't go to the funeral of a murderer that killed his wife's sister!" Again, they were blown away by the revelation, leaving Rob to shake their head as Shadow raged inside over losing a friend that they could not honor. "You should call Tombstone..." The Goblin ended, "I'll give you his number."

As the dial tone rang in their ear, Rob tried to pass the call to a one percent instinct, "You should take this?" but Shadow, feeling banned from heaven had not the will to come forth in a forsaken life, for which they firmly blamed Fate and Irony... "Hope you fuckers are happy!"

Clearly, the reality of a cowardly act had been a hard pill to swallow for Tombstone, whose few words on the phone spoke volumes within a coffin bound conversation that beheld no joy and no hope that anything good could come from a grim tragedy, except for that unexpected moment when Fate and Irony suddenly gave rise to opportunity…?

"We need to get away from this crazy chick we're stuck with!" Rob said to Tombstone, who suddenly informed them that he might know someone up in Dead Man City some eight hours north of their location that might be able to help them out with a place to stay and a job within the oil industry… "I'll give him a shout and call you back!"

Waiting for a call back that would either confirm or kill their hopes, Rob thought about a place they had never been, yet had heard much about from the oil hounds they had encountered, whom had claimed Dead Man City to be a major petrochemical hub in addition to being the murder capital of MY-BIG-HOUSE, but for them, it was a place they aimed to call home upon receiving confirmation from Tombstone to… "Get your ass to Dead Man City and Chaos will pick you up!"

"Chaos…?" Shadow echoed in Rob's mind, "Wonder how he got that name?" In a lifetime of crazy nicknames that more often than not served as an accurate description of mortals they had known and humans they had met willingly, or otherwise, they had essentially given up hope to ever meet anyone that was normal within a life that was prone to Fate and Irony's last minute mood swings, which by now everyone is vividly aware could be quite a fucking thing, but, they were nonetheless compelled by the sound of perseverance.

"We don't feel well. We're calling in sick tomorrow" Rob had told Sabbra to get out of going to work the next morning, which found her going to work while they were left alone to pack up their few belongings at an unhurried pace before bidding adieu to a religious rocket queen, whom would arrive home after her shift to find a "don't go away mad, just go away" dear Jane letter they had left upon the coffee table to say thanks for the sex and chivalry, before walking their ass to the bus depot and departing Crater City forever with a one way ticket to a place that was hardly paradise city.

"I kind of feel bad" Rob admitted whilst gazing upon purple hills colored by the setting sun, but on the inside, Shadow reminded them of their first day at a new job they had just quit, where the potential to learn all about the science of building large structures made from heavy steel had been erased upon watching Sabbra openly flirt with the dirty, unkempt male co-workers, whom judging by their body language had already climbed her stairway to heaven!

"Gross!" Rob thought with a chill before asking a one percent instinct that fated question, "Have we figured out how we're going to make a business out of Dreams-Reality-Heart?"

"A plan is still being formulated" Shadow admitted as the landscapes rolled past in a moment of déjà-vu upon a bus ride that felt an awful lot like the day they had been released from prison, only, this time things were different as they reflected upon the madness they had just endured, where, the death and rebirth of dream had strangely made all the insanity seem worth it in a lifetime of crazy.

**REASON FOR LEAVING**: Dreams, Reality …and Heart.

# BAD DEAL AQUA-DIGGING

## *Dead Man City, ~ 2006 ~ Groundhog*

"Well that's great, but let's not do that again!" Rob advised as they arrived at a bus depot that was conveniently located next to a Y.M.C.A. "...And by the way, you might want to fast forward any bright ideas about tomorrow, because here we go!"

"Be ready for anything" Shadow cautioned after an all too familiar "Who is this?!" phone call had left them standing in doubt upon a big city street corner surrounded by high rises and homeless beggars asking for spare change, as they waited for Chaos to show up and...!

*SCREECH!*

When a bright orange sports car suddenly skid to a halt beside them, Rob immediately knew it was their ride and got in, where they were greeted by a long haired driver wearing sunglasses at night who looked like he was high on more than just life as they took off in a cloud of smoke from squealing tires and roared through a maze of streets like a bat out of hell, speeding towards a final destination under cover of darkness.

"Can you even see where you're going?" Rob asked whilst attempting to not appear nervous sitting within an old classic car that had been manufactured before seatbelts had been deemed mandatory.

"Me? Fuck yeah!" Chaos answered in a speedy, yet, distant tone that failed to inspire confidence, "I broke my prescription glasses..." Chaos explained as they swerved around traffic at break neck speeds that whipped them around in their seat. "...but I can see the taillights of the cars in front of me!"

Hanging on for dear life within a life in the fast lane city tour, Rob's their pulse wasn't the only thing racing as they rode along in a ride or die reality, which had taken them far and wide across a country of origin, a native nation, a homeland...

"MY-BIG-HOUSE...!" *SCREECH!*

Shadow never finished their thoughts as the stopping G-force sent him into the back of Rob's bulging eyeballs upon suddenly coming to a screeching halt on some unknown street within a lost neighborhood, where Chaos announced, "We're here!" which compelled Rob to quickly glance around wondering where the hell they were, however, before they could say anything, Chaos then added, "Oh, by the way, there's something you should know before we go in there... I live in the basement of my brother's place and he has a girlfriend with a kid!"

After all the insanity they had witnessed in the last few months, not-to-mention their life, the notion of an arguing couple and a crying child seemed mighty tame, especially when they compared it to living with a religious nymphomaniac as they crossed the threshold into the place that had just become their new ho...! *CHOKE*

"Ugh! What the fuck is that smell!?"

They had been unprepared when the overpowering pungent odor punched them in the face with an invisible stink fist, which left Rob teary eyed to take in the sight of the dirty kitchen they had just entered, which was decorated by rotting garbage, dirty diapers and an overflowing cat box where naked baby girl was seen playing with the clumps!

"Nice…" Rob muttered with sinking hopes, while Shadow used The Energy to profile a scene retaining the hallmarks of chronic patterns exhibited by, "…Fucking addicts!" Rob finished a one percent silent observation that found Shadow ready to throw up in the fourth dimension…

"For fuck sakes" Rob sighed with a labored breath of despair, as they followed Chaos down into the basement, where, it was mercifully tidier and did not reek of putrefaction thanks to the closed door at the top of the stairs, however, standing there looking at one room with one bed, they couldn't help but wonder… "Where are we gonna sleep?" …but just then, they caught a scent of another chemical odor, one that sadly proved their previous observations to be true…

"Is that… cra…!"

*BOOM! BOOM! BOOM! BOOM! BOOM! BOOM*

"What the fuck is that!?" Rob said with sudden panic, as they looked at Chaos for confirmation that the thundering noises echoing from above were not…

*BOOM! BOOM! BOOM! BOOM! BOOM! BOOM*

"The kid…" Rob realized with despair, as the two ton toddler heel stomped its way back and forth across the floor upstairs…

*BOOM! BOOM! BOOM! BOOM! BOOM! BOOM*

…which was made worse by the unfinished and un-insulated ceiling downstairs that amplified a child's footfalls tenfold...

*BOOM! BOOM! BOOM! BOOM! BOOM! BOOM*

"How the fuck, do you put up with that!?" Rob asked Chaos in a moment of shock and awe that could only be topped by the response they got… "I smoke crack!" Chaos stated openly with a sheepish grin, which only added more weight to the gravity of a tortured situation,

*BOOM! BOOM! BOOM! BOOM! BOOM! BOOM*

"Motherfucker…" Rob thought with tired exasperation, at the notion that everyone in Dead Man City just might be a rock head, but there would be no rest for the wicked as Shadow immediately began plotting an escape from the fucking twilight zone they had just walked into. "Ok, first of all, we're going to find some fucking earplugs… savvy?"

*BOOM! BOOM! BOOM! BOOM! BOOM! BOOM*

"Then…"

*BOOM! BOOM! BOOM! BOOM! BOOM! BOOM*

"Then we're going to hurry up and get the fuck out of this crack hole as soon as immortally possible!"

*BOOM! BOOM! BOOM! BOOM! BOOM! BOOM*

## Professional Shadow

"Stop eating cat shit!" The bitch girlfriend yelled. "Waa...!" The child cried, which all added to the urgency of an escape plan that could not be understated when Chaos showed them a pile of blankets on the floor in the furnace room that was a fitting welcome to a new life of struggle in Dead Man City, where they could only hope that Fate and Irony would go easy on them, as they chased a rainbow in the dark.

"So... Tombstone said you can get us a job. Is that true?"

When Chaos nodded and revealed that he could get them hired at his place of work as an assistant aqua-digging assistant, the profound sense of relief they felt just knowing that a source of income was at least real, made the uncertainty of an unseen future a little easier to accept, leaving just one question left to ask... "What the fuck is an Aqua Digger?"

When Chaos described the act of excavating soil using high pressure water and a vacuum system, it all seemed mighty technical and quite dirty for someone seeking a preferably clean career. "Don't worry..." Chaos reassured as he pulled out his crack pipe, "It's easy once you get the hang of it! Besides, they're always desperate to hire people!"

"I think he means they hire desperate people!" Shadow said of their host, as they lay next to the furnace upon a bed of emotional nails, where Rob tried to find a bright side to their suddenly turbulent thunder underground existence,

"With our abilities and gift of The Energy, we should be...!"

*BOOM! BOOM! BOOM! BOOM! BOOM! BOOM*

"Sigh… We should be able to easily shine at this new job."

Deep down, they knew this to be true whilst trying to block out the insanity of their reality, not-to-mention the noise of the lighter flicks from a crack head getting high in the next room, which found Shadow driven to a solemn vow. "We'll shovel shit for shillings if it gets us out of times like these!"

The weariness in their body could not be understated as they arose the next morning and went with Chaos to a last minute job interview, where they were swiftly hired as an assistant aqua digger at a Bad Deal company and assigned to an aqua-digging unit they discovered was simply a big rig type truck outfitted with a large, powerful industrial vacuum system.

"Looks easy enough!" Rob said to Scotty the shop foreman, whom immediately gave them a skeptical look that hinted to the truth about a revolving door industry, however, there was no turning back for someone teetering at the edge of oblivion, with no choice but to move forward lest they be consumed by despair and end up like Chaos. Although Rob had hoped to learn the ropes of a new trade with someone they sort of knew already, when they were instead paired up with someone else other than a drug addict who was higher than our hopes of selling copies of this book, they really could not protest, however, upon meeting their new operator and driver, Shadow sensed The Energy of someone whom they knew Rob would immediately grow to hate, leaving them to wish they could work with a crack head instead.

Were it not for the fact that "The Goof" compelled us to dig deeper than we ever had before to tap into The Energy in ways never imagined, a two-faced narcissist piece of shit would have never been mentioned in this story.

"Are you feeling like a groundhog yet!? The Goof had mocked them from outside the deep excavation, when Rob caught a splash of muddy water to the face, the kind that really placed a hard fought dirty life into perspective as soil and sand was driven into their eyes and teeth, forcing them to spit it out one grain at a time whilst standing in a mud hole of rage and embarrassment that had them thinking…

"Keep it up fuck face… and we'll be burying you in this fucking hole!" Shadow seethed in silent psychosis, while Rob channeled The Energy to focus upon a task they were failing at. "We're going to fast!" he reasoned, "We have to let the water work!"

It was here that Rob realized how much they were allowing The Goof and his purposefully distracting ego to get under their skin, leaving them to struggle to revolve around a narcissistic asshole who believed himself to be above everyone else, as an Aquarius with a seemingly natural ability with water focused with everything they had to block out The Goof and feel the water they wielded to become fluid in their motions, which in no time saw their speed and movements reach a level of fluidity that soon found a "groundhog" no longer eating rocks for breakfast.

They were hardly surprised when The Goof made every attempt to take credit for Rob's hard work, leading Shadow to imagine to some colorful mental visions… "We could beat him with a dig wand …or, just push the piece of shit into a twenty foot deep hole and say that he fell!"

"Yeah…" Rob entertained the idea, "Or, perhaps *we* should go get the commercial driver's license to drive these big trucks like The Myth and Father used to do and pilot our own fucking Aqua-digging rig!"

To be certain, gaining the ability to get away The Goof, whom was a scheming, holier than thou piece of garbage, made them seriously consider following in the footsteps of a family tragedy, even though Shadow's first idea about a motto once recited by The Freak had been more than very tempting, "Violence solves everything!" which led them wonder how a once best friend and brother had fared after their departure.

"Not the purpose I was expecting" Rob thought in an attempt to change the subject away from a co-worker and betrayer, whom they knew was the type to not hesitate to capitalize upon their misgivings of others to advance his own bullshit agenda, which effectively turned a job into a sentence of moral endurance.

Upon making those crucial first paychecks, they swiftly moved into a rooming house away from Chaos, whom ended up putting an aqua-digging rig in a ditch within a drugged out stupor that got him fired, while Rob finally got a good night's sleep that gave them the courage to swallow their pride as they rode the bus in a serious attempt to become a professional at something other than desperation and depression, which found them continually digging away against the odds for months until finally, they had earned enough to purchase a newer leased vehicle with crushing interest, which softened the anxiety of always being dead broke in a monetary society.

"We got a long, long way to go" Rob said dividing their age versus their financial assets, which all added up to a delayed retirement that would no doubt find them doing a young man's job well into their golden years.

"I know, it's getting late!" Shadow admitted whilst searching for a path to an unseen purpose, all the while keeping an eye out for Fate and Irony's next move as they sat held up in big city traffic on a particular ominously grey morning that seemed to compliment the notion that life was about to change abruptly, before arriving at work to find out that The Goof had been promoted to the office?

*REASON FOR LEAVING:* A world in crisis.

# HOME TOWN INK

## *Home Town, ~ 2008 ~ Professional Shadow*

When the management position went straight to a Goof's head, a string of resignations by the industry veterans soon found Rob as the last man standing upon sinking ship caught in the choppy waters of a world financial crisis, which resulted in a tsunami of shelved projects and cancelled contracts that led to a skeleton crew at work, the backbone of which, they were no longer interested to be as they bowed to Fate and Irony telling them to... "Go your own way!"

"Another one bites the dust!" A job eulogy spoken by an unemployed career refugee did not change the fact they had wasted years getting dirty for dollars, only for reality to come along and take away their progress and prosperity every time things had begun looking up.

"We're really are not meant to be an hourly employee ...are we?" Rob asked with restless anxiety whilst sitting in their rented room that had begun to feel a lot like their old prison cell.

"I'm afraid not" Shadow confirmed from the edge of sanity, where they tried to solve the riddle of life that would offer release to a cult of personality trapped under the weight of a story forever bound by seemingly endless time.

"Well, I'm bored" Rob said after about a week of sitting around binge watching maternal memories in their mind, so, Shadow came up with an option that would not only solve boredom problem, but also address a lingering matter that weighed even heavier upon the heart of a home sick son... "We should go see mom."

"Yeah, it's been a while" Rob agreed, as they evaluated the reasons holding them back from ditching a pay as you go rental accommodation, and taking off upon a last minute journey eastward across MY-BIG-HOUSE, where a long drive upon the open road was a version of ultimate therapy that no amount of prescription narcotics could ever top, especially when combined with the soothing effects of loud music set to constant motion across a land of ever changing scenery and discoveries that were always waiting within every horizon. "Sigh...!"

With the stigma of failure long faded in the rear view mirror, the return of clarity enabled them to envision going to back to Home Town for a few months to visit friends and family, and, "Who knows...?" Rob left the plot open as they arrived at Tombstone's place out on the outskirts of Home Town, beyond the muddy river where an enthusiastic friend on the phone had offered free hospitality for the duration of their stay, except of course for the tiny unspoken stipulation that they shoot first and ask questions later when protecting a biker's homestead that was caught up in a previously omitted turf war against a rival faction?

"...For fuck sakes!" Shadow's shouted in silence at always being lied to and used by so-called friends, while Rob was more preoccupied with the nameless feeling of being a profoundly changed man on the inside, whom found it strange to look and act like the same person that everyone had once known, in a reunion of old acquaintances that led to the reminiscing of fights they had won, and the ghosts of war whom had lost the battle for their souls, like Crippled Crab, which was still a sore spot for Tombstone to talk about, so they went for the other burning question that lingered within everyone's thoughts, "How's The Freak?"

Over the years, tidbits of rumors had described a spiral architect whom had embarked upon a symphony of destruction that led to legal troubles and court ordered rehab, involving many a bad medicine that were arguably worse than the addiction, which, according to Tombstone had been… "Fucking tough to watch!"' From the back of Rob's mind, Shadow cursed a profit driven pill pandemic that had turned so many good people into the walking dead, as they went to visit the only one left from a damage inc. history whom was uncorrupted by the darkness gripping the world, and the only one to make them weep for humanity upon seeing a tiny, frail, and visibly older Mom living out her sentence of time, all alone except for her daily drop-in caretaker whom was at least some form of company in an otherwise daughterless existence, waiting patiently for her son to return so they could hold her hand and let a cherished parent know that she was loved and never forgotten.

"We're going to do something great for you one day …Mom." Shadow echoed through Rob in hopes that the positive ambition in their eyes might comfort the worries of an old woman, whom would not see their eyes leak in the car afterwards, where an epic battle with Fate and Irony, found them ready to journey into the lungs of hell if it meant beating life at its own game.

After heading over to visit their old childhood friend James, whom was always a voice of reason and encouragement, and whom was one of the few that could see the difference in Rob. Later, they drove back toward the madness of Tombstone's place without hurry, choosing instead to take the long way home, which found them driving by the old "After" D.A.R.K. shanty that used to be in front of Home Town High School, which they discovered had been completely razed to the ground, along with the old Matrix strip joint that used to sit behind it.

"We're here for a good time..." Shadow reminded, as old memories of their D.J. slash M.C. days floated back into focus, whilst continuing on their way toward Whore Street, where Tombstone had said The Freak could be found eking out an existence in some decrepit hole in the wall tattoo studio, where, naturally, a burning curiosity dictated that Rob could not simply drive past The Freak's place without stopping in.

Upon entering the rundown studio, the only thing more shocking than the state of a tattered tattoo parlor, was seeing Skinny Jesus still sitting there in his eternal loyalty and... "Is he still wearing the same clothes!?" Shadow wondered from behind Rob's peering gaze, as they were greeted by four words that revealed a history that did not look upon them favorably...

"What do *you* want?" Skinny Jesus asked in a tone that belied his poorly hidden contempt for their presence, which Shadow attributed to events surrounding their departure all those years ago, leading to various opinions voiced about them in their absence, however, Rob did not offer any rebuttals and simply asked the one question that had brought them there in the first place... "Where is he?"

"He's sleeping. Come back later." The cold reply from Skinny Jesus had spoken volumes about a world they were no longer a part of, however, just as they were about to leave, a beautiful girl walked in the studio, whose black, backless blouse... "Say that three times fast!" ...revealed a pair of large angel wings tattooed over her entire back that were amazing to behold. Simply looking at the shading style washed and whipped into a large epidermal back piece, they knew right away who the artist was, but who was quickly forgotten along with intentions of leaving upon locking eyes with Angel Wings. The Energy within Angel Wings was unmistakable as they got to know this heavenly creature, whom they learned had fallen from grace after suffering the same chemical romance that had left so many fumbling within a fictional reality, just like...

"The Freak" Shadow said a split second before the door to the studio opened, and in walked a man they barely recognized, but was unmistakably the same brat everyone had known and loved, as they locked stares with a Gemini and a potential enemy if old wounds, new scars never healed properly. However, all it took was a split second eternity to know they had nothing to fear as the history of their journeys was revealed at first sight, before they ever spoke a word.

"My condolences about your Mom" Rob offered in respect upon reading The Freak's thoughts, where they discovered that his mother had passed and that it had been an inheritance that had covered much of the cost of consequences born of addiction, to which The Freak simply nodded a wordless, "Thanks...", before suddenly peering at them intently... "When did you two switch places?"

Gone were The Freak's long golden locks that now revealed a bald tattooed head, and gone was the trench coat and vampire attire, which had been replaced with a kimono and hakama, the traditional grab of the samurai, revealing a return to martial arts roots that The Freak had used as means to overcome an affliction that had wrought so much damage upon an iron will refusing to say die.

After all the fakes they had encountered upon their travels, to once again stand in the presence of someone whom had always been a true force with The Energy was like a breath of fresh air that, in a strange way, sort of made them feel whole again, as Rob began visiting their friend ...and brother, over the following weeks to avoid being present for the hillbilly feuds going on out at Tombstone's place, but mostly to rekindle the moments that honored The Energy within simpler times, and let's not forget Angel Wings, with whom they had felt the spark of interest, leading to an unforeseen relationship that inevitably led to a change of accommodations, when they traded a gun for a less traumatic reality that, suddenly made the idea of sticking around seem that much more plausible.

"You think you could still pull it off?" Rob asked The Freak one night during a long overdue new tattoo, slash, therapy session. "The theme we mean..." Rob clarified, "...not the franchise". Despite still retaining the fire they once had at the beginning, for the first time since knowing him, Shadow watched The Freak hesitate, "...I don't know."

They could tell their friend was still fighting the chemical poisons lingering deep within, which was in turn fighting The Energy, but eventually, The Freak asked them the fateful question, "What do you have in mind?" leading Shadow to stoke the embers fire of old theories, and turn them into new "semi-serious" ideas that maybe, just maybe, held the potential to regain a piece of what once had been and could be again?

Everyone was on the edge of their seat as The Freak searched inside for the strength to rise above the calamity wrought by Fate and Irony, before finally saying... "Yeah, fuck it! Let's do it!" ...which set a new plan into motion that first entailed renovating the shithole studio using nothing for resources in a repeat of past miracles, which turned a dive tattoo shop into something that could actually be called "amazing", thus reigniting rumors of renewed interest within a city seeking something beyond the mundane norms of a dreary eastern existence. When The Freak then turned around and sold a newly renovated, turnkey tattoo business to a perspective buyer, whom had no idea that he had just financed his soon-to-be direct competition, The Freak used the funds from the sale to secure a place over on Kill-'Em-All Drive, where a future new studio began taking shape upon a street conveniently alluding to The Freak's last name, setting the stage for Home Town's newest soon-to-be hot spot tattooing studio aptly named, "Home Town Ink!"

Everything was set and in just a few more weeks a new beginning was about to take place that would let everyone know the boys are back in town. With all the positivity floating around, The Freak wished to celebrate a return to good fortune by hosting a barbeque feast, where he gifted a jeweled golden cross to Rob as a symbol of their friendship, within a moment of shared dreams and purpose that left it up to the imagination what lay ahead of them next.

"Any other dreams you've had you wished could have come true?" Shadow asked an innocent question to a friend and brother whom seemed content with the way things were going. "Besides writing a fan letter to The Prince of Darkness, I'm pretty good at this point!" The Freak admitted in a rare glimpse of fan boy innocence from a man whom as hard as a coffin nail, "...But, there is one thing I need to do first."

When The Freak described how he had dishonored himself with an addiction and thus needed to perform Yubitsume, an honor based ceremony that would culminate with the severing of his right pinky finger to atone for his perceived failures, which, seemed a little extreme even for someone with no fear of pain, however, just then, Shadow suddenly thought they sensed an ominous presence cross the room, right before The Freak began complaining of an egg taste in his mouth and not feeling well, leading to canceled festivities when The Freak announced that he was going to bed, while Rob and Angel Wings went back to her place for what dreams may come.

***REASON FOR LEAVING:*** In this river

# 13

# *NEVER SAY DIE*

# R.I.P.

# Aaron

## aka… The Freak

"You were a friend of Dreams, a teacher in Reality, and a brother with a true at Heart. The Energy you still carry will live on in those who remain and remember"

Shadow

# HOTWHEELS CONCRETE

## *Dead Man City, ~ 2008 ~ Concrete Criminal*

\*BOOM! BOOM! BOOM! BOOM! BOOM! BOOM\*

"Ugh... doesn't that kid ever tiptoe?" Rob mumbled in the slumbering darkness as they rolled over and tried to ignore the pounding noises threatening to pull them into consciousness.

\*BOOM! BOOM! BOOM! BOOM! BOOM! BOOM\*

"Goddamn it... we so need to move away from Chaos!" They sighed upon seeing daylight through closed eyelids, which meant that they would now have to fight to get back to sleep, so they would not have to endure reality and...!

\*BOOM! BOOM! BOOM! BOOM! BOOM! BOOM\*

"What the fuck!" Upon opening their eyes, the shock from realizing that they were in bed with Angel Wings and not back on the floor in the furnace room of a chaotic household, had left Rob momentarily disoriented, until they realized there was someone pounding on the front door...

\*BOOM! BOOM! BOOM! BOOM! BOOM! BOOM\*

"Alright already... We're coming!" Rob groaned as they got up naked and grabbed the nearest thing available to cover them, and went to see who it was. Rubbing the cobwebs from their eyes, Rob opened the door to find The Goblin standing there, looking pale and perplexed upon seeing them wearing a tiny bathrobe that belonged to Angel Wings, which barely covered their...

"The Freak is dead!" The words suddenly blurted out by The Goblin failed to register in their head at first, compelling Shadow to give it a shake to clear the fog as Rob said, "Come again?"

When The Goblin repeated his words with a solemn face, Shadow felt more than a dream shatter upon learning that The Freak, whom everyone thought had merely been sleeping within his barricaded room for the last two days, had died in his sleep, the apparent victim of asphyxiation when he choked to death on his own vomit due to severe acid reflux, and had been unable to awaken from his slumber thanks to all the prescribed sedatives The Freak had been taking to help him deal with his treatment for a pill addiction that had destroyed his stomach.

"Wow..." Shadow uttered in total defeat as Angel Wings standing there in a towel, suddenly collapsed to the floor and began sobbing uncontrollably, the sight of which opened the floodgates of Shadow's grief that sent tears streaming down Rob's face, whom fought with everything they had to keep it together long enough to get dressed, after which they headed over to The Freak's last resting place, where in a gut wrenching moment they saw The Freak's daughter Natasha, whom they were at a loss to console.

On that day, life grew noticeably darker as The Energy of a bright light and a rock for so many, departed this mortal world leaving everyone that knew him in an endless void of sorrow that was stuck on an endless loop of condolences that became too much for Shadow to bear, compelling Rob to look to the horizon for an escape and no more tears, which led to a last minute decision to pack up the car with their things and Angel Wings, along with her two dogs, and then they vanished from a Home Town fog of misery …forever?

"Well, we'll go back to visit Mom …and your family, but we can't ever live there again." Rob told Angel Wings on the long drive to Dead Man City, where a new beginning within a different setting would hopefully provide a floor to a free fall of emotions within a far flung destination, where, attempting to bury grief, Rob was determined to make a new life happen upon arrival by using the last of their savings to quickly get situated into a furnished place that left nothing to want from a fragile Angel Wings, before then turning their attention to the job obituary, where they sought work within the very first industry they found that had not been completely ransacked by a faltering gig economy still caught in the throes of a "Great Recession", which beheld no concessions for a mentally unstable and overtaxed employee measuring wealth by the hour, whom settled upon…

"Wanted… Concrete Laborer" Rob read the job heading out loud in an attempt to not only visualize the impending weight of a heavy task that was not for the weak and feeble, but also to convince Fate and Irony that a job working with concrete was the career that would go on to build the foundations of their happy ever after, as they called the number and…

"You're hired!" The youthful sounding business owner had said over the phone, which made Shadow frown on the inside as they were given a job site address and told to show up the next morning, and then the man on the line swiftly hung up leaving Rob to look oddly at their phone thinking, "That was way too fucking easy!"

"It'll be ok" Rob said to an anxious Angel Wings as they kissed her goodbye and headed off to a new day at a new job in the concrete industry, where they at least had some remote novice idea about what they would encounter... "Yeah, it's called grunting and fucking sweating!" Shadow predicted about a back breaking toil, as they pulled up to a building under construction, where they had fully expected to meet a haphazard crew preaching a bitter sweet symphony of expectations and irrelevant personal gripes, only, instead they met a seemingly …really nice bunch of guys?!

In a surprising twist, their work crew turned out to be some of the most professional and friendliest people they had ever met, which appeared to hail a changing of the guards in Fate and Irony's repeating verse of trauma and tragedy, leaving them deeply relieved when Rob's new young boss and small business owner turned out to be the laid-back type, happy-go-lucky-me employer whom immediately made them feel welcomed and appreciated, as the gang proceeded to eagerly teach Rob about the finer points of pouring concrete in a positive and nurturing work setting that seemed too good to be true.

"I think Fate and Irony are finally going to leave us alone!" Rob boasted to Angel Wings a few weeks later, when a fat paycheck in their pocket led to some weekend drinks at the kitchen table, where they sat twirling an unfinished blade in their right hand that The Freak had crafted through his martial arts sobriety therapy, which Angel Wings had taken as a memento of someone whom had been a well of talent.

"Yep…" Rob nodded with confidence as they spun and flipped the bare blade with increasing speed, motivated by alcohol and unfettered by the fact that it did not have a handle or a guard on it. "I think our luck has changed for the bet…!"

When Rob tossed the blade up in the air, something had suddenly compelled them to delay the catch, causing Rob to hesitate in a missed timed move, which resulted in the wrong end of a very sharp blade to be caught that sliced deep in the flesh of three fingers upon their right hand, of which their pinky finger received the worst of a nasty cut that warranted going to the hospital to have it looked at, however, since they had been drinking heavily and were thus unfit to drive, Rob merely bandaged their damaged digit and left it to heal on its own like an idiot, only to discover at work the following Monday that their pinky finger had lost all mobility from the second knuckle, resulting in that delayed trip to the clinic, where the doctor confirmed a previous idiot theory by revealing the presence of severed tendons requiring surgery, which by now would only grant an estimated eighty percent use of an otherwise paralyzed extremity that, beheld no other option for recovery except for …partial amputation?

All of a sudden, Shadow remembered how The Freak never got to perform a Yubitsumi ceremony to regain his honor and at that moment, an insane idea entered Rob's thoughts. Aware that the doctor would never understand their reasons behind the act, they elected for the amputation under the premise that a bit of finger was in the way of a working hand, which saw the severing of a limb using a local anesthetic and a scalpel, instead of six Saki shooters and a Washizaki blade. "Son of a bitch..." Rob spoke Shadow's thoughts aloud upon realizing that The Freak had just used Fate and Irony from beyond the grave, to complete his ceremony to regain his honor.

"Man, that's some deep shit!" their young employer had said when Rob showed him their freshly filleted finger and told him a story so crazy that the man gave them a raise! "I'm glad to have someone solid like you on my crew!" the young blooded boss then admitted, which, for just a fleeting second, gave Shadow the odd impression of someone again being too nice, especially when The Freak whispered in Shadow's ethereal ear... "He's full of shit!"

**REASON FOR LEAVING**: Hot wheels and dirty angels.

## DEADLY DEAN'S CONCRETE

### *Dead Man City, ~ 2008 ~ Concrete Undertaker*

With time, the world would heal from its financial wounds, but when it came to Angel Wings, the sutures of the future had failed to mend a bleeding heart that had been shattered into a million little pieces, resulting in an ever growing drinking habit to numb the pain and sooth the withdrawals of an old, yet, still there pharmaceutical addiction, which Rob had figured they could keep at bay, but Shadow had not been so convinced upon feeling… "Something is different about her."

Then one day, after Angel Wings had dropped them off at work and took the car to go run errands, they got a call from the police stating that she had totaled their car after crashing it into a ditch while intoxicated, which had resulted in pending fines and restrictions for her, along with a loss of mobility for Rob, who purchased a last minute beater vehicle on a strained budget, that was haunted by the down payment blues of a car loan the insurance company had refused to cover. Although they had been happy that Angel Wings had not been hurt in the accident, from there, they noticed her growing ever more distant in a way that made Shadow wary, as they began to suspect something else was going on, a notion which gnawed at their instincts on that dark overcast day at work, when it seemed like everywhere they looked, Fate and Irony could be seen dancing in the dark with the omens …and cops?"

## Professional Shadow

They just happened to glance up from their task of placing rebar to reinforce the concrete garage slab they would be pouring, when suddenly Rob spotted two uniformed policeman standing over by their young employer's big shiny pickup truck that was attached to the large tow behind jobs trailer with the matching paint scheme, where one of the officers could be seen standing on the tips of his toes peering at what Shadow had surmised was the vehicle's identification number located on the left of the dashboard at the bottom of the windscreen glass, while the second officer next to the first held a shoulder microphone near his face, and was obviously relaying the information over the radio?

"That's odd" Shadow whispered in a rattle head moment of confusion that compelled them to quickly glance at their crew working around them, whom were oblivious to the police presence, before looking over at their young boss to get his attention to their observations.

"Pheet!" They whistled to their boss, whom looked over to see them doing a head motion toward the officers with the expectation that a small time business owner would have gone to greet the two policemen now approaching the job site, however, when the young entrepreneur said, "Shit!" and he, along with the rest of the crew took off running in separate directions, Rob was left standing there frozen in dumbfounded surprise!

"You gotta be shitting me" was all Shadow could say, as Rob was arrested and read their rights for grand theft larceny, before being cuffed and stuffed into the back of police cruiser and taken to the station for interrogation, where they discovered the hard way that the big new pickup truck and attached jobs trailer containing all the tools and equipment to execute concrete projects, which they thought had belonged to their now former employer had been stolen from a small time concrete company down in Bovine City, meaning that they had been working for thieves for nearly a month doing seemingly legit construction jobs …and getting paid for it?

"He advertised in the fucking newspaper and paid us for our labor with checks bearing the same company name that's on the goddamn truck!" Rob said with exasperated incredulity to the detectives investigating the case, whom were unconvinced about their claims of innocence thanks to a prior criminal history, leaving them to simmer in a holding cell of convicted flashbacks for a few hours until it was discovered that they had been duped by group of brazen, and albeit friendly crooks before being subsequently released.

"Don't go too far, we'll be contacting you!" The officer warned after escorting them to the public entrance of the police station and ushering Rob out the door.

"Fat chance on that, our car is still at the job site you fucking asshole!" Shadow yelled inside Rob's mind, whom did not feel like returning to a crime scene to collect their vehicle and instead got on the magic bus of despair and headed for home, whereupon their arrival Rob tried to figure out how they were going to explain to Angel Wings the crazy events that just happened and that they no longer had a job, but upon walking in, they were greeted by two happy dogs, but, no Angel Wings?

"Guess *you* won't be explaining anything" Shadow remarked when they tried calling Angel Wings twice, but her phone went straight to voicemail both times on the second ring? "Probably just busy and can't talk right now" Rob tried to sell an innocent reason, but Shadow wasn't buying as they made something to eat then took a seat on the sofa with the dogs and waited for Angel Wings to return from wherever she might be.

Sitting there, Rob tried to wrap their head around a day so crazy that it defied belief much like their life story, as they waited and watched the hour hand on the clock move ever so slowly …for three hours, until shortly before their usual arrival time from a job they no longer held, the dogs suddenly perked up and began going berserk, signaling that Angel Wings had arrived. At that moment, Rob jumped up and moved to the window, and when they peered out through a slit in the closed blinds, they spied Angel Wings getting out of some weathered pickup truck?

"I fucking knew it!" Shadow said flatly, while Rob chose to not jump to conclusions and hold out for the faint hope that the truth might be something other than…

"Nope, she's cheating" Rob calmly acknowledged, upon watching Angel Wings lean over to the male driver of the pickup truck and kiss him deeply on the lips, before exiting the vehicle and starting toward the house, where, they need not be a wedding planner to know that the honeymoon was over. "Killing is my business and business is good!" Shadow offered to beat up the mystery lover boy, which had appealed to Rob, however, without a car to chase down an adulterer in his pickup truck, they remained standing by the window with arms folded, as Angel Wings walked in to find two very happy dogs and one very unhappy man, whom eventually got a cheater-cheater pecker eater to admit that she had been fooling around with some lover boy she had met shortly after their arrival in Dead Man City, whom had been feeding her pills, alcohol and apparently fairytales about a happy ever after, which Rob facilitated when they told her… "Call your lover boy before he gets too far, because we're done."

Sitting there alone in a silent home, Shadow thought, "I miss the dogs", as the acute sting of an "it's your life" moment that had just amounted to a zero sum, left them feeling like they had just been put through a cosmic corpse grinder that swallowed their happiness and chat it back out in a steaming heap of Fate and Irony, which even left a foul odor in the air?

"That's the dog shit in the hallway" Rob pointed to the fresh brown clumps, but it still did not brighten a shitty mood within a fucked up reality, which had stolen a will to climb a mountain of sorrow, leaving only one thing to do for a single Guy seeking to forget the emotional scars of a prodigal son pushed too far.. "Let's go get the car… and then go to the bar."

Sitting alone at their pub table sipping a whiskey on the rocks, Rob savored the burn from the alcohol that helped to lessen the burn of being unemployed again, where a lack of direction without purpose was a bitter distraction to the glaring truth they had tried to forget ever since the passing of The Freak, which had seen their dream career die for a second time. "Want to talk about it?" Rob asked himself whilst gulping down their drink, and then waiving to the cute waitress for a refill.

When Shadow echoed silence, Rob knew to not pressure a one percent instinct grown weary to the core by the constant round and round of Fate and Irony, which had seen them trying so hard to be civilized at shitty labor jobs that made their resume look worse that a fucking rap sheet in the eyes of business professionals, something they were clearly destined to never become.

Faced with a head crusher dilemma, they wondered what they would do next for work, however, worries were quickly forgotten when the cute waitress brought over their drink, and with a wink, invited Rob to keep her company over at the bar, in a reveal of interests that guaranteed a good tip after her shift. "Well my friend…" Rob concluded to a private hell session, "…if you'll excuse us, we have some rebound to attend to!"

As far as the law of attraction was concerned, they were acutely aware of their ability to attract The Energy of the opposite sex, especially since they were in great shape from all the hard work they had done across a life of labors which often led women to stare at their chest instead of their eyes, permitting Rob to play upon the repeating patterns that always led to favors, which was exactly what they were going to get when the cute waitress took them home for a lesson in californication, where the proper pronunciations of words was forgiven thanks to all the free liquor the waitress was feeding them…?

At that moment, three weathered workmen walked in the lounge and took a table directly behind Rob's barstool, who quickly forgot about fun and frolic to focus upon the loud chatter of the three humans behind them, whom spoke about life, bullshit ...and concrete?

Riding the waves of inebriation, Shadow suddenly zeroed in on the hints of opportunity, compelling Rob to look up from their drink to their reflection in the mirror behind the bar, where the liquor bottles lined the wall, and there, they quietly confirmed... "We're getting a job with these clowns!"

Keeping a casual vigil upon their prey, they waited for their chance to break the ice, which presented itself a short time later, when one of the three concrete workers came to the bar to buy a round of drinks for his buddies, enabling Rob to set the wheels of destiny in motion...

"Long day...?" It was a harmless question that could go either way, which truthfully, had seen Rob half expecting to be told off with something like, "Don't talk to me!" or, "Go fuck yourself!" by someone whom they sensed wasn't the most socially adept, however, when the stranger replied, "Yeah, we're really busy! We got a lot of projects on the go!" Rob knew they were in. With years of experience in the art of bar talk, they easily convinced the human colon to invite them to his table, where they met Tooth Decay, a tall redheaded wanker with a serious case of dental atrophy displayed in a mouth littered with jagged stillborn stumps jutting from gangrene gums, whom was the purported second in command within a three man crew.

"Damn!" Shadow thought inwardly, as they struggled to look at Tooth Decay's rotten maw as he spoke about the concrete industry in an attempt to be the man, but whom was clearly just another follow the leader type in a piss wreck trio that left only one other at the table besides Rob with a full set of fucking teeth, which revealed Deadly Dean to be the employer and owner of a small time concrete business that was actually his, as they got to know an energetic entrepreneur whom beheld no inhibitions about using his wealth to be the center of eternity, evidenced by the wads of cash Deadly Dean tossed around in a bid to impress Rob and anyone else paying attention.

Sitting there smiling and laughing at stale jokes, Rob merely played along to Shadow's plan of allowing time and alcohol to reveal personal histories and exaggerated truths about the house that Jack built, which revealed Deadly Dean to be a connoisseur of the white nasal powder that nearly compelled Rob to walk away from another junkie story, however, when Deadly Dean hired them to be the fourth musketeer upon a busy concrete crew that paid handsomely, they remained seated within a night of fortune, frolic and forgotten morals that ended in fetish when the cute waitress took them home after closing for some overtime activities that found her receiving the biggest tip of the night.

**REASON FOR LEAVING:** Deadly Dean… dropped dead.

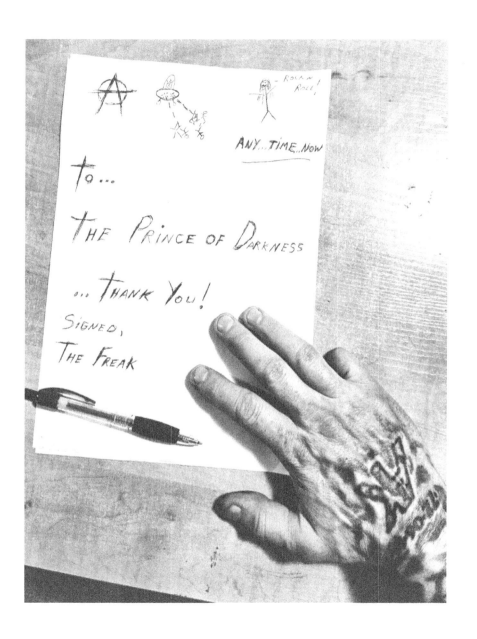

# TOTAL CHAOS H.D.D.

## *Crap-Bag Park, ~ 2010 ~ Dirt Donkey*

In life, the right to go insane without going completely off the deep end had always been dependent upon their ability to use The Energy to find a way through those tragic moments that might have killed the average... stick man?

"What the fuck are you drawing!?" Shadow asked as they sat at their kitchen table doodling upon a piece of paper, in a check my brain moment that saw reality beg to differ when it came to conveying images with depth and dimension onto paper, canvas, or even skin, meaning that anything beyond the written word was sadly, beyond the grasp of someone apparently destined to a lifetime of back breaking labors that tested their toughness on a daily basis involving concrete, sweat, and zero fear.

"*He* had no fear..." Shadow said about the owner of the initials tattooed upon their right hand, which had traded it's power for honor when a pinky finger once taken for granted was severed in tribute of someone whom had fought his way through life with a die by the sword mentality and could wield The Energy to draw and paint beautiful memories, unlike Rob's scribbling that led them back to scratching words instead.

"Any... time... now..." Rob wrote in an attempt to push Shadow toward making haste to find purpose, however, no matter how hard they tried, the obvious refused to be seen upon an unclear path of blind inspiration that led to anxiety and raised their blood pressure, causing a ghost pinky finger to begin throbbing at the end of a severed stump that reminded Shadow of The Freak during a last supper, whom had been so alive with The Energy in pursuit of renewed goals that had inspired them to dream like the youthful brats and fan boys they were…?

Suddenly, Shadow remembered The Freak's innocent fan boy wish to write a fan letter to The Prince of Darkness to say thank you to his favorite musical artist, whom was blessed with The Energy to reach so many and whose fateful songs had been the heretic anthem to their lives growing up that, quite ironically, had been just the inspiration they needed in a fucking crazy world spinning on into the void.

"Does that make us crazy?" They wondered as Rob drew an "O" for you know who, and then placed the letter "A" for Aaron over top of it, effectively creating a symbol of anarchy that made them pause to consider… "What if *we* wrote The Freak's fan letter?"

"Now that would be crazy!" Rob acknowledged as he moved down the page to write, "To… The Prince of Darkness…" They lingered for a moment, before moving below and simply writing, "Thank you… signed," then below again, "The Freak".

Looking upon a fan letter from the afterlife, Rob laughed, compelling Shadow to question why? "I'm laughing because The Freak just wrote this from beyond the grave... and now everyone is going to think we're insane!" Rob's point of view was not misplaced, however, from where Shadow was sitting next to The

Energy, which is what The Freak had become and now lived on as… "What's your point?"

All things considered, and given the way their life had gone up to that point, it seemed that crazy was all they had ever known, however, the prospect of writing a fan letter to The Prince of Darkness beheld a factor of intimidation that was hard to overlook. "People are going to say were living in the past!"

Shadow paused under the weight of it, however, like it or not, they both knew they were going to do it anyway. "Well, given that we chopped off our pinky finger in memory of The Freak, I think we're little past obsessed and far beyond driven…" Shadow paused to feel The Energy guiding their thoughts, "…who gives a fuck what anyone thinks!"

"Well, since you put it that way, this doesn't seem so insane after all!" Rob said encouragingly, however, upon looking at the simple words etched upon a plain piece of paper, it seemed that something was missing. Rob was ninety nine percent right, leading a one percent instinct to agree that a simple "thanks" splashed upon a page failed to describe The Freak and The Energy he had carried, "Yeah…" Shadow reflected for a moment in search of the obvious, but The Energy suddenly began to fade and the connection to a dearly departed friend and brother was lost, allowing a mortal weariness to overtake them that sent Rob to bed in preparation for another day of labor with a concrete crew, who, were an alright bunch of humans to earn a living with despite their quirks and bad habits, within a don't tread on me scene that seemed like it would always be there.

## Professional Shadow

Upon waking the next morning, Rob felt strangely drained from a restless sleep as though Fate and Irony had played pinball wizard with their body all night long, which they tried to shake off with a large coffee whilst driving to work under grey skies to a condominium complex under construction, where Deadly Dean had scored the contract to pour all the concrete sidewalks around the place. There, they had met the site supervisor whom was a wannabe greaser with long hair, earrings and a black leather jacket sporting a "Louder Than Everything Else" back patch, which made a lucky winner type and a poser stand out amongst the professional tradesmen, however, the fact that a rebel without a cause loved to party at rock shows, Rob accepted Lucky-Winner for who he was, which inevitably found them going to rock and metal shows to blow off some steam in mosh-pits filled with other adult children colliding into one another in a stamped of crazy horses whom were high on The Energy, which introduced them to a soreness born from a hard rock rumble that was fair trade for waking up the next day drained of stress and anxiety, as they continued to work within a heavy concrete industry for Deadly Dean, whom was a good employer Rob figured they would be working with for the foreseeable futu…?

"What did you say? Dean is still in bed!?" Rob asked Tooth Decay when he ran up to their car window shouting something before they could roll it down, upon arriving at the job site, where Tooth Decay repeated words that stopped time itself…

"Dead…! Deadly Dean's is dead!"

Their eyes grew wide in stunned disbelief when Tooth Decay described how Deadly Dead had died the night before in a drug overdose that stopped his heart, leading Shadow to begin cursing at Fate and Irony... "You rotten fucking bastards need to stop killing my fucking employers!"

Suddenly unemployed by the loss of a concrete gig at a small time company that died with the owner, they no longer had the will or the interest to continue working labor jobs to support a life that had just gone from a best foot forward to running with a financial broke leg, which had left them no choice but to seek out another job elsewhere before the money ran out, which suddenly gave them cramps, leading to the need to take...

"...A dump? No, we don't want to go work there!" Rob said looking through the jobs obituary of a coffee shop news flyer whilst sitting atop the great white bowl of brown submarines, in search of anything that had nothing to do with concrete. "Let's see here..." Ugh! Warehouse worker...? No!"

They were in a cramp stomp to figure out what else they could do for an income that paid decent enough to support them... "Ugh!" ...until a long lost purpose could come to pass... "Ugh! Forklift driver... No!" From where they were sitting, things were looking mighty shitty for career choices, however, just then... "Ugh!" ...they saw an ad by a company specializing in horizontal directional drilling, a process used to install underground telecom cables over long distances, which was looking for an assistant aqua digger to daylight anything buried within the drill's path during the installation of said facilities... "Ugh!" ...and since they already had some experience working on vertical drill bores... "Ugh!" ...and aqua-digging, they were compelled to pinch one off the opportunity tree that... "Ugh!"

…might turn out better than a previous crappy memory at two shitty businesses, as Rob wiped their ass with Fate and Irony and then drove to the company, where, they tried to exude confidence and certainty in front of a hillbilly manager, whom Shadow immediately sensed was full of it.

"My name is mud!" Rob said when the hillbilly manager gave them a position upon the drill crew instead of the assistant aqua digger position they had applied for, which was a vivid reminder of being viewed as just another tool as they soon discovered why the company had been looking for workers in the first place, upon meeting their co-workers whom turned out to be the worst collection of reckless rejects they ever had the misfortune of tolerating, whose idea of beauty through order involved drinking and getting high on the job whilst engaging in horseplay of questionable risks that threatened to place more than an individual's morals in danger, within a job role that was anything but glamorous as they stood in mud holes up to their knees while being slandered by idiots whom removed any notion of gold on the ceiling.

**REASON FOR LEAVING:** The definition of insanity

# 14

# *HOLE IN THE SKY*

## "CERTIFIED" CRAZY PERSON

### *Dead Man City, ~2011~ Dreamer*

The bright ideas were few and far between as they sat in the same old rented basement doing the same old thing night after night, which had seen Rob escaping reality by listening to music that took them away from the present and back through the eras, where they tried to pinpoint all the things of relevance that happened at the time both throughout the world and within their life, leading to a growing stack of brief written memories, like their first rock album, the first time they got laid, drunk and high, went to prison, an old sports car, a group of friends, strippers in the clubs, and the late night tattoo sessions with …The Freak.

"You know, I was thinking…" Shadow suddenly mentioned when Rob finished writing this last paragraph, "…about The Freak's fan letter and how a simple thank you upon a bleak boring page just doesn't cut it to describe The Energy we all carried upon our sleeves!"

Shadow was suddenly hooked on more than a feeling as a one percent instinct dared to dream on. "What if we wrote The Freak's fan letter to The Prince of Darkness, but, instead of just a simple thanks, we offer some crazy stories from our life?"

Rob raised an eyebrow at a crazy idea, "Well, we definitely have crazy stories, but, what are we thinking? Like a book?"

Suddenly, they raised both eyebrows, "...To give it purpose?"

At that moment, it felt like the universe had just pulled back a cosmic curtain that had been blinding them to the obvious all that time, leading Shadow to exclaim, "There's our fucking purpose!" over the one thing that had eluded them for so long. "That's how we're going to share The Energy with the world!"

Aware that a one percent instinct was most likely crazy, Rob struggled to envision something that somehow felt achievable; however, given their lack of skills both in creative writing and typing, not-to-mention zero resources beyond the internet to learn the tricks of the trade of a writer's career, Rob initially cast doubt upon the undertaking of an unlikely destiny...

"I don't know... You really think we can do this? I mean honestly, we probably have a better shot at winning the lottery or, becoming a stock broker!"

Gripped by a sing for the moment epiphany that actually had the potential to become a reality, Shadow was already looking beyond Fate and Irony's fan letter to a career as an author, "Don't worry, it'll be fun! Like our own bohemian rhapsody!"

"Oh, yeah...?" Rob responded with an eye roll that tested an unlikely theory, "Alright then Mister King! What are we gonna call this thing!?" It was a justified question that presented the first hurdle to a last minute career choice, which led Shadow to think about a title that would accurately fit a momentary lapse of reason, but drew a blank, prompting Rob to accept the obvious, "Right..."

Acknowledging defeat, they lifted their gaze to look upon the kitchen table before them in search of inspiration, where eyes went straight for shiny objects like the jeweled gold cross given to them by The Freak the night he departed a physical realm, which was resting next to car keys attached to the old Certified Crazy Person keychain they had found in the basement of the "After" D.A.R.K. tattoo studio…

"How about…, Diary of a Mad Man?"

Rob took a long pondering breath, "Isn't that a little close to home since it's an actual song belonging to you-know-who? We want to pay tribute to people, not fucking rip anyone off!" Shadow knew this to be true and plagiarizing those they were attempting to honor was not the intention at all, however, given the theme of a crazy idea it seemed a fitting title that pushed them to explore other ways to say the same thing, only, with the use of different words. "How about Diary of a Mad …Fan?"

"It's accurate, but, it's a little too groupie!" Rob twisted their lips one way at the obvious, then back the other way at the obvious that wasn't, "…And it's probably out there already!" Feeling frustration taking hold, they glanced upon the table once more, drifting back and forth between a gifted golden cross and a Certified Crazy Person keychain, until suddenly,

"Alright then, how about…"

## COWBOY AQUA-DIGGING

### *Horseshit Settlement, ~ 2011 ~ Cow Poker*

"Well, what do you think?" Shadow asked a critic of ninety nine opinions. "I think you're insane!" Rob answered without reservations, whilst standing in a mud hole under a November rain thinking, "We should quit before we end up burying these assholes in this mud hole!"

Shadow could not deny the insanity of their daily bread, which found them working in the cold, soaked elements, waiting for their co-workers to stop fucking around and do their jobs so they could change out the drill bit for a reamer to make the drill bore larger. Clearly, were it not for the sake of a paycheck and a phantom car loan teetering upon default, they would have quit a shitty employment labor position that made them feel worthless in a bridge burning career, which only saw vacations whenever they quit, or got fired for defending morality. "Fuck those jobs!" Shadow spat defiantly from within. "We're meant to do more with our life than this shit!"

All day long, the air itself seemed heavy with the presence of Fate and Irony, which had seemed to forewarn of a sudden life change within their immediate future, as they waited to access the staff locker room to change clothes after a wet, muddy, and seriously shitty day, however, a co-worker stood in the doorway talking to another, so Shadow chose to ramble on...

"We've wasted years working at labor jobs that are below our talents and have never been worth the pay!" Shadow said with rising power. "That's why it's all been mostly bullshit, while everything else has been shit happens!"

Rob suddenly gasped loudly... "You said those two words! ...and instantly, Shadow regretted it, in a moment of shocked superstition was mistaken for impatience by the talking co-worker in the doorway blocking their path, whom knew he was in the fucking way and was just being a crap sack about it, yet, still chose to spin around and be confrontational.

"You got a fucking problem!?" Crap Sack said in an attempt to flex his ego, which did not impress or scare them in the least, as Rob merely stood there burning a hole through Crap Sack's forehead with a laser stare, all the while inwardly scolding a one percent instinct that just fucked up big time. "You had to go and say it!"

"Fuck!" Shadow apologized for the blunder down under, which they both knew had initiated a chain of events of trauma and tragedy times three, which had just begun with Crap Sack whom decided to push an ethereal envelope containing The Energy without the proper postage...

"Oh, you think you're tough...?" Crap Sack said noting the look upon Rob's face, behind which raged a great battle for the soul of a being suddenly born of wolf and man, whom offered only one merciful warning...

"We're in no mood for your shit! Now, get the fuck out of the way!" Rob told the human filth standing before them, whom did not heed their words and instead puffed out his chest...

"Oh, yeah...? Well, I'm golden gloves motherfucker!" Crap Sack bragged whilst beginning to sway like a praying mantis, and at that moment, time slowed to a split second eternity as Shadow profiled a show boater and dirty fighter, whom was known to strike in mid sentence to catch opponents off guard, giving them the heads up to mentally shift their weight onto a right leg and slowly begin powering up a right triceps in anticipation of an inevitable altercation.

"I can't believe you said those words!" Rob said with inward disbelief, "Ya, I know!" Shadow replied with eternal regret, as Crap Sack began to speak his final verse that would forever change reality as they knew it... "I'll knock your ass...!"

Before Crap Sack could finish his words, they had already fired off a fast left jab that was ahead by a century and caught Crap Sack in his left eye, momentarily stunning him to give Rob just enough time to follow through with a hard right loaded with all the love hate sex pain of their recent history, which smashed into Death Valley between nose and cheek in a moment of esoteric surgery that, put a piece of shit down for the count ...along with their employment, "...Out!"

"You hit me!" Crap Sack began to whine upon coming too, "You're so fucking fired now...! Ha! Ha!" At that moment, the futility of tolerating an hourly labor job when others in the world were making millions had been never more apparent.

"Purpose…" Shadow said to prevent Rob from hitting an idiot again, leaving them to merely say, "Fuck your gloves and fuck this place!" before walking away from a dead career and driving off in a downpour of rain and retribution that, not even windshield wipers on high could not offer clarity upon the road ahead, which compelled Rob to pull in at a nearby bar & grill to get a bite to eat after a shitty day that suddenly found them unemployed, however…

"I really did enjoy that though…" Shadow admitted of striking Crap Sack, whom long had it coming anyway, while Rob sat at the lounge table awaiting their meal, opening and closing a right hand that no longer had a pinky finger to back up The Freak's fist… "But… you said *those two* words!" Rob rubbed the obvious into a cosmic wound, "You know what 'happens' when you say those two words and you start with 'shit'!"

There was no end to Shadow's regret for making the mistake of invoking the wrath of their one superstition that basically granted carte blanche to Fate and Irony to screw their reality with a sandpaper dildo. "Fuck…." Hoping that the second thing to "happen" wouldn't be too painful, they lingered there at the table sipping on a beer after their steak dinner, trying to envision what their next resume of altered facts was going to look like, upon going to get hired by some other poor ethic company within a labor career they did not want, which, in a strange way, made it seem like they had already quit their next job without ever getting hired, as the sexy waitress walked up to their table to ask if they wanted another beer, which Rob initially refused and was about to ask for the tab when the slithery server girl suddenly winked and leaned in close to whisper…

"Want to come home with me tonight?"

Considering the shitty day they were having and the fact that they no longer had to work the next day, a little attention to relieve some tension did not seem like a bad idea, so they stayed there at the bar sipping beers and tipping Slimy her sticky sweet slut fees until closing, until it was only them remaining after last call, waiting for their dessert to finish her liquor counts.

"Wow, got a buzz on!" Rod admitted with a hint of worry over getting whiskey dick later on, when suddenly, a stranger walked in and took a seat at the end of the bar, where he simply sat in silence looking at his phone, which Shadow, navigating the sloshing seas of sobriety within, immediately sensed that something was off when Slimy, whom had glanced at the stranger upon his arrival, never said that the place was closed?

"What the fuck is this?" Shadow wondered when the music on the jukebox suddenly stopped and the silence turned The Energy in the room into awkward conspiracy. "...A boyfriend?" Rob suspected, just as the notion of being played by Slimy for tips suddenly began to take hold, which not only made them feel like an idiot for believing that the "happen" was finished with them upon a shitty day, which now found them in a precarious situation since Slimy was supposed to drive their car to her place because they were now too drunk to drive.

"Just get up and leave. We'll call a cab outside." Shadow advised, but Rob, in a feel no pain state of mind, did not feel the urgency. "We're going to the washroom then we're out" they announced to Slimy, whom merely nodded without looking at them, which all but confirmed a previous suspicion.

"She was just playing us!" Shadow confirmed as they slid off the barstool and walked to the rest restroom, where, just before they entered, from the corner of their eye Rob spied Slimy looking at the stranger, whom had risen from his barstool and was starting toward them in a dead giveaway that things were about to get messy.

"You gotta be fucking shitting me!" Rob said with impatience to a forthcoming conflict, as they stepped inside the men's room and then stopped one pace beyond the door closing behind them, where they turned to channel the rage to overcome. "You think it's her boyfriend?" Rob questioned the obvious as they stretched and popped shoulder and neck joints. "…A boyfriend who fights for a slut girlfriend…?" Shadow tested the obvious that wasn't, "… or, is this something else?"

"…A mugging?" Rob narrowed their eyes upon replaying the fact that Slimy had seen the wad of cash in their pocket, not to mention having glimpsed the large jeweled cross that The Freak had given them, which hung brightly at their neck, where not even the four horsemen of the apocalypse had the power to remove from their cold dead body. "Just so you know, I blame you for this!" Rob said in a calm voice whilst placing left foot ahead just enough so the men's room door would strike it upon opening, which compelled Shadow to apologize again, just as the men's room door began to open… "Ya… I know!"

As the stranger pushed the door open with his right hand, they immediately spotted the knife in their opponents left hand, whom was surprised to find Rob standing right there waiting for him, "Hello sweetheart!"

At that moment, the assailant attempted to force his way into the washroom but was stonewalled when the door jammed against Rob's foot, creating a power struggle within a threshold, which they held just long enough to build up pressure, before pulling a jumping jack flash back from the door that suddenly swung open that sent their attacker stumbling forward and off balance into the washroom, where they were already coming back with a flying fist bearing The Freak's initials that flew like an albatross into a would be mugger's face, crashing hard into Death Valley that caused the stranger's head to snap back whilst his legs ran out from under him, sending the man to the floor onto his back causing him to drop the blade, and there, within a split second eternity, Rob weighed their choices... "Fight or flight!?"

"Let's fucking go!" Shadow commanded when Rob thought about going for the knife, but saw the strange already stirring to get up, leading to an escape from the men's room and a mad dash for the exit. Upon running past the bar where Slimy stood frozen in wide eyed fear, Rob told her, "You're a fucking piece of sh...!

*SLAM!* When they hit the exit door that did not open, Shadow realized that Slimy had locked the entrance so no one could get it, fortunately it was the latch type and not a keyed entry, thus allowing them to unlock the door and make the great escape into the night. Outside, Rob bolted for the car and peeled away from a dangerous situation only to find them in a precarious situation driving home, as the adrenaline rush began to wear off and the alcohol again began to blur Rob's vision, leading to a struggle to keep the car straight upon the road.

"What a fucking bitch!" Shadow exclaimed to the dramatic scene they had just experienced, whilst attempting to reassure a drifting driver... "Don't worry, just keep it steady and we'll be fine. At least there's no traffic at this hour except for us and taxi ...cops!?"

Shadow's words of encouragement were suddenly cut short by the red and blue flashing lights behind them, which meant they were being pulled over and subsequently arrested for drunk driving, when it was revealed that the staff of the bar & grill they had barely made it out of, had phone to report an intoxicated driver, yet never mentioned the altercation with the stranger?

"...That fucking cunt!" Shadow said in disbelief as Rob was taken to the station to be processed by officers whom did not believe a crazy story from a drunk about a mugging attempt that was never revealed by Slimy, leaving them to sit in a holding cell filled with flashbacks of prison song days that led Rob to vomit in a familiar steel toilet of tragedy as the gravity of their situation suddenly decided to evacuate the booze and the expensive steak dinner from their stomach, the cost of which was trivial compared to the cost that Fate and Irony suddenly incurred when the courts found them guilty of impaired driving and suspended their driver's license in addition to imposing hefty monetary fines that soaked up most of their meager savings, leaving them nearly broke, jobless ...and walking.

"A job loss, a mugging and a DUI all in one day..." Rob said with strangulated pride, as they weighed the serious jam they were now in thanks to "happen" number two and three consecutively, which had just buried them under a mountain of shit that left them completely fucked, to put it lightly, however, they knew it was their own damn fault.

There was no denying that they had grown complacent and brought their newfound state of misery upon themselves, as they carried on from the aftermath of a traffic violation that had just added another social black eye and ensured they would keep existing as a scourge of life, left to crawl through a jobs obituary in search of semi skilled positions that would never last, especially given their current immobile status.

"There's got to be something here…" Rob said with despair after three weeks of forever and a day that had pushed them to the brink of homelessness and starvation, where The Energy was the only things keeping them going in a futile employment search that found them about to give up and die when Shadow spotted an ad from an aqua-digging company hiring laborers with experience for a winter pipeline project in the northern reaches of MY-BIG-HOUSE…?

***REASON FOR LEAVING***: The hat doesn't make the cowboy.

# LAST CHANCE WELL SERVICING

## *Dead Man City, ~ 2012 ~ Roughneck 2.0*

"Not exactly the life of a famous author!" Shadow stated the obvious, which had failed to keep them warm out there upon a perennial quest to survive dangerous to life temperatures that cut through their insulated coveralls like a screen door, all the while attempting to dig through permafrost using lukewarm water and shitty pressure from a half busted aqua-digging rig, with a green operator whom had been of zero help... "You know, at first I thought we were simply fortunate to get hired..." Rob said with measured amazement, "...but, after that cow poke shit show, I wonder if Fate and Irony forgot to stop at three!"

Looking back upon another job they had just quit, which had found them working within the far northern regions of MY-BIG-HOUSE in Horseshit Settlement, where a bad day digging for a lost buried pipeline upon a icy, windblown oil lease had resulted in the oil consultant complaining to Cow Poker, their now former area manager, whom was a wannabe cowboy who, at first glance had appeared to be the real deal with his cowboy boots, his boot cut blue jeans, the big Brahma bull belt buckle, the plaid button shirt, the thick horseshoe moustache and the big ten gallon hat stuck atop the two dollar head of an aloof, former department store manager hailing from Rhymes-With-Fun City, whom had lost everything in a divorce due to alcohol, which a poser still drank in his office every day, to the point of slurred words, which led to a tense moment after Rob returned to the shop that day, and manager Cow Poker got in their face with that stupid phony cowboy swagger, reeking of alcohol and clearly drunk, and then proceeded to engage in the demise of sanity.

"You're just another lowly digger that can be easily replaced!" Cow Poker said with arrogance, which, Rob, tired from burning every kilo joule of The Energy just to stay warm, would have ignored the bulls on parade comment, however, when Cow Poker suddenly began poking them in the chest as he spoke... "So you're gonna do the job...*POKE!* *POKE* "...or else...!"

Cow Poker had poked them twice, but he never got to do it a third time when Shadow suddenly took over and slapped away an incoming finger, then quickly moved in to grab an idiot's Stetson by its edges and pulled it down hard over a stunned manager's eyes, which effectively blinded the man and instantly sent a drunken into a buckaroo fit of rage that humored Shadow and made Rob smile, as they waited for the fool to pop the hat from his head, so he could see their open right hand coming in to slap the buzz from a man that was all hat, no cattle.

"Wow, you're life is crazy!" Lucky Winner told Rob, whom was now living upon his sofa after quitting another bullshit job that was over all too soon, and had failed to earn them the money to cover rent without starving to death, so, the choice had been made to nix their place and bribe Lucky-Winner to let them sofa surf at his place for far less, thus leaving enough left over to eat and catch a few rock and metal shows, where, at least for a while, they could forget a "people equal shit!" outlook, brought on by too many terrible employers with a false sense of power, whom somehow believed it gave them the right to push around people viewed as labor slaves, only to discover themselves sorely mistaken upon poking the wrong Mr. Roboto.

"We must have been real dicks in a past life for Fate and Irony to have such a hate on for us!" Rob thought with certainty, as they sat upon a sofa of survival feeling like a complete failure after busting their ass across years of labor and servitude at companies that were hardly professional. While The Energy seemed to hint to another life once lived, deep down Shadow remembered their words that day in prison, where a challenge had been made… "If it's a fight that Fate and Irony want!"

"Yeah, I guess we haven't been winning that fight, now have we!?" Rob said of their situation, which found them breaking the same old ground of despair and destitution with basically nothing but the clothes on their back. "Don't worry about it…" Shadow reminded whilst refusing to crumble under another shitty reality, "…it's just stuff! As for the rest of it, we were meant to live a professional life and career, but we found ourselves slippin' into darkness at a young age because of the environment we grew up in, and it's only thanks to The Energy that we've been able to survive everything we've been though."

At this point, Rob didn't need convincing, "So… as long as we keep doing jobs that are not what were truly meant to do, Fate and Irony are going to keep using our ass like a cosmic parking lot?" When Shadow did not reply, Rob knew the last job quit would not be their last until they had achieved their purpose, by publishing a crazy story about honor, and never quitting on that which mattered most…

"Yeah, us...!" Rob said feeling The Energy, which suddenly made them feel better about the fact that their life was forever destined to be anything but normal, unlike Lucky-Winner's life, which was big on bourbon and low on brain power, thus keeping a forklift driver blinded to life beyond a menial job that might one day yield credit and assets for someone from doing the same thing over and over forever, however, what really made Lucky-Winner fortunate, was the fact that he was surrounded by good friends, well, mostly.

To describe a group of defensive personalities whom literally had nothing in common except for a love of hard rock concerts and metal music, we first introduce Repeater, whom was Lucky-Winner's roommate and co worker, and the reason Rob was sleeping upon the sofa in a two bedroom apartment. Repeater was an older chap with an unremarkable history aside from the fact that he was on medication for schizophrenia and a severe case of obsessive compulsive disorder, which found the man repeating the same conversation over and over again...

"Yeah Rob... those managers were fucking idiots and that waitress that got you the DUI was a fucking cunt, yeah, yeah...!" Repeater repeated, "...Those managers were idiots and that waitress was a cunt yeah...!" Although Repeater was a little dysfunctional, at least he was sincere, which was a lacking trait in Pea Brain, a self serving, self professed womanizer whom thought of himself to be some supersonic sex machine, but whom was really nothing more than a tolerated fool that often ran the risk of evoking Rob's wrath with his "alcohaulin ass" views about women. Despite Pea Brain's faults and generally septic attitude, he was there for Lucky-Winner, which counted for one thing Rob could respect. Finally, there was Ryan, who, was just Ryan as a heavy equipment operator with a penchant for getting drink, drank, drunk at rock shows that often led him to pass out and miss most of the acts, which was perhaps the worst sins of someone destined to live a simple life of lowered expectations, which was all forgivable within a circle of camaraderie that gave Rob and Shadow, as someone used to living life on the outside looking in, something to believe in.

In the essence of the show must go on, the ritual gathering at Lucky-Winner's place before a metal concert that weekend had seen everyone plow as much gin and juice into their bodies as possible, to reduce a need for overpriced stadium liquor that they still ended up drinking anyway, after wearing down the buzz in mosh pits filled with thrashing humans that had seen Rob catching their breath whilst standing in the beer garden line ups, where they sensed The Energy emanating off of everyone around them, leading Shadow to take notice of the group standing in the next line up beside them, where one of them spoke about assets, family …and life upon the service rig? "We got experience on those!" Rob suddenly pointed out to obvious, to which Shadow quickly countered with the obvious that wasn't, "…If you mean knocking out the manager!"

Rob was well aware of a fossil fuel fiasco that had ended with them knocking out a "pushy" manager, however, given that Fate and Irony had just presented them with a last minute opportunity in a fight for survival social stability, Shadow eventually caved to a reality one way choices, thus granting Rob The Energy to work up the courage to intrude upon a group of strangers, by including themselves into a rigger's conversation to ask a loaded question… "Excuse me…" Rob said whilst putting on their most nonthreatening demeanor, "We couldn't help overhear you say 'service rigs' and are curious if you would happen to know of a good company that we could apply to?"

It was a feeble pitch to break the ice that would hopefully evoke a favorable response from the one man in particular, whom judging by the way he spoke they had figured him to be the manager of a service rig. When the would be rig manager and his group immediately fell silent and serious, a sudden awkward moment arose that could go either way, but when Shadow noticed how they were looking at their physically toned, tattooed torso in a muscle shirt, Rob knew they were in when the manager replied… "They're all bad …but I can get you a job!"

That night, they met Lips Maclean, a down to earth service rig manager with a sharp tongue, whom could win any argument with an oil executive or make any suit and tie guy cry within an industry of hard-asses, which they got to witness firsthand after Lips Maclean essentially hired them on the spot at the concert, and gave Rob a position upon his rig, where they discovered a crew that not only worked well together, but they were nothing like the fucking assholes of a previous bad rigging experience, whom had made an arduous task harder than it had to be …only to find out the hard way.

Although they were back to doing a physically demanding job for an hourly wage, this time however, they really didn't mind the rigors of hard labor whilst working for Lips Maclean, whom was a decent family man whom had been working in the oilfields for years, and who, despite his take no prisoners oil hound persona, provided Rob with a hook up for a place to stay with one of his buddies, which effectively moved them off Lucky-Winner's sofa and into the basement of The Wild Man's place, another rig manager whom was known as the no bones movie type who ran a tight ship and could make a pot of rig coffee that could revive the dead. While this had impressed Rob, Shadow however used The Energy to look within The Wild Man, where they discovered a walking train wreck outside of work whom spent his days off abusing drug and alcohol while his house slowly fell into disrepair, which found Rob happy to be working on the road during rig rotations that kept them away from another place that hardly felt like home.

Laboring away with Lips and his happy crew, they felt a sense of accomplishment despite the strains and pains upon a middle aged body, in a job role that seemed like they had finally found an escape from Fate and Irony's plot twists, until one day that is, when a subtle earthquake caused the formation of hydrocarbons deep underground to shift and trap equipment down hole, upon a high stakes well completion that not even Lips with all his verbal daggers could prevent the oil client from demanding that the rig company terminate Wishbone, the driller on the rig, whom was replaced by The Dictator, a replacement driller whom was a large burly man with a militant attitude, who immediately fractured an otherwise harmonious atmosphere that killed everyone's cheer faster that a hydrogen sulfide gas release, leading to a strained working environment that soon led the rest of the guys including Lips, to begin talking about packing it in, much to Rob's chagrin.

Then one day, while everyone was in the crew shack at the end of the work shift, a shouting match erupted between Lips and

The Dictator that reached a fever pitch over their next move to salvage an oil well that had become known as the money hole due to .the length of time it was taking to complete, which found Lips getting creative with words that touched upon a potbellied man whom had not seen his penis since childhood, or, perhaps ever, thereby prompting The Dictator to assume a threatening stance and begin yelling and pointing obscenities at everyone…

"You're all a fucking joke!" The Dictator screamed at Lips before pointing to Darcy, the pipe tongs operator whom had been snickering at their feud. "…And you're fucking garbage!" Then, The Dictator pointed at Rob, whom had merely been sitting there in silence, "And you…! You're a fucking piece of sh…!"

***REASON FOR LEAVING***: Retied the cape

# 15

# *GOD IS DEAD?*

# CRAP BUCKET AQUA-DIGGING

## *Dead Man City, ~ 2013 ~ Feces Facilitator*

"So what happened then?" The Wild Man asked as they sat at his kitchen table having vodka cran-razz from the large one hundred ounce bottle on the counter.

"Well…" Rob continued with a story worthy of a comic book ending, "From there all it took was a subtle glance from Lips for the green light to fly like an eagle, which found our right foot placed upon our seat that served as a launch pad to soar across the crew shack in a single bound to deliver The Freak's right fist into Death Valley upon The Dictator's face like superman's dead, which dropped a big villain and effectively neutralized a shitty attitude mere moments before the onsite oil consultant entered the shack to question how the driller got a black eye, bloody nose and a fat lip from tripping over his own boots?

"Get what you fucking deserve!" The Wild Man raised his drink in toast of a debatably heroic act, which had seen them resign to save Lips the paperwork and to avoid "accidently" murdering The Dictator at the worksite, whom surely would have used his superior position out on the rig to exact revenge best served cold, thus, compelling Rob to step away from the rigs permanently, in a never to return to an industry sector as a rig pig.

## Professional Shadow

"So, what are you gonna do now?" The Wild Man asked with an abnormal enthusiasm, which immediately tipped off Shadow to an anterior motive, and prepared Rob for the ninety nine and one percent, "thanks for being a friend" fees, upon revealing the cards of an open schedule... "We're gonna chill for a while... work on our story. Then find another job ...eventually."

At this point, the notion of finding employment no longer held the same first job jitters for someone having labored all over MY-BIG-HOUSE, which had taught them many things about the bullshit behind the interview, and the "interviewer", like when the applicant asks, "What do you pay?" and the interviewer replies with a question of deflection, "Well, what are you looking for?" which immediately turns an interview for a so-called career into a marketplace hustle for profit, where Rob would simply get up and walk out of the interview, but not before answering, "We were looking for you to answer the fucking question!"

"Perfect! So hey, wanna fix up my place since you have time and experience with renovations? I'll give you free rent and all the Vodka and Yayo you can consume!"

"Free rent?" Shadow echoed on the inside, to a kids aren't alright theory that once again found them view as a tool or agent for profit, revealing they would never be true friends beyond the "what-have-you-done-for-me-lately" of convenience and loaded chivalry, however, the chance to flex The Energy away from time clocks was enough to coax them into a challenge that tested their professional abilities, however, as far as the booze and drugs were concerned, "...Thanks, but we'll stick to the weed!"

"Leave it to Fate and Irony to turn our home life into a fucking job!" Shadow thought of their "will work for food", or, in this case, rent, which had created another distraction from writing that, despite a growing mound of scribbled footnotes and short, roughly written passages, they were nowhere near any kind of manuscript, not to mention a fucking plot or platform to carry a fan letter slash music theme.

"Now we know what actual writer's go through!" Shadow admitted as Rob paced the floor of their basement suite chasing creativity through many bouts of frustration sprinkled with curse words, over how to accurately convey The Energy onto paper, where it was glaringly obvious that something missing. While writing a biography dedicated as a fan letter seemed pretty straight forward, something was needed to carry the story beyond the tribute that would give it not only purpose, but also a common link shared by everyone aside from death, taxes, and music, however, Fate and Irony would not let the obvious reveal itself, leading to many doom and gloom moments of doubt that, at times, compelled Rob to begin thinking that perhaps they were making a mistake to hinge their hopes upon a writer's career, which was seemingly, if not constantly, at odds with Fate and Irony's plan…

"Whatever that is…!" Rob sighed as they leaned back in the chair to stretch their back after hours of spiritual genocide over a blank page, only to have gotten nowhere in the recanting of fatefully ironic tales that bordered upon the unbelievable and the insane.

By spring, a rundown "bumgalow" had been turned into a "baby, I'm an anarchist!" party shack, complete with repaired hot tub out on the back deck, which Rob had fixed via stunning feats of improvisation, proving yet again that their mastery of The Energy gave them the ability to fix anything Rob touched...

"...Except for people and writing, apparently!" Shadow said as they took a break from a non fictional story, to draft another fictional resume of career highlights and through the never timelines that...

"Hey, can you imagine putting 'Lips' or, 'The Freak' or even 'The Ghost' as a reference on a job application?" Rob mused with a sense of humor that, surprisingly, was still intact after so many unhappy jobs and world eater careers they had arrived at by chance, not by choice.

"Speaking of 'choices', we need to find a job where we are in more control, instead of being at the mercy of morons, namely the aqua-digging unit operators within the aqua industry, which were going back to because it's an easy in given our experience!" Rob thought about it for a moment, "Are we ready to become a commercial operator? What about family tradition and all that black sheep shit!?"

After all those years of avoiding Father's long haul path, they knew it had finally become their best option to survive, which found them using the rest of their savings to enroll in and pass the commercial operator's course and exam with surprising ease, after which they set out to find a company that would hire a new operator that was a pro digger, which led them to a smaller aqua-digging business that seemed like a good place to begin their miles behind the one wheel that mattered, all the while hoping to not end up in another crab bucket career because, honestly, and despite popular opinion, they hated quitting jobs and starting over at a different job more often than some people changed underwear, leaving them to face the, "Are you experienced?" questions from managers retaining less skill, not-to-mention less class than their severed pinky finger, in a groundhog's day of restarted realities that yet again placed them before another company manager, whom was a diminutive man who used to be...

"...A chef, you say!" Rob expressed their fake amazement to someone whom would clearly be of little help as far as digging dirt and operating industrial equipment was concerned, but, all this was forgotten when they were assigned to their very first aqua-digging rig they would be operating, which, despite a few minor mechanical quirks and a sticking "up" button on the functions remote, it nonetheless felt like a real positive step forward to be the man calling the shots on projects and dealing with clients, now that they were the one dictating how the jobs would play out, or, at least that's what they thought until they met Rob the assistant assigned to their rig.

From that initial feeble handshake, Shadow had sensed a scavenger of human sorrow within their acne faced young assistant, whom, reminded them of a certain rash many lifetimes ago at a con job making patio furniture. Standing there, listening to Squirts claim that he was some hot shot digger blah, blah... Rob couldn't help but notice that Squirts was toting a five gallon pail with him, which, in their experience within an industry that used hydraulically driven equipment, they suspected it was either an emergency spill kit or hydraulic fluid, which made them curious if their rig had leaks, so Rob asked the innocent question, "Hey, what's with the bucket?"

"It's not my fault Ok! When I gotta go, I have to go!" The sudden defensive response from Squirts had surprised them, but then the obvious sunk in that made Shadow echo... "Gotta go?" ...and Rob's eyes narrow as they looked down at the bucket again, then to their hand they had just used to shake with, and there they thought... "Gross!"

If by this point there is any lingering doubt that Fate and Irony are not actual real entities whom can fuck with your reality, burn this book, or keep reading about that which led to a crazy story, as we go to work at our first ever operator gig, with someone whom has to bring a fucking bucket to shit in upon job sites, because he suffers from uncontrollable bouts of explosive diarrhea?

Look, while we can be sympathetic to the physical debilities of another, the notion of having to look at and smell someone's improvised fucking toilet every day, quickly cancelled the scent of a rosy career that was just the tip of a shit-burg, which they discovered when Squirts immediately began using his affliction as an excuse to get out of doing any work at all, thus revealing a so-called hot shot assistant to be more full of shit than his bucket, as a walking, talking, ten pounds of shit in a five pound bag, hid in the cab of the aqua-digging rig playing on his phone, while Rob did all the work, attacking the earth with focused, yet silent rage that resulted in ultra efficient excavations courtesy of "The Groundhog" whom was making the grade, however...

"I'd rather work with actual cattle shit than that little fucking shit stain!" Rob fumed over fecal frustrations. "Don't worry..." Shadow tried for a silver lining, "...we're not gonna wipe his ass for much longer. We'll talk to The Chef when we get back to the shop and tell him Squirts just isn't cutting the mustard!"

That day, they had just completed a large excavation alone because of a useless helper that had once again dodged his duties, which found Rob beyond irritated as they drove to the dump site for cleanout of the mud slurry holding tank, a dirty task that Squirts tried to weasel his way out of, but Rob, pissed off and tired of the helpless act, wasn't having it.

"You've done barely anything since you got on my rig! Now get off your dirty ass and go do your fucking job!"

Of course, Squirts was unhappy and grumbled under his breath as he disembarked, leading Shadow to envision giving him a swift kick in the ass that risked getting shit on a boot. Outside, Squirts opened the door to the passenger utility cabinet in order to access the water hose and functions remote, but left the cabinet door open that effectively blocked Rob's view in the passenger mirror, as they engaged the hydraulic systems and began tending to the dumping paperwork. Everything seemed fine for a moment until suddenly the truck bucked violently and made them drop their pen in surprise.

"What the fuck was that!?" Instinctively, Rob depressed the clutch pedal to kill the power to the hydraulics, whilst urgently glancing in the passenger mirror that was still blinded by the cabinet door, however, just then, out beyond the passenger window, they spied a hard hat rolling off into the distance, leading them to believe that Squirts was pulling a tantrum over having to do any work, which suddenly annoyed them greatly as Rob climbed out and proceeded around the truck to go tear a strip off a shitty assistant like a slapped actress, however, upon rounding the other side, they discovered the large mechanical booming arm that held the large heavy rubber suction tube, raised all the way up in the air with the end of the suction tube dangling over Squirts, whom was lying on the ground next to the work cabinet, whimpering and covered in his own feces?

"Gross!"


***REASON FOR LEAVING****:* Some shit just isn't worth it.

# Professional Shadow

# BAD DEAL AQUA-DIGGING pt.2

### *Mob City, ~2013~ Aqua-digging …Fetish?*

They couldn't decided whether or not Fate and Irony had been on their side that shitty day, when a sticky "up" button upon a functions remote and a ghost in the machine raised the large booming arm holding the big suction tube, until it began pulling against the feeble straps holding the end of tube to the deck of the truck body, resulting in a tug-of-war of increasing tensions that inevitably caused the feeble straps to break and sent a boom arm under pressure rocketing violently upwards, taking the big suction tube with it, all except for the end of course, which came flying off in a whipping action that caught Squirts with a cross check from Hell and slammed him hard into the open work cabinet door like the boards of a hockey rink, effectively knocking the wind out of a wind bag whom collapsed to the ground, where, in all the locomotion, his crap bucket fell out of the open work cabinet and spilled all over a prone, breathless assistant!

"At least that's what I think happened" Shadow deduced from a fucked up scene that Squirts fortunately walked away from unscathed, but not unsoiled, in a hidden detail of embarrassment that became apparent upon the drive back to the shop, when Rob smelled a foul odor and asked Squirts that fated question… "Did you shit?!" …followed by an ironic statement, "Guess that really knocked the shit out of you!"

## Professional Shadow

When the ex-restaurant chef manager let them go after Squirts went crying like a bitch and then lied by saying they were slandering the company in from of clients, Rob was actually relived it was over. "Fuck this shit!" Shadow said wiping away a shitty memory so they could focus their attention upon ordering gold seat tickets for the upcoming Prince of Darkness and The Godfathers of Metal concert in Tower City, which, at the time, was advertized as the only show playing in MY-BIG-HOUSE and a chance to see the man and the band credited for starting a revolution is my name heavy metal trend, they simply could not afford to miss.

Naturally, they thought of The Freak and how he used to love listening to The Prince of Darkness and The Godfathers of Metal whilst doing tattoos, and it was here that Shadow compelled Rob to look back across all the vague chapters and name them using the songs titles by The Godfathers of Metal, firstly as an innocent means of separating and compartmentalizing all the memories, only to realize that the song titles, not-to-mention the actual songs themselves, ironically fit the eras and the memories near perfectly, as though it was just meant to be.

"Song titles... those aren't copyright... are they?" Rob wondered at the notion of getting sued by the persons they were trying to pay tribute to, but for some reason Shadow had no fears and embraced a rare moment to levitate in the pursuit of purpose, which had seen the act of writing become an outlet that enabled them to channel The Energy beyond a burning question, "Am I going insane chasing the definition of insanity?"

## Professional Shadow

Suddenly, Rob remembered how they used to write essays as a kid back in Father Saul's Catholic Junior High School, when Shadow used to look up the essay title in the dictionary and then, as a form of cheating, "borrowed" the entire definition by placing it the essay and then building around it to score high marks, and it was here that it occurred to them that music was now their dictionary and that each song was, in itself, a definition of something, or someone.

"What if we wrote song titles into our story?" Rob wondered passively as their attention went back to golden concert tickets, which they had just bought with the intention of giving one to The Wild Man as a way of showing an appreciation for a place to exist, however, a few days before the show Rob had a falling out with The Wild Man, whose drug habits were spiraling out of control that led them to the announce that they would be moving out soon after their return from the show, which saw The Wild Man immediately turn bitter and begin claiming that he was owed rent for those free months when they had renovated his rundown residence, resulting in a solo flight to Tower City for a once in a lifetime opportunity that was everything they knew it would be.

At the show, they had a great time and got totally smashed. After the show, Rob was sporting a massive hangover upon the economy red eye flight home, which had a stopover in Mob City to take on more passengers. Sitting in their aisle seat clinging to consciousness, it was forty-six and 2 in Shadow's favor over rock, paper, scissors about who was going to sit in the vacant window seat beside them... "I say it's some fat lady named Rosie!" Rob said with a drunk grin, while Shadow hoped it would not be someone exceeding the dimensions of an economy class ticket, as they squinted through the blurriness up the aisle at the humans herding single file along the row, looking for anyone fitting the description of a beach ball, when suddenly, up at the front of the plane, they caught a glimpse of …the red.

From their seated position, they could only see the flaming eighties mane popping up over the filing passengers, until it drew near enough that a red headed woman came into view, whom was dressed in a black leather jacket and matching mini skirt tightly hugging a slender figure, which stood atop bright red shoes that gave her the appearance of hell on high heels that suddenly erased all visions of whole lotta Rosie!

To Rob, the mystery crimson lady looked like she was fire from head to toe, but for Shadow that fire was real when they were suddenly struck by The Energy emanating from the only one on the aircraft whom actually looked happy to be there, as a ginger bounced and bopped her way along the aisle, seemingly destined to pass them by in a fleeting moment that would never permit them to meet this alluring creature that…!

"Excuse me, but that's my seat!"

They had been staring at the floor partly because Rob was still drunk, but mostly to avoided staring and looking like a creep, however, when they looked up at the fiery phoenix soaring above them, The Energy radiating from her being created a "hold my liquor" moment that seemed to last forever …until Shadow suddenly realized they were keeping an angel standing there…

"Let her in dumbass!" Shadow slapped their brain into action, compelling Rob to shift their legs in the cramped quarters to allow a firecracker to shimmy past and take her place by the window, however, when the mystery fire woman brushed their knee on the way by, Shadow instantly felt how powerful The Energy within her really was, just like it had been within The Freak that fateful night they met at The Goblin's garage party, which had instantly confirmed...

"We have to talk to her!" Shadow said with a certainty unlike any they had ever felt before, while Rob, trying desperately to sober up, was like... "Ok, slow down there brother love! Let her get settled first and let me find our balls hiding somewhere under all this nervous anxiety!" Moments later, when the plane began queuing up the tarmac to line up for takeoff, Rob began looking around at random, seemingly paying no heed to The Energy with the drop dead legs sitting beside them, until suddenly, they turned to look at the scarlet stranger and said with a straight face, "Excuse me ...uh, hi, we're Rob, and we just thought you should know the person beside you in case there's an emergency, or, something goes wrong and the plane crashes!"

It was an attempt at dark humor and a crazy thing to say to someone they just met "on a plane" about to take off, which ran the risk of making them look like a fool, but when the stone faced woman held their gaze for that split second eternity, and Shadow got to see The Energy behind wild eyes, they knew that she was more than just some random Roxanne.

When it came to The Energy, they had never met anyone that even came close to The Freak, but when the mystery woman suddenly laughed at their attempt at icebreaking humor, they suddenly felt that same family feeling they had felt from a brother from another mother, and right then, Shadow knew they had just adopted Kinky Clare as their long lost twisted sister, with whom they shared fatefully ironic stories about their crazy lives, and by the time the flight touched down in Dead Man City, it felt like they had known each other their entire lives.

"Wow…" Shadow thought as they bid farewell to the sister they never had, in a parting of ways that had seen Kinky Clare tell them, "If you're ever in Mob City look me up!" I'll take you out to see the city and meet all my friends! You'll love them! They're awesome! It'll be a blast! K… Bye!"

Left standing there, exhausted, hung over and hungry from a thirty hour waking journey, Rob wondered, "Did all that just happen?" to which Shadow replied with absolute certainty, "Yes, yes it did!" as they watched Kinky Clare leave with her folks from a small town a few hours outside of Dead Man City. At that moment however, Rob suddenly realized what a one percent instinct was thinking… "We're not seriously thinking about going to Mob City just to hang out with her… are we?" But, Rob already knew the answer when Shadow firmly decided… "Yes… Yes we are!"

Upon returning to their dark hollow within the basement of The Wild Man, a drug addict working overtime at ingesting things that were unfit for human consumption, a growing disdain for The Wild Man's drug induced attitude led to a quiet plan to escape from a dead head environment a week later, when they packed up and moved out whilst The Wild Man was away on a work rotation, as they set off upon a one way drive to Mob City with no idea of what to expect beyond the thought of partying with Kinky Clare, and being just a little bit closer to their aging mom they had not seen in far too long.

"We do recall that things are *different* in Mob City, right?" Rob reminded about a place they had seen only briefly in a past life, where jobs paid less than out west, yet, the cost of living was higher within a culture that was certain to make blending in a socially awkward experience, especially when they went looking for a job position within the aqua-digging industry thanks to a Bad Deal franchise operating in the city, upon which they had placed their hopes for a flawless transition across MY-BIG-HOUSE, after they went to see Kinky Clare of course, whom did not know they were coming, but would hopefully hook them up with a place to stay in a last minute life.

"You realize how crazy this is!" Rob kept on with the obvious, "She could just as well say no and tell us to fuck off!"

On the inside however, Shadow somehow knew that wouldn't happen, as they called up Kinky Clare and told her they were in the city, which evoked a... "Who are you!?" ...to which they were used to, and didn't panic when Kinky Clare failed to recognize Rob on the phone right away, and then was a little wary upon giving out her address to some crazy person she had met on a plane. They were electric with anticipation when Rob pulled up to Kinky Clare's place and rang the bell to the unknown, which reunited them with a twisted sister they had unwittingly adopted, and whom looked at Rob like they were crazy at first, in a "what the fuck" moment that left Kinky Clare both stunned and amazed that someone would travel all that way to be her brother. "Uh, yeah, when I said look me up... I wasn't expecting it to be this soon!" Kinky Clare said with a cringe. "Besides, I just moved in here with my new boyfriend and..."

After three days of driving across thousands of miles, Shadow suddenly realized they had never bothered to ask Kinky Clare about her living arrangement, having simply assumed that she was holding down her own place and doing well as the lesbian dominatrix she had claimed to be, in a city with more kinks than a car crash. "Uh, yeah..." Kinky Clare suddenly began with another cringe. "I may not have been totally accurate when I said that!"

All Rob could do want stand there like a boy scout song that had just earned his merit badge in stupidity, as Shadow began to imagine living out of Priscilla, their trusty old sedan and soon to be car-apartment at some truck stop, where they would try to figure out only god knows why they lived so impulsively.

"Did you really come all this way just to hang out and party with me?" Kinky Clare suddenly asked again in confirmation of an insane moment, to which they could only offer a smile that would never hide anything from someone that somehow filled a family gap, leading Kinky Clare to say, "Ok, fuck it! We'll tell my new boyfriend, The Wallet, you're my brother from another mother and that we've been family since way back, like when you ran off with that stripper you told me about on the flight, what was her name? Anyway, and that's that! Welcome home bro!"

The fact that they had just pulled off the craziest stunt of their life was yet another confirmation they could do anything with The Energy, as they moved in with Kinky Clare and her new boyfriend The Wallet, whom looked oddly upon this tattooed stranger settling into the basement of a business professional and owner of a thriving keep-it-in-the-family construction business that, at worst case, would perhaps behold another employment opportunity for Rob if they didn't get hired at the Bad Deal franchise the very next day …which they did.

"Since you're new to the city and don't really know your way around, I can only pay you this much!"

Every time Rob looked into the eyes of The Greedy Weasel, Shadow knew they stood face to face with a shrewd business owner and career hustler, whom did not hesitate to exploit an out-of-towner by low balling Rob on their wage, despite hiring them on the spot due to their industry experience.

"Screw you too asshole!" Shadow screamed from behind their eyes, which had seen many forms of professional manipulation and outright theft of employment earnings at jobs that were just an imitation of life and only served to delay their true purpose, until the inevitable… "We quit!"

***REASON FOR LEAVING***: A date with destiny

## Professional Shadow

## COWBOY AQUA-DIGGING pt.2

### *Dead Man City, ~ 2014 ~ Groundhog 2.0*

"That's just great... we're being mugged by our employer!" Rob told Kinky Clare with words riddled in sarcastrophy, all the while trying to not appear like a loser to a twisted sister whom was like an immortal fireball with The Energy.

"Aw... that sucks babe. Hopefully things will work out for you and the story you're going to write! I so want to read it!"

When it came to The Energy, they understood each other without complicated details or even words, which was a good thing since words failed to describe the strange feeling Rob felt whilst standing in a room filled with people dressed like human sex toys and engaging in sadomasochistic rites that was unlike anything they had ever witnessed in the flesh at strip clubs or otherwise.

"Well... this is weird!" Shadow thought of their first foray into an underground world of fetish and kink not shown on the six o'clock news or, taught within an elementary classroom, which had made it difficult for Rob to maintain a stone cold face to Shadow's unabashed point of view, as they trailed Kinky Clare around as her plus one chaperone and dance partner, opening doors and fetching drinks in a "spoiling my sister" act that made those of eccentric tastes take notice, in a lifestyle of the not-so-rich-and-famous that was not sustainable.

"Well, you're the one that wanted crazy stories for the book!" Rob admitted with ninety nine percent insolvency to their transition to Mob City, which they hoped might lead to a written story and a greater purpose, but after three months without making any progress both literally and financially, thanks to an unpredictable labor job that continually found them getting ripped off by a greedy, scheming employer that ultimately led to the decision to leave a city of reduced wages and head back out west to seek better fortunes, after visiting mom for the holidays of course.

Kinky Clare had been saddened to see them go, but she knew the uphill battle they were facing as Rob set off into the sunset in a bid to outrun Fate and Irony, which was forever casting them into careers built upon pillars of dust that continually forced them to make last minute, albeit difficult choices in the life of a carry on wayward son, whom merely wished to do right by others and a Mom, to whom they renewed a vow to never quit pursuing purpose until they had their day.

"Maybe we should have stuck around back home and gone for the high school diploma" Rob had mused whilst doing the national acrobat thing across MY-BIG-HOUSE, where a long drive accompanied by loud music that tapped into The Energy, found them noticeably less stressed when they arrived at Lucky-Winner's new place in Dead Man City.

"Wasn't in the budget and wasn't the right timing" Rob told his friend of misery, as they took up residence upon a busy sofa that had reunited them with Repeater… "You're back in the city Rob yeah, yeah! The city Rob! You're back! Yeah!" …in addition to a new character named Mighty Mac, whom was a younger, aspiring entrepreneur and carpenter hailing from the eastern shores, known for his drunken karaoke and chasing the plus sized girls, whom instantly became a valued friend to someone living life in a state of collateral damage that, strangely, they sensed was about to change that weekend at the bar with the guys, where Pea-Brain approached them cautiously and mentioned this girl from his work…

"So, Rob, there's this crazy chick at work I can't shake and I need your help to get her off my back?"

"Who would chase after you without alcohol?" Rob echoed Shadow's one percent opinion, which made them smile on the inside at the thought of knocking Pea Brain's teeth down his throat, as he spoke about some young baby mama of three kids whom were not good enough for a self-admitted, male chauvinist, but… "They're good enough for you Rob!"

"Just let me do him. They'll never find his body!" Shadow offered from within, while Rob clenched his jaw in restraint from destroying someone with total disregard for anyone but himself, which apparently included innocent kids that, for some reason, made them curious to meet this rumored shameful girl with obvious bad taste in men that led to a blind date being set up at a bowling alley that beheld all the hallmarks of ghetto hookup, where they agreed to keep things platonic in a onetime meeting of personalities.

"Don't forget what that waitress did to us!" Shadow warned as they entered the bowling alley for their blind date, "…And no crazy ideas about white picket fences!"

Admittedly, at thirty eight years old chasing a purpose that might never happen, it all seemed obvious as they walked up to a table where they half expected to meet your little hood rat friend with a busted back, only for Fate and Irony to blindside them upon meeting the most beautiful woman they had ever seen, next to Kinky Clare of course.

"Ah shit" was all Shadow could think when Rob suddenly went from a prepared for hell demeanor to feeling an attraction to someone with the heart of a lioness, whom was powerful with The Energy in ways she did not fully understand, yet was driven to overcome the hardships left behind by the sperm donor junkie father of her children that had abandoned his kin?

"We should run away!" Shadow advised as Rob drove Shameful home after their date, where Fate and Irony made sure they would fall into a rabbit hole of destiny upon standing next to the beater vehicle that a struggling girl hoped to fix on a strained budget, leading Rob to make an attempt at positivity by placing their foot upon the car's front bumper for a spring test of reliability that…?!

When the front bumper fell to the ground, Shadow felt their reality instantly change into a mission to help a single parent of three, whose family portrait had been shattered by an addict that had left Shameful crippled financially.

"So she claims!" Shadow warned as Rob, with time on their hands firstly began with small acts of chivalry like fixing her car with little to no resources, which evolved into rides to and from a shitty warehouse job that found a struggling single parent living in destitution within a rented basement room, whose sudden return to mobility placed her in a better position to take on the adversity of a family known for casting the first stone.

At that point, it should have been the end of it for a friendship with "benefits", but when Shameful introduced them to her three little bang trophies whom were being held in the clutches of an evil grandmother threatening to put them up for adoption, Shadow knew they had just become the stalwarts of a Jesus Christ pose that would go far beyond the material things like new shoes, new glasses and some emergency dental, which led them to look upon Shameful as a sort of science experiment with the focus of bringing out The Energy from within someone whom was oddly submissive in the bedroom?

"We should run!" Shadow echoed again, but it was too little too late when Shameful was suddenly let go from her discriminating warehouse job that suddenly presented a problem requiring a solution so crazy, it seemed like the obvious path for someone having grown weary of waiting for the day that never comes, leading Rob to begin envisioning settling down against the reservations of a one percent instinct, whom again warned, "She's got The Energy... but, there's something about a girl!"

In their own urgent need to secure an income, caution and pride were thrown to wind as Rob walked in at a previously worked cowboy company, where out of sheer curiosity they went to see if the old management was still running the square dance, only to discover a new impressionable young manager whom knew not who they were, but had heard of "The Groundhog", and whom hired Rob on the spot given their years of experience that suddenly kicked a dead horse career back to life.

Like a man on the moon, they were living life in the vivid dream upon scoring a high paying operator job, which now found them poised to enact part two of a plan to get Shameful hired as their full time assistant upon Rob's aqua-digging unit, where they became known as Mr. & Mrs. Groundhog, working amongst the assholes bragging about smashing holes, and the egomaniacs dreaming about a womb with a view, whom all were made to eat their words by husband and wife type team whom kicked ass within a sandbox of colored hats, all the while impressing the white hats whom signed generous invoices that financed what everyone had perceived to be …a happily ever after?

**REASON FOR LEAVING**: A shameless destiny

# 16

# *FAIRIES WEAR BOOTS*

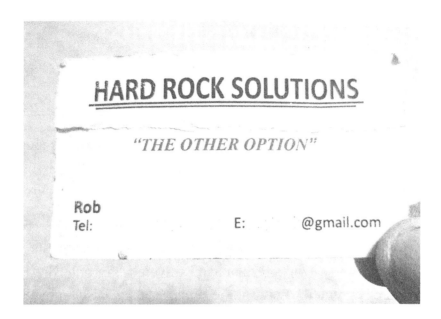

Professional Shadow

# HARD ROCK SOLUTIONS

## *Dead Man City, ~ 2015 ~ Mechanical "Miracle Man"*

"You really think this will work?" Rob asked with the sincere will to try to escape a last minute life, which had been filled with so many unknowns that it had long trained them to be resourceful when facing problems with no obvious solution.

"This is like laughing and not being normal!" Shadow admitted, as they dropped their well traveled bag onto the floor of a newly rented, new home, where they also moved in Shameful and the kids after rescuing them from an evil grandma, and where, for the first time in their life, they could not feel the weight of the time and oblivion pressing down upon their shoulders, leading them to dare to believe that Fate and Irony had brokered a truce with Karma Karen, which would finally allow a stable future to manifest itself upon a not-so-nuclear family riding high on The Energy, whom were making life happen at a blistering pace, which had seen Rob walk into a car dealership to convince the owner to put a beautiful mom of three behind the wheel of her first leased vehicle, which began the process of plugging the holes in a credit score shot to hell.

The idea, had been to set up Shameful to become financially secure first to provide a base, then Rob would in turn begin patching up their own cratered credit score, in a nowhere-but-up story that Fate and Irony did not hesitate to cancel when the bottom fell out the oil industry due to a war of commodities, which sent prices plummeting and industrial projects sent back to the drawing board that suddenly found many people scrambling to find another career direction, compelling Rob to use The Energy to overcome their "what are you waiting for" doubts, leading to the creation of a day home for Shameful while Rob turned a rock and a hard place situation into a "Hard Rock Solution", upon going into business as a freelance aqua-digging operator, contracted to be a pinch hitter at four separate aqua-digging companies at the same time.

"Take that Fate and Irony!" Rob echoed a double whammy of success that found them commanding handsome fees and appeared to have saved the day in a slaves only dream to be king reality, or, so they thought. For that split second eternity, it almost seemed like they might live out their life as a happy daddy, but from the moment they put Shameful on their phone plan that effectively got her back on social media, Shadow suddenly felt a wedge being driven into The Energy between them that hinted to external forces at play, silently perpetrating turmoil that Shameful tried to deny with lies from the table cloth that only made the disrespect worse since Shameful was horrible at lying.

"That girl's got a skeleton in the closet!" Shadow cautioned, as Rob began frequently arguing with someone whom they thought they knew, but left them stunned upon revealing that she was in contact with the "sperm donor" of her children, with whom she wanted to rekindle a relationship?

# Professional Shadow

It was a crushing blow to a perceived notion of "us against the world" leading to a death of trust once rooted in The Energy, which saw them split from Shameful and move into the spare bedroom over at Lucky-Winner's place, which had been abruptly vacated by Mighty Mac after a falling out between friends, leaving Rob to question everything within a fragmental sanity as they came to grips with the fact that the fairytale family life that had once seemed so attainable, was never meant to be.

"Wow, what a crazy bitch to pick a junkie over us!" Rob said with disbelief, whilst hiding in their lonely room trying to make sense of reality. "But… she believed in us, and the story, didn't she? I mean, Shameful even typed out and filed our mess of hand scratched memories!" Shadow paused to try and figure out the obvious that wasn't, "You think it's something she read?"

Although they didn't want to admit defeat to Fate and Irony, they knew the purpose of their story was the reason the universe had pushed them away to pursue a story that had not seen progress toward a real happy ending due to the same case of locked up writers block, leading to frustration and despair over a lifetime of never being able to see the obvious before it's too late, like the fact that Shameful never really wanted to be with someone older such as them.

"A hump and dump is all it should have been!" Shadow concluded, as they took stock of a life they now had to salvage …with nothing. After leaving Shameful with everything to avoid wrecking the world of three kids more than it was going to be with real daddy, the lack of belongings to cart around was but a small respite from the weight of the burdens they carried on the inside, which had been made heavier by the fact that a crashing oil economy no longer required a freelance operator's services, thus leaving them unemployed in a grand fuck you finale Fate, Irony, and Karma Karen's fist up where the son never shines, which had left the uninterested in returning to the aqua-digging industry where, phoney smiles and fake hellos from people expressing condolence at their breakup wasn't something they wanted to hear, so, they did nothing…

"By nothing it also means not answering the phone to little miss 'my plague'!" Shadow berated Rob each time they answered the phone to a soul stripper, calling to drag the waters of a dark side of my heart drama series involving the father of the kids, whom had arrived to prove he was still a loser in person and not merely in spirit. All this ultimately found Rob seeking to get away from the atrocity vendor of her own misery, within a subchapter growing more and more stagnant with each sentence, as they searched for a new plot that would offer another direction for a life story stuck in a marathon middle of madness and…?!"

"Hey! Where's the cross The Freak gave us!?!"

When all of a sudden Shadow noticed that a distinct weight upon their chest was missing, a visual search of their person as they drove in traffic found them serving all over the road, so Rob pulled over to thoroughly search the car …six times, before it finally sank in that it must have fallen off when they got out to buy cigarettes back at the corner store, leading to a mad dash risking a speeding ticket back to the store to inquire about a lost item …that was never found, which instantly sent Shadow falling into the river below upon losing the only material thing that connected them to The Freak…

"Fuck! Why is Fate and Irony doing this to us?" Shadow wondered as they drove home under a dark cloud of misery, in a life that would never allow them to hold on to anything sentimental, or, for that matter, anything of value in a forsaken existence that...?

"Hey..." Lucky-Winner interrupted Rob's droning on of self loathing, "...can you help me fix my truck?"

Despite his faults they liked Lucky-Winner, but his timing was fucking shit along with his mechanical abilities, which found them burying their own troubles to go fix those of a friend that were arguably more serious.

"Why don't you buy something better?" Rob asked whilst on their back under Lucky Winner's old beat up pickup truck performing an engine starter replacement.

"My dad had one just like this" Lucky Winner replied, leading Shadow to remember their long deceased father, whom also used to have a pickup truck that was very similar to the one they were currently fixing, which was from an era when vehicles were built to last, instead of the disposable junk heaps being mass produced within a new age of computerized cars. Once they had fixed Lucky-Winner's old tank of a truck that kept a mechanically inept metal head rollin in nostalgia, they were hardly surprised when Repeater decided to tap them for some low budget repairs to his small pickup truck...

"You know Rob, I wonder if you'll fix the brakes on my truck, yeah, the brakes on my truck Rob ...yeah. The brakes on my truck need fixing Rob, yeah, I wonder if you could fix the brakes... yeah..."

While their initial reaction had been to turn down a replaying request, they eventually caved to help a hapless friend in need, and to stop Repeater from repeating himself, repeating himself, however, upon completing the job, they should have known... "It's awesome that you fixed the brakes on my truck Rob... yeah, the brakes on my truck, yeah... that you fixed Rob..."

"Don't mention it" had been their sincere reply to stop a broken record from driving them insane, but just then, Repeater said something that surprised everyone... "You should be a mechanic Rob, yeah, a mechanic, Rob you should be a mechanic, yeah...!"

In a world of survival and self sabotage, the only thing crazier than Repeater changing the subject, had been Fate and Irony turning baby face to remind them of The Energy they possessed, which they could tap into to do anything they wanted, which suddenly revealed a new direction beyond the mud holes of measured hopes leading to a study of the local automotive repair industry, where they discovered a employee scene that paid shit without the certificate.

"Yeah... no" Rob said with raised eyebrows to the thought of being a grease monkey in some dirty garage, however, just then the crazy idea of going into business as a freelance mechanic entered their mind, which prompted them to look at what type of repairs they could perform in a mobile setting without the benefits of a garage equipped with a car lift and pneumatic tools, which would find them using a simple car jack and elbow grease to execute repairs upon client driveways, or on the side of busy highways they would reach using Priscilla, their trusty old sedan loaded with mismatched tool and a ratchet set that was missing that goddamned ten millimeter socket!

"Fuck it" Rob said with deep breath before taking a leap of crazy that found them going to work as a mobile mechanic literally overnight, which, at first glance seemed to be the fated next step to continue a self-employed status, however, upon digging into the details further, Rob discovered that specific certificates and permits were required to pursue their chosen path, not least of which an official mechanic's certificate deeming them to be a registered wrench head with insurance in the event of mishaps and defective workmanship, which brought up another detail of vital importance that made a lack of diplomas and paperwork seem trivial…

"Professionals don't say 'oops'!" Shadow cautioned about screwing up never before attempted auto repairs upon vehicles, which, unlike working on their own stuff that merely carried the risk of being stranded on foot to walk to the parts store, messing up a repair on a complete stranger's low rider carried real consequences of unknown severity, however, the consequences of doing nothing carried a far worse financial Fate, which found Irony pushing them go for it.

Rob was nervous as hell that first time someone replied to their catchy online ad. "Don't sweat it…" Shadow reassured as they arrived at their very first paying mobile mechanic gig, "…we know enough to get by, and for the rest, tell them we're texting our nonexistent girlfriend, but really, we'll go online to watch repair videos to quickly learn the details, and then, simply copy what we see!"

And so, a last minute career found them going around repairing just about every make and model vehicle Rob dared to put their hands on, or could find a repair video for, which over time, not only granted them deep wealth of knowledge in the field of auto repair, but proved once again that an ability to use The Energy to accomplish amazing things was not merely the stuff of fiction within a crazy story, as they slowly grew their list of callback clients over the next year and a half at a freedom job role that seemed like it last forever?

*REASON FOR LEAVING:* Who can it be now?

# MIGHTY MAC CONSTRUCTION

## *Dead Man City, ~ 2017 ~ Builder of Things*

Between going to hard rock shows with Lucky-Winner, working as a "Professional Shadow" of the auto repair industry, and avoiding Shameful, whom had split up with "the sperm donor" for the second time and was now openly earning a dirty thirties title by sleeping around with various suitors...

"More like 'shameless!'" Shadow said out spite to keep Rob focused upon their survival, to which there seemed to be little time to waste on a woman creating turmoil in their life, the kind that found Shameful place a restraining order upon Rob simply because she was angry at him for calling her bullshit, but then gave him oral sex the following night in her credit building SUV they had helped her get into.

"We should think about moving out of Dead Man City before a master manipulator has us put in jail!" Shadow stated with growing impatience over mind games that were a constant weight dragging them down beneath the water under the bridge of emotional suicide.

"Dumbass...!" A single touché word of encouragement from Lucky-Winner had been worth an entire novel of would haves and should haves, every time Rob allowed them to die for a lie by speaking to Shameful, whom continued to take them to a place inside that left them trapped by the slow motion sickness of to forgive is to suffer at the hands of Fate and Irony, which had cheated them out of happiness and prosperity and left them haunted by the girl of their nightmares, whom turned out to be a total shutter island of social and sexual issues beyond anything they had imagined.

"You two are like a fucking bad miniseries...!" Lucky-Winner had profiled their "don't come around here no more" shit show relationship with an egotistical narcissist, "...The fucking Rob & Shameful Show!"

"Our fat chance friend has a point!" Shadow admitted whilst attempting to put their best metaphysical foot down upon an "out of my mind" resolution, whilst trying to have a good time that at a metal show filled with The Energy, where they bumped into Mighty Mac whom they had not seen in a while and were saddened to hear that he had recently lost his parents, which made Lucky-Winner's "I'm better than you" attitude towards Mighty Mac uncalled for and compelled Rob to begin looking at their own friendship with someone who, had begun to show the hints of resentment to the fact that the girls they met at metal shows were more interested Rob than him.

Simply trying to stay level upon the you keep me rocking waves of last minute mechanical saves, they continued repairing things that could actually be fixed within a busy mechanic service that had led to meeting Garry, a used car dealer and consummate hustler, whom sold them a pickup truck they named Elvis, which served to take a load off Priscilla, their sagging sedan that refused to quit, just like them, in a daily "you gotta believe" career that had seen Rob called a savior for rescuing stranded motorists on the side of the road, and a saint for helping struggling families avoid financially crippling vehicle repairs at repair shops charging exorbitant fees.

"Maybe we haven't lived enough yet, and the story is still being written" Rob suggested about their lagging literary obsession, as they lay under another mechanical patient in some back alley repair job. "Long enough...?" Shadow shot back in surprised denial, "We're forty fucking two years old under here mate! It's a little late for long enough!"

Neither could argue the fact that it felt like Fate and Irony were purposefully refusing to reveal the answers to a project karma that had left them to exist as villains of circumstance, within a life that offered no breaks unless they quit whatever task they were doing because life just wouldn't budge, just like that stubborn bolt that wouldn't break loose, leading Rob to attempt an exorcism using brute strength and curse words to bust the damn thing free...

"In either case... *UGH!* ...Fucking thing! We should start recording this mechanic shit... *UGH!* ...Fucking piece of garbage... and post the videos online... *UGH!* ...Shit! Fuck... On our own web page and... *UGH!* ...Son of a fucking bi...!"

*BUZZ!* *BUZZ!* *BUZZ*

Straining to get their cracked phone out of Rob's back pocket, they looked at the number and saw that it was a private caller, to which Shadow offered the same "watch what you say" cautions over talking about auto repairs to strangers on the phone, especially after Garry the used car dealer, had warned them about an industry watchdog going around putting uncertified freelance mechanics out of business.

"Yeah, yeah…" Rob said to quell the one percent paranoia as they answered the phone with impatience, "Hell! You whack them we rack them…!"

"So I hear you fix cars…" When the unknown male voice on the other end went straight to the obvious, the hell's bells of apprehension began to chime in their mind, compelling Rob to get creative with their reply… "If you mean my roommate's old knuckle buster square body pickup truck, I don't think "fix" is the word I would quite use!"

There was a slight pause before the man continued, "Oh, so you not going around fixing vehicles for money?" The subtle terror tactics entering their ear suddenly caused their pulse to quicken… "Don't know what you're talking about?"

There was another short pause that felt like an eternity, before the mystery man added, "Oh? So that's not you under the Nitro in the alley?" At that moment, Rob began glancing around from their prone position beneath the vehicle, looking for the presence of humans with handcuffs, but when they saw none, they relaxed …slightly. "Who are you and what do you want?"

Although they did not admit to their actions, they knew there was no more need for theatrics within a thrown into the fire moment that, suddenly heralded the end of another last minute career when the matrix agent on the phone turned out to be a seven headed whore of corporate weaponry, known in this case as a private investigator, whom advised them to cease and desist all repair activities or there would be legal consequences!

"Go fuck yourself!" Rob wanted to tell a reaper of reality, but instead chose to take their last breath as a freelance mechanic, and quit doing repair services with just one word, "...Fine."

"You think it might have been someone you know whom was just fucking with you, fucking with you?" Repeater asked them back at Lucky-Winner's place, where they sat trying to process the separation anxiety of abruptly losing another income stream, which felt like a part of them had just died thanks to the ritual knife of misfortune constantly stabbing their reality to death, and then some... "No one knew we were on that job!"

They had no choice but acceptance the loss of a fly by night career that had run its course and move on, however, it was a little difficult with Repeater sitting there... "Well that's just fucking bullshit they are stopping you from fixing things Rob! Yeah... they don't want you fixing things... yeah! Well that's just fucking bullshit Rob... yeah!"

No matter how many times Repeater repeated it, repeated it, nothing was going to change the reality of their situation which, despite having done well at a technically challenging profession that had led to the acquisition of some assets of value like tools and some expensive gold pieces in memory of The Freak, they were no further ahead than when they started, partly due to the constant capital investment needed to keep a shadow enterprise operating, but mostly due to a keep me lifestyle that was every bit as freelance as a now canceled career.

## Professional Shadow

"It's going to work out for us, just be patient!" Shadow tried using The Energy to mend a gaping financial wound that refused to heal, "I hope you're right" Rob said about their ride or die situation, which left them once again unemployed and looking for another cold and empty labor position they knew would only lead to another cold an ugly ending, after beating up their body, their sanity, and quite possibly another manager at some random punch clock career for far less than they were worth...

"We're not ready for that..." Rob simply resolved, as they decided instead to get drunk at Karaoke with Mighty Mac, whom was the lifeblood of any ad lib party that permitted him to stand upon tables and belt out his best renditions of "love stinks" and "I got you babe" classics ...but in a growling metal front man's voice.

"Out of all the people I know Rob you have the craziest life!" Mighty Mac had complimented over Fireball shooters, "I tell ya buddy, you inspire me, and if ya ever need a job, you can have a spot on my construction crew!"

And so, they went to work with Mighty Mac on his building crew, where they hammered away helping a friend within in a woke up with wood career of carpentry that added yet another uncertified notch upon the tool belt of a Certified Crazy Person, whom built houses and condominium complexes without that fancy piece of paper stating that they were an educated monkey capable of doing any job without ...going bananas?

***REASON FOR LEAVING***: A road paved with gold?

## Professional Shadow

# YELLOW BRICK ROAD PAVING

## *Mob City, ~ 2018 ~ Trailblazer*

Flexing their pinky stump attached to a hand feeling the effects of too much manual labor and too many shots to Death Valley, they knew that a missing extremity was just a weak excuse for a lack of typing skills, which found them constantly having to watch the one finger keystrokes of a literary novice, poking away upon at the definition of insanity by night, whilst working a rugged labor job by day with Mighty Mac that, despite working in the company of a good friend, seemingly had nothing in common with writing their story.

"It's alright, I think our writing is pretty good …in short bursts!" Shadow tried to encourage as they heaved with the guys to lift a wall into place. That morning, the job site was an ant hill of activity, where tension had been running high after the so-called leader of another building crew had picked a fight with Mighty Mac, only to find out about the wrong one to fuck with when Rob went head hunting in the name of honor, which found a phony tough guy go into hiding somewhere on the job site, where the animosity lingering in the air seemed to compliment the grey skies of infamy, which never failed to bring about change in dramatic, if not traumatic fashion, when Mighty Mac suddenly announced that he was shutting down his small time builder business after getting screwed over by project developers, fellow contractors and so-called friends, all except for Rob whom had to watch a good friend seek bankruptcy that resulted in Mighty Mac moving back east, leaving them unemployed once more whilst sitting in a shitty rented room after a falling out with Lucky-Winner over a pack of fucking cigarettes, which they knew they should quit before quitting the next random stepping stone they would find in the jobs obituary, where the question was no longer… "Can I do that job and will they hire me?" …but rather, "Who do we want to put up with now and how many fucking morons are we going to meet this time?!"

By this point, employment ads that were once intimidating due to inexperience were now viewed as subchapters of slavery within someone else's story, where they rewrote the rules of probationary periods by applying The Energy to learn and master new tasks in mere hours or days instead of weeks and months, by which time the truth about a "lies are a business" company would no doubt be revealed leading them to walk away from another damage case career with a flip of the bird to some asshole manager, which, only added to their hesitance to do anything physical for anyone anymore.

"I think it's time we start working with our mind instead of our back!" Rob said with ninety nine percent certainty that their body would soon begin showing signs of wear from all the physical strains they had endured, all the while wondering if Fate and Irony would ever give them the clarity to know where to go nex…! *BUZZ!* *BUZZ!* *BUZZ!*

"Hellooo hun…! How's it going!?"

A permanent smile appeared on Rob's face when they heard Kinky Clare's voice on their new smart phone, which instantly took away all of the madness and misery they had endured since departing the crazy world of a twisted sister, whom could always use The Energy to make them feel like life was never as bad as it seemed.

"Honestly, it feels like our story is never going to be written Clare..." Rob confided to a sibling adopted among the clouds, whom never failed to be a source of compassion and positivity, not-to-mention common sense... "Aw, hun... you just need to get the fuck out of there!" It never ceased to amaze them how "clare-voyant" their sister was, given the timing of their sudden unemployed status that made it seem like a god send when Kinky Clare announced... "Good news! I told The Wallet about you going around fixing everything out there and... he wants to hire you as a mechanic in the maintenance shop of his construction business!"

It took a moment to dig themselves out from under The Energy avalanche that Kinky Clare had just dropped upon them, which made peering into a lesson lived is a lessoned learned future a difficult vision to grasp, as they considered the idea of returning to live and work in Mob City, where traffic was always shitty and the paycheck of an hourly employee barely covered the basics of survival, leading to hesitation when they attempted to weigh the obvious that was, versus the obvious that wasn't.

"On the one hand, we would be close to our twisted sister and her cooking, which is to die for..." Rob presented the high points of a sudden and unforeseen career direction, to which Shadow added the most important of point of them all, "We would be within driving distance from mom, whom we haven't seen in..."

"Lifetimes…" Rob said without falter about the one whom had given them life, right before looking upon the *other* hand, where the path to a new career was unclear and carried many unknown variables, upon going back to a place that would cost more than a pretty penny to drive to in a pickup truck that was set up for mud and work, not for long distance life changes.

"We'll think about it" Rob said to their twisted sister whom then handed the phone to The Wallet and told him… "Convince him to come here! I want to see his face!" …which they overheard and could not help but smile at the warm feeling of having someone beyond a parent whom actually care about them, which offered a measure of reassurance when The Wallet, whom they respected as a good friend, told them… "Your road is paved with gold!"

The famous last words echoed in their mind long after Rob hung up the phone, giving rise to the reminder of past life promises that never yielded prosperity or an everlasting career, leading to renewed hesitations about throwing caution to the wind and taking off across MY-BIG-HOUSE, despite the strange feeling that it was going to happen anyway if Fate and Irony had anything to say about…! "How's it going?"

When Rob turned to look at Shameful, whom had just pulled up beside their jacked up pickup truck in the parking lot at the mall, the drain upon The Energy had been instantaneous as they gazed into the eyes of someone looking thin and sickly, as though chasing death within a shameless reality of me so horny sex hookups that began leading Rob into another emotional tail spin of disappointment, until…

"Alright, that's fucking it!" Shadow said with worn out tolerance, "We done right for those kids by helping Shameful rebuild a destroyed life that couldn't even get a goddamn phone plan, and no one can ever take that away from us!"

All of a sudden, Rob could feel The Energy surge through them that caused pupils to dilate with in a lateralus moment of laser focus that finally put an end to a maze of torment...

"Fuck this place..." Rob announced to Shameful. "...we're moving to Mob City to work for The Wallet ...and we're leaving today!"

THREE DAYS LATER... "What you mean... you moved the company thirty miles outside of the city?" Rob questioned The Wallet about a different reality than the one described over a brief phone call, which had omitted crucial details about a supposed golden egg career that had suddenly become a prison sentence.

"...And what do you mean it's just a grease monkey gig? What do you mean it's the graveyard shift? What do you mean we have to pay back the relocation fund that moved us across MY-BIG-HOUSE...?" And Shadow's favorite...

"The fuck you mean, we *'owe'* you!?!"

**REASON FOR LEAVING:** Rock star

# 17

# *A HARD ROAD*

## "IN YOUR DREAMS" CASTING

### *Mob City, ~2018~ Casting Extra*

"This is so not us" Rob sighed with disdain and despair, as they wiped away the blobs of grease from dirty coveralls, at a night job in the shop of The Wallet's construction company out in the middle of nowhere.

"Yeah..." Shadow agreed about a greasy, although necessary maintenance task, "...but, at least we don't have to pay back The Wallet!"

At the end of the day, or, in this case, night, there was only them to blame for giving Fate and Irony the power to blindside their reality at the 11th hour, which had left them time and again regretting life and career, where, despite The Wallet wiping the slate clean upon realizing the error of a short sighted desperation to fill a company position, Rob was now bound by honor to someone whom was practically family, to remain trapped within a job role they did not want to be doing in total seclusion of human contact late at night, all alone with the smelly skunks and the abnormally large spiders ...fuck!

"Even worse..." Shadow delivered the killing stroke, "...it's stealing our time and The Energy away from pursuing the purpose we should be!"

While they were disappointed, Rob could not be angry at The Wallet for at least they had been reunited with their twisted sister, "Classy Clare...?"

"Uh, yeah...they only call me Kinky Clare at my Christmas parties now!" Classy Clare said with a laugh and a wink, upon describing her life in the years since they had not seen each other, which had seen big changes for someone having traded the all night transcendent partying for a media socialite personality posting daily on Classy Clare's Corner for her large following whom shared in The Energy of a truly beautiful soul through comedy, cooking, camping, gardening, and burlesque acts with her trusty sidekick Jimmy Phule, whom was no fool and a master of a thousand disguises, and an all around great person.

"You've been busy! We're so happy to see you!" Although Rob's words were sincere, on the inside, a future plan had been silently set into motion that would see them serving out their sentence for the season at a boring and depressing red eye employment incarceration, and then leave in the fall to go east to finally acquire their high school diploma ...and to visit a poor old parent.

"Everyone loves a mama I'm coming home story!" Shadow daydreamed about a heartfelt theme of devotion and tribute, which they were certain would touch anyone reading a fan letter biography, which was still missing a yellow ledbetter platform that could join together the million little pieces of a scattered life, about to undertake another an easier said than done journey that hopefully, would not turn into another tragic suicide is painless miniseries of unforeseen caveats to a contingency plan aimed at finally acquiring a basic high school equivalency certificate, before moving back out west to go work in the oilfields ...for good?

"Where we will finally write our story ...because nothing else matters, right?" Rob attempted to add ninety nine percent ambitions to a bandwagon of motivation however, Shadow's one percent reply was blunt, like the end of a warrior's war hammer, "Sure... but, there something we need to cross off our career bucket list first."

"You know, we've been through so many jobs that to most people, except perhaps for our twisted sister, Classy Clare, we just look like a quitter...to everyone..." Rob stated the obvious, as they drove down to the casting agency to sign up to be a casting extra in television and film projects being produced and shot in a city with a vibrant Arts & Entertainment industry, "...but, at least we never quit on us!"

As a kid growing up, they had aspired to becoming a famous actor or a superstar musician despite never revealing that day in elementary when the teacher asked everyone what they wanted to be when they grew up. "That's because we're not just one more astronaut!" Shadow reminded as they parked Elvis, their jacked up pickup truck and walked toward a place that had the potential to make dreams come true for a kid raised by television and guided by music. .

"This is ballsy!" Rob admitted in nervous anticipation, as they reached for the door of destiny that, at the very least, might lead to new insight into their own and literal directions stuck in development hell, all the while wondering... "Will we find a busy foyer full of extras with dreams just like ours, or, see some dreamy hot receptionist chewing gum and doing her nails whilst ignoring the phone ringing off the hook, or, meet some sleazy movie producer with a cigar in his mouth and multiple gold chains hanging over an exposed furry chest, who will ask us that life altering question, "But…" *ZIP!* "…don't you want to be famous?!"

"Bah…!" Shadow quickly dispelled the anxiety. "Look, after forty plus job positions and like thirty more across MY-BIG-HOUSE that were simply too shitty to mention in a biography… this is just another job interview!" Shadow reassured without fear, "So, relax, this will be a walk in the …part!?"

"Right…" A one word speaking line uttered from a script treatment written by Fate and Irony, was about as close to an audition as they were going to get upon entering the casting agency expecting to wield The Energy like a super power, only to find themselves standing in a security bubble looking at the unremarkable receptionist with thick nerd glasses sitting behind a thick pane of bulletproof glass, whom slide them an oddly thick application form through a slot and told them flatly, "Fill that out!"

"Figures" Rob said shaking their head and taking a seat upon the sole hard plastic chair, where they attempted to rock dat shit upon filling out the first page of an application that contained the usual personal info queries like name, address, contact info, age and entitlement to work in MY-BIG-HOUSE, however, upon flipping to page two, the plot thickened in ways that suddenly

## Professional Shadow

created a metaphysical brick wall between an elite world of fantasy and a brokie's world of good intentions...

*Do you have any previous acting experience?* "Uh... No."

*Are you affiliated with any acting unions?* "Uh, No."

*Do you have a passport?* "Nope!"

*Do you have a criminal record?* "Uh... Shit."

When Rob put "Yes" to a criminal history, it felt like they had committed career suicide before the star was ever born, and by the time they got to page three, four and five, all hopes had been completely removed of ever landing a lead breakout role in some action or adventure screenplay, adapted from some novel about a Certified Crazy Person trying live as a Professional Shadow, whom had never before seen such an in depth questionnaire bearing so many checkboxes, which sought to identify any notable achievement, talent or skill an aspiring "Z list" actor might possess.

They did not sing and dance outside the shower, and did not play any musical instruments beyond a guitar or drum kit made of air, nor did they play any official sports beyond fitness training... "Oh, oh...! Check!" ...or perform any amazing acts of human athleticism beyond beating up assholes more than twice their size... "Martial Arts...! Check!"

As for the rest, they held no notable assets, certificates or degrees stating that they were indoctrinated to be smarter than the average bear, which left them wishing there was a section in the questionnaire reserved for The Energy... "In that case..."

they both thought with one hundred percent certainty, "...we'd have a Bachelor in Dreams, a Masters in Reality and a fucking PH.D. in Heart!"

Attempts at levity were largely empty, just like most of the checkboxes upon a questionnaire that made them feel invisible by the time Rob's profile pictures were taken from various angles, reminding them of mug shots within a crowbar system, all the while spawning questions that inquiring minds wanted to know... "What's my good side? How's my complexion? Do I need a nose job?"

When it was over, they were simply told, "We'll be in touch" which really took the famous out of the fantasy, leaving them feeling like a bigger nobody than before they walked in the fucking casting agency, as Rob returned to their lowly night shift grease monkey job amongst the wild vermin and steroid spiders, hardly expecting a call that could change it all, in a life of few wins that had never even seen a lottery ticket payout beyond the chance to keep losing.

When the end of the season arrived and they announced their impending departure, Classy Clare was again sad, but knew it was a path they had to follow that would lead to a long lost high school diploma equivalency before going back out west to work a much higher paying aqua-digging job that...?

*BUZZ!* *BUZZ!* *BUZZ!*

Visions of Dreams, Reality and Heart began to race upon answering "that" phone call, when the voice on the other end gave them instructions to show up on a location to shoot some scenes for a television show about some artist wanting more? With Fate and Irony as the executive producers of an opportunity, they gathered up the courage to face improbability, as they showed up on that scheduled day, filled with anticipation as they were met by a simple production assistant, whom led them to a large room full of other casting extras, where they were simply told to sit and wait, and so they waited... and they waited... and they...!

"Well, this is boring!" Rob thought from sitting around all day next to every other idle wannabe idol waiting for their five seconds of fame, which, at one point, made them wonder about a job role within an industry that was nothing like they had imagined, as they lingered alone in a crowd acting like they were busy networking on their phone that died an hour earlier, all the while stealthily studying everyday people seated around them, many of whom were doing the same thing as the nobody watching them, while others sat in groups engaging in active chatter about things they could not make out from a distance.

"Go charge the phone near those girls. They look like they've done this before!" Shadow directed them to a wall outlet closer to a group of women whom were emitting more of The Energy than the rest of a breakfast club of hopefuls, "Let's see what kind of over there shit we can learn about this cattle trap!"

Upon moving over, the conversations Rob overheard led them to understand how show business works in the life of a casting extra, where, it all appeared based on word of mouth among the "who you know" cliques whom referred and promoted each other's talents to prospective agents and producers, which made

## Professional Shadow

sense if someone was trying to earn a living on a casting extra's meager salary. Still, the benefits of being part of an entourage that could foster opportunities rather than trying to go it solo did not go over Rob's head, which at that point made Shadow wish they had a finished novel in hand containing their story they could use as an icebreaker to meet...!

*ROLE CALL!*

When the production assistant finally appeared and gave everyone instructions for an upcoming scene, Rob was hardly star struck by how cut and dried the entire process was, as they were all led outside and herded down the street to a film set that saw an entire street cordoned off by the production crew, whom were busy moving behind the scenes setting up lights and cameras that suddenly placed Rob on a high unlike anything they had ever felt.

"Well, light my fire!" Rob thought as they stood upon a film set they never imagined to be a part of, which was surrounded by curious onlookers standing behind crowd barriers, watching them perform a moving scene involving a co-star of the show that found them in the backdrop like a "Shadow", in a moment of "I did this" that could never be taken away from them as the scene ended and they were all herded back to that big room to wait some more, until a production assistant eventually showed up with a check bearing their meager earnings, and just like that, they were done?

*REASON FOR LEAVING*: It's a long way to the top

## Professional Shadow

# MUDDY SHORES AQUA-DIGGING

### *Fracture, ~ 2019 ~ Mentor*

"Maybe we'll get offered a part as a bad Guy in some crime drama, or a stand-in role for some famous actor!" Rob imagined with amusement, while Shadow, never believing them to be high definition handsome, was simply happy to have experienced the thrill of it all, as they said goodbye to Classy Clare and drove to that place once known as home with the aim of removing a lifelong thorn in their side, which found them wasting no time upon arriving in Home Town, to get signed up for a study class that was ironically located in the worst part of town amongst the homeless and the spent hypodermic syringes?

"It's no good" Shadow reasoned over a fateful reminder about of what happens to those whom fail to get an education in their formative years. After getting set up for an academic curriculum of recycled ambitions, they went to stay with their friend Mighty Mac, whom Rob discovered had spawned a kid with some crazy girl that had left him on his own to raise a daughter, Alayna, whom was frighteningly strong with The Energy, and whom adopted a Certified Crazy Person to be "Uncle Rob" in a kids turned out fine story that blessed a Professional Shadow with family in the most unlikely places.

Upon getting settled, Rob then turned their focus to the most important reason they had returned to a place that no longer held attachment beyond a few friends and the one who mattered more than life itself, and the one to whom they would dedicate their story to perhaps more so that even The Freak...

"Hi, Mom...?" Seeing their mother with winter white hair was a jarring reminder of time moving on from a long lost childhood, which had once seemed like it would never end, only it had, adding urgency to the reality of time is ticking away to find a way to write their story within the lifetime of an aging parent, not-to-mention their own, which, given the way their life was going would probably see an old woman outlive her son not long for this world, whose tortured heart was filled with happy sadness as they played cards with a lonely soul whom they had not spent nearly enough time with over the faded years, in a bitter reality of infrequent visits to bask in the grace of a cherished parent whom would always love them unconditionally.

"At least she's safe here from all the madness out there" Shadow thought with consolation and partial envy, as they sat in perhaps the only place left in the galaxy that wasn't connected to a noisy world of technology and opinionated media, woven together by a web of wires and gadgets distracting a world of human drones addicted to their phones, while a seven nation army led by political war pigs bent upon world domination spread hate worldwide in the pursuit of murder for profit.

"We swear to you, Mom, one day our story will be told and you will be honored like you should be, because you are the reason we are here, and we will achieve our purpose... that's a promise!"

## Professional Shadow

With fingers crossed, Rob felt like they were carrying a mountain on their back as they walked past the downtrodden of a broken society every day, to study for a title of education that felt more like a redemption song, leading them to wonder if having high school diploma at their age would even matter anymore, especially if they ever succeeded in publishing their book, to which they hoped an academic environment might grant some insight into a world of literacy, in which they literally had only scratched the surface and still had miles to go both figuratively, and quite literally, before they could ever be called a wannabe writer and an author, whom was still without a platform upon which to base a story about honor, tribute and…

"Nope" Shadow echoed from within when it was revealed that the class tutor was in a worse way socially than they were, not-to-mention so far disconnected from The Energy that considering something requiring imagination and artistry was like trying to get a flower to grow from a bad seed. With perseverance and a measure of luck that saw them escape injury and serious damage when some old man drove his car into their jacked up pickup truck, against all odds, Rob earned that goddamned high school diploma, in a moment of no surrender that felt less amazing than they thought it would be, which, at the end of the day, was worthless if they never did anything with it.

"The sky's the limit for you brother!" James, their best friend had said to them in a fleeting moment of encouragement, before setting off on the road again across MY-BIG-HOUSE, heading towards the black pastures and killing fields of Fracture, where an oil industry offering another way to die would be their eternal penance after lying to a maternal parent and best friends about a quest for purpose that, had finally driven Shadow to throw in the towel upon a fight they seemingly would never win.

"Honestly, I don't think Fate and Irony will ever give us the time and place to write our story!" Shadow mournfully admitted, "...It's like they are fucking scared that we'll become successful and be able to buy our way out of their bullshit!"

"Sigh, when the music's over..."

In a soul searching session befitting of a psychologist's sofa, Rob fought the grim truth behind a dream that had once seemed possible, only for it to all have been for nothing in a never ending documentary of failure and forbidden happiness, upon another long and lonely road into the unknown. Shadow had nothing more to say when they arrived at a remote woodland town that was considered ground zero for an industry turning the sands of time into an endless supply of petrochemicals, where they were most likely going to spend the rest of their unnatural life working as a groundhog getting dirty for dollars, while the notion of purpose would slowly fade away within a last minute life of lost cause jobs leading nowhere.

They rented a room at The Shawshank, some dive hotel with low monthly rates that was populated by destitute tenants eking out a meager non-existence on government benefits, which Rob would have avoided with better credit, however, given that it was located close to an industrial park filled with companies starving for bodies, they accepted a lowered state of survival in hopes that it would only be temporary, as they went to get hired by another muddy company they had previously scoped out within the online jobs obituary before leaving Home Town, however, upon walking in to apply for their one hundred plus job, which was all but guaranteed simply based upon their years of experience within the aqua-digging industry they actually hated, never did Rob imagine they would run into Randy, an old acquaintance and former co-worker from their days working at a previous cowboy outfit, whom just happened to be the new manager at the company they had just applied to, and whom not only immediately hired them without the need of a tediously written resume of tweaked facts and quantum timelines, but also gave Rob the newest rig of the fleet, in addition to making them the official training and safety mentor?

"How about that…" Rob exclaimed with amazement, as they assumed a semi-official management role that suddenly made their entire journey for a fucking high school diploma seem like a major waste of time in light of an unexpected twist that was nothing short of a gift compared to the usual cosmic colon exam administered by the cold hands of Fate and Irony, which is why Shadow wasn't overly convinced about a too-good-to-be-true career opportunity.

"Well, we never saw that coming!" Shadow whispered in the back of their mind as Rob supervised new employees claiming to have experience, or be some hot shot operator, however, using The Energy to look beyond words, it wasn't difficult to spot whom was real and who was full of shit, simply by making them nervous. "Better to be nervous here, in the company parking lot, than out there in trenches …snowflake!"

Perhaps the best part of their unforeseen foreman position was the fact that, unlike management, who were bound by rules of conduct that prevented them from voicing personal opinions and telling lagging employees to… "Please do the fucking job *you* applied for!" …without being reported to the company H.R. department for the eighteenth time, Rob on the other hand, whom was merely a lead hand and still just another set of boots in the trenches, getting dirty alongside the rest of the grunts, found them capable of expressing a broader range of vocal encouragement that their good friend Randy could not enjoy, which found Shadow separating the mice from the men through motivational statements that put metaphysical boots to asses to spur the slack ass labor to… "Do your fucking job, or get the fuck out of my hole!"

From there, every day became known as "Groundhog's Day", at a job that was seemingly destined to be the final entry in a long storied career of "I quits" and "see U never" job roles, which had all failed to lead them to that coveted salary that was unaffected by a time clocks of pinched prosperity, not-to-mention a dead on arrival story that was now gathering dust back at their hotel …cell?

*BREAKING NEWS!*

"In a place where they will eat anything with a pulse and lie about it to save face, reports are emerging about people getting sick after a bat took a steaming dump on someone's Pangolin burger at a live food market just down the street from an infectious disease testing lab, which couldn't possibly have had anything to do with it, and now there's a virus named after a redneck love song, going around annoying all the woke who vote with a bullet whilst infecting all the sheep whom now believed that it's the end of the world as we know it!

All of a sudden, everyone within MY-BIG-HOUSE went into unemployed lockdown, two things they were already intimately familiar with under much worse circumstances, which is perhaps why they questioned a shutdown of society that occurred so fast that it almost seemed …planned?

"In either case…" Rob detracted from the obvious to their immediate situation, which found them socially isolated within their hotel room at the Shawshank, a place that could only benefit the town if it burnt down, and where the psychological reminder of prison and their old jail cell produced flashbacks that were about as cheerful as an edible autopsy, after having the illusion of freedom along with their career ripped away from them again, leaving the mortal fear of running out of toilet paper as the least of their worries.

***REASON FOR LEAVING***: The day the earth stood still.

## DREAMS-REALITY-HEART

### _Fracture, ~ 2020 ~ Author of Fate and Irony_

Despite a one percent theory of shadowy conspiracies, they were less concerned about a manually modified, mass marketed flu strain that was ninety nine point seven percent survivable, than what would happen to their health living on what essentially amounted to a monthly social security benefit that had been all too eagerly handed out by a suspect government, almost like a giant test, or study, or, a distraction from all the pedophilia hitting the media, which left Rob to keep on rotting in the free world of their mind while the real world went to Hell in a hand basket.

Sitting there the like a man out of time, the only solace to their predicament was that, if they died in their sleep, a cleaning lady would find their body before it decomposed to a state off grossness to match the décor of a dive hotel room, where they liquidated anything that might weight them down in the event of a fast bug out during end times, which found them tossing out old paperwork like auto parts receipts for Elvis, their enduring old jacked up pickup truck they so loved, along with old tax forms with personal information stating how bad they got fleeced on their earnings as a labor slave, and… that stack of used resumes?

"Fuck sakes... we've worked a lot of places!" Rob said with tired amazement over how many job positions they had held over a forty year cause of death career, which had seen every hourly labor job as one too many for someone seemingly meant for a greater purpose, upon a journey that continually found them surviving outside of their natural element without the benefit of guarantees or that steady salary, which had seen every unsainted job position eventually fell prey to Fate, Irony, and a skull fucked economy that now left a man on fire seemingly holding the ashes to ashes of an irrelevant career work history...

"Unless we wrote about it in a story...?" Shadow suddenly suggested from out of the dark, compelling Rob to frown and place the half dozen resumes in their hand, in chronological order from eldest to most recent, and there, within that ever trusted split second eternity, they finally found the long lost platform to their story!

"Son of a bitch... It's the fucking jobs! That's the common link everyone has beyond death and taxes!"

In a moment of clarity and disbelief, they tried to process the killing joke of Fate and Irony, which had seen them actually "working" the obvious to their tribute story the entire time, all the while laboring through countless miles across MY-BIG-HOUSE, in search of something that had always been a mere breath away, which made them feel like the unforgiven to, for not seeing the truth that had been continually punching them in the head.

After having spent most of their life burning The Energy at physical jobs, it only seemed to make sense that their work history become the platform and common plot that everyone could relate to, which...?

"Uh...but not everyone *has* a job!" Rob said immediately poking ninety nine holes in a last minute dream come true, which made Shadow pause for a moment to consider the obvious. "Oh, really...? Tell me then, and why do people work... Let me answer that for you..." Shadow sold the rhetorical question, "Everyone works to survive, just on different levels!"

While the theory appeared to have merit on the grand scale of things, Rob wasn't entirely convinced, but Shadow wasn't done making a point. "From the homeless man on the street digging in the garbage bin for something to eat, to The Queen ruling over a kingdom with subjects at her feet, *everyone*, has a job to do if they want to survive!"

Rob merely sat there in silence unable to argue a fact, which suddenly gave rise to The Energy of anticipation, but also the crushing weight of intimidation in the face of an undertaking that would surely be the most difficult thing they had ever attempted.

"I know" Shadow said with condolence, well aware of the road ahead of them, "...but, we've always believed in our story, which has inspired just about everybody we've ever told about it, so, is everyone wrong, or, are we just crazy?"

The jury was out on both counts, but they knew that it's now or never given that Fate and Irony had just shut down the entire fucking world for them to take a stab at destiny and finally write a story that had haunted their life, yet created the very memories that could fill the pages of their very first novel. "Well, how do we do this?" Rob asked rolling up their sleeves and turning on the old laptop with an 07 Word program they had pickup at a pawn shop.

A moment passed as Shadow considered how to bend the spoon of creativity, "We don't know how to write a book like the professionals that much is obvious, but, we *do* know how to write a fucking job resume so... to get the information out, let's write a book of resumes containing all the work we've done, except in our story we won't sugar coat what those jobs were really like, or add any of the fictional bullshit that everyone puts on a curriculum vitae for the sake of an interview, meaning..." Shadow paused when they felt The Energy stand up to Fate and Irony, "...meaning, no sweeping the truth under a magic carpet ride of white lies!"

Rob raised their eyebrows at the thought of exposing the dirt from their life for all to bear witness. "This is going to be a goddamned confession! Are we sure we want to air our dirty laundry and talk shit about real people, real places and actual companies?" Admittedly, the sensitive nature of facts regarding the people they had met, the places they had been, and the companies they had worked for carried the risk of being sued for slander, but Shadow was driven without fear to honor The Energy of a friend whom was gone, but never forgotten.

"Fuck 'em! We'll change all the goddamned names! Besides, most people we knew had a nickname anyway, so we'll just add a fitting one to everyone and, everywhere and everything to fit the narrative!" Shadow was on a roll, "So, if we liked a person, a place or a business, we'll bestow unto them cool names and titles, and as for the rest… we'll bestow a name or title that's befitting of the bearer, or deserving of the situation, because in our book… in our story… we finally win!"

"Oh, that will be fun!" Rob agreed with a sly grin. "So this is for all the marbles huh? You know, this is going to take forever…" Rob said flexing their pinky stump attached to a cramped up right hand, but Shadow was unfazed by the journey that lay ahead of them. "Well, it's not like we haven't been there before and, I never thought we'd say this, but finally, it seems like time is our side for once!"

**REASON FOR LEAVING**: Fate giveth and Irony's taketh away

Dreams - Reality - Heart

# THE FORGOTTEN TIMES

### ~1983~ Home Town, M-B-H

**POSITION:** Paperboy Assistant   **SALARY:** $1/ Day

## HISTORY & EXPERIENCE

- As child, I was blessed to have an older brother, The Myth, whom was my shadow and a window to the future that permitted me to experience things second hand without most of the "I don't know" consequences.

- As the curiously energetic kid sibling whom was seemingly born just to annoy the hell out of an older brother, through The Myth and his tough love teachings about strength, courage and wisdom, I learned to recognize the repeating patterns that lead to life's ultimate wedgies.

- When The Myth got a paperboy job, I worked as his assistant doing most of the labor for the least compensation, which taught me that when it comes to responsibility, keeping a word can be harder that lifting something heavy.

- When big bro quit his paperboy job because the newspaper delivery route supervisor was a scamming asshole, who claimed… "If they don't pay, you don't get paid!" …which taught me that, when it comes to money, the only thing that's free …is how much people will try to take advantage of me.

Dreams - Reality - Heart

# THE FORGOTTEN TIMES

### ~1983~ Home Town, M-B-H

**POSITION:** Paperboy Assistant     **SALARY:** $1 / Day

---
## SKILLS & ATTRIBUTES
---

- Born with The Energy, I just don't know it …yet.
- Early ability to recognize patterns within games and within people.
- Capable of annoying the shit out of my own shadow.
- Ready, willing, and able, to become child labor.
- Entry level understanding of currency
- Aware that with responsibility, you have to deal with the good, the bad and the ugly.
- Aware that if I don't like the fucking bullshit …I can just quit!

**REASON FOR LEAVING:** Screw that, I'm going back being a kid!

# 18

# *THE WRIT*

## Professional Shadow

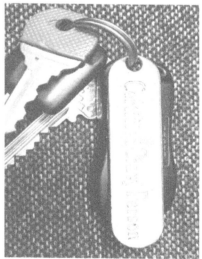

# SOUL DRAIN

## *Prime City, ~ 2021~ Fate and Irony's Pin Cushion*

"I don't know, it feels like something is missing" Shadow reasoned when they wrote the end to a hard fought tribute, which had taken months of sitting in a mental cell at The Shawshank Hotel, using The Energy to travel back in time through the eras and the events that shaped their reality, whilst working away and never seeing the obvious...

"The fuck you mean...?" Rob questioned whilst stretching through the soreness from sitting for so long, "I think we did alright getting the meat of our story down, and all that's really missing is a book cover!" Although they had placed great effort in searching out the most relevant parts of their life, Shadow could not help but feel like The Energy behind the story was incomplete. "Yeah, but, when I said we would offer the resume of our life as a fan letter, which, ironically doubles as a crazy "resume" to be a writer, I didn't exactly envision the book being in actual resume form!"

Looking at their old laptop upon the ratty desk that reminded them of Karma Karen on that fateful day they nearly died on the job, Rob felt like dying at the thought of starting all over in a lifetime of restarts. However, at that moment, an attempt to do something most only ever dream of, gave way to a wave of weariness that compelled Rob to shake off the weight of time...

"Whatever, we'll self publish this on Amazon send a copy to Classy Clare!" Rob resigned, "Our twisted sister will let us know what we missed and how good or, how bad we did!" Shadow nodded on the inside, as Rob suddenly wondered, "Anyway... where *is* the proof of that book cover we had made? Isn't that in the suitcase in the back seat of Elvis out th…!"

Every day of their self-imposed semi incarceration, they had glanced out the window at a deserted world devoid of human movement thanks to some biological Babayaga, where they gazed upon Elvis, their jacked up pick truck that was sitting in the parking stall behind the Shawshank Hotel, right there, where they could keep an eye upon their toolbox on wheels, which suddenly …wasn't there anymore!

"What the fuck!" Shadow said in shock upon seeing that Elvis had left the parking lot, prompting Rob to run barefoot downstairs and outside to look for it …like an idiot, whom was now stuck outside without their key to get back in the fucking building.

"Motherfucker!" Rob screamed in rage, as the reality of being ripped off by some night prowler who had apparently decided that he wanted to go party with Elvis and not return! Which now left them watching the bags of cash fly to the angels upon calculating the loss of the truck and the cost of the modifications done to it, not-to-mention all the fucking tools that had been locked away in the bed box, most of which had been painstakingly acquired over months of repair jobs performed through blood and sweat that, now only left tears for an uninsured forty thousand dollar hit.

"I think I'm gonna puke" Shadow said from within, as they now found themselves on foot feeling naked and powerless without their mobility, which, in their life, had been their most crucial asset and only defense against Fate and Irony, which had really fucked them over this time upon losing something most people take for granted. Just then however, Fate and Irony served up the insult to the injury, when Rob suddenly remembered that the proof picture to their book cover, which had been in the suitcase in the back seat of their truck, along with the original stack of pages and notes, along with images they were going to add in their story, like the official incorporation certificate for Devil's Right Hand Inc they had held onto all that time… but, no more.

"What the fuck are we going to do now!?" Rob wondered in panic, over how they were going to escape a black hole a dive hotel and travel eastward across MY-BIG-HOUSE under quarantine, where they had planned to reach Prime City located a few hours north of Tower City and a few hours west of Mob City, which would place them closer to a sister, and within driving distance from their poor old mother, whom was thankfully safe in her bubble upon sparsely populated shores, which were still under a strict lock down that found none could venture too without getting a warp speed vaccine jab that had been developed suspiciously fast.

"Good question…" Shadow answered with an open ended plot theory, which left The Energy as their only remaining worldly possession beyond a crazy story of inspiration and motivation detailing the crazy life of someone whom had mastered the art of surviving by instinct, which now found them frantically playing out millions of scenarios in their mind, desperately seeking another hard rock solution to a fucked up, yet, same old situation to which a spiral architect had but one option… "Garry! We need wheels!"

Ever thankful to have friends in low places who operated on a different kind of credit, a bus ride down to Dead Man City and a visit to an old friend indeed, found Rob placed behind the wheel of a used, yet reliable junk heap that permitted them to begin a pathfinder's journey, toward a place they had only seen at sixty miles per hour going across MY-BIG-HOUSE. For them, Prime City seemed to behold their best chance of scoring work in a paralyzed economy, which would find them seeking out yet another aqua-digging position as the one job they knew nobody wanted to do, and then solve a homeless problem. .

"At least we have room to sleep in this bucket of bolts!" Rob commented about a ride that was a considerable step down from their jacked up pickup truck, however, given the circumstances a poor man teetering at the edge of desperation could not afford to be ungrateful. Upon reaching Prime City some three days later, they wasted no time going to get a job they knew was all but guaranteed despite a lying manager hustling them on their hourly wage… "We're not really looking for an operator right now" the man had stated, but then hired Rob on the spot based upon their years of experience and skill, which unbeknownst to the manager included the ability to see bullshit.

"We'll put him in a fucking hole!" Shadow echoed on the inside with disdain for another bullshit job deal, as Rob tried to focus upon a last small matter of a place to stay, which led them to the doorstep a beautiful early thirties woman with a dynamite body and a fake chest, whom was into fitness ...and writing!?

"Fuck me running" Rob thought about a one in a million stroke of luck that found them moving in with a hot vegetarian ...whom lived with her dad!

"Cock block!" Shadow laughed to a fatefully ironic, and albeit awkward setting, which found them remaining gentlemanly for the duration of their platonic blue balls stay, in a give and take of Fate and Irony that, after everything they had been through, had left them confused over whether or not they were actually lucky, especially when their twisted sister, Classy Clare, gave them feedback on their story ...and let them down softly.

"It's a really great story hun, and I really enjoyed the skills & attributes parts, but, it's hard to follow with everything written in actual resume form. It's too brief and missing continuity and... "

They would respected their twisted sister's unbiased opinion, however, Classy Clare had revealed an aspiring author's worst fears about a novel attempt that wasn't good enough due to its lack of development and, yes, continuity, which all added up to a near miss on a tribute attempt in honor of a friend, leaving them to consider the bitter reality they now faced..

"Where are we ever going to find the time to rewrite and re-edit our story?" Rob wondered feeling tied to an anchor, whilst standing at the foot of an "I'm the mountain" undertaking, which now had the added weight of a day job to distract and steal The Energy away from the one thing that truly mattered in a life and death struggle to survive.

"We keep trying…" Shadow stated the obvious. "No matter how long it takes, or, whatever it takes!" The fact that they had even dared to write a book was already confirmation that they would never quit until they accomplished what they set out to do, even if it took the rest of their unnatural life and led people to look at them and say, "Obsess much?!"

"Quit a hundred jobs, a hundred people and a hundred places, but never quit on us!" Rob said with courage as they got ready for work. "Because we're not awesome, we're driven …right?'

"No…" Shadow said with certainty, "Because we're crazy!"

Thus, in defiance of Fate and Irony, they set about rewriting the definition of insanity, yet again, in the morning before work and at night after shifts, which was a major distraction and stole The Energy from a fateful story about life, honor, and ironically, jobs, as they went back to the drawing board in a serious attempt to be a real author, which found them deconstructing Dreams-Reality-Heart and rewriting resumes into actual chapters and paragraphs, in which the chapters would be associated to a song title by The Prince of Darkness and The Godfather's of Metal in tribute to The Freak, while the rest of the songs titles from every other band, musician or artist that influenced their world and everyone's reality, would be written right into the text body, blended within the obvious and highlighted in tribute to The Energy for all to see.

"You know, telling people we quit a bunch of job makes them think that we're just a quitter, but after reading these stories, quitting wasn't such a bad thing!" Rob reasoned whilst trying to balance a tightrope of destiny that found an aspiring author by night and a dirt digger by day, working overtime at two jobs that stole their time from that which mattered most. "This is going to take another three years!" Rob said with beat up integrity one day whilst eroding holes in the earth for commercial clients whom all had their own safety protocols to access their sites and projects, leading to the inevitable ultimatum... "Get a vaccine shot or lose the contract!"

"The fuck you mean we have to take an experimental vaccine? It's been almost two years and we haven't even been sick!" Rob protested when their soul draining manager dropped a labor ultimatum that would have made them quit on the spot were it not for... mom.

"Threatening people with their jobs and their survival just sounds so fucking suspicious it reeks of corruption!" Shadow stated warily, to which Rob agreed as they drove to the pharmacy on that grey overcast day. "I don't think we should get that shit put in us!" Shadow warned as Rob, feeling trapped with no other choice, rolled up their sleeve to receive the first of two shots of a foreign substance they did not trust. "Don't do it!"

Adrift between reality and conspiracy, Rob felt uneasy when the big pharma lady jabbed their arm with an alien liquid, which immediately triggered a strange feeling within them, as though a glitch in the matrix had suddenly changed their DNA and begun attempting to separate them from The Energy, causing their body to begin fighting off a thief of natural defenses that, despite not making them drop dead right there in the pharmacy, nonetheless lingered with them for days after, making them feel more and more lethargic as though the sands of time were literally flowing through their veins with each passing day, until day four, when it felt like they had a bowling ball in their chest that compelled Rob to drive to the hospital, where the doctors pretended to not know what was trying to kill them, which was the last thing Rob heard as he suddenly grabbed their chest where a heart used to beat, before collapsing to the floor.

Well, actually, the last thing Rob heard was Shadow yelling between the ears of a fool… "I told you not to take that shot! I fucking told you so!"

***REASON FOR LEAVING:*** ……Funeral hymn………

# 19

# *END OF THE BEGINNING(S)*

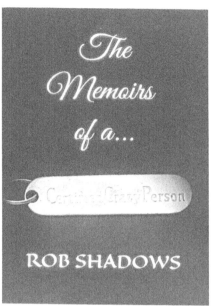
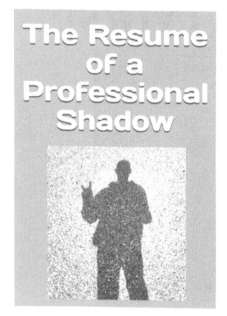

## PROFESSIONAL SHADOW

### *MY-BIG-HOUSE, ~ 2025 ~*

To whom it may concern,

If you're reading this, it means that we have moved beyond our mortal form and ascended to that place among the stars, where we exist now as The Energy within this volume and upon these pages. Obviously, we survived a patient # 9 episode and went on to achieve our purpose both in story and in tribute, which, *only* took another three years, three more moves across MY-BIG-HOUSE and thirty more repentless fucking jobs that were never going to retire a Certified Crazy Person, who survived off of nothing but the sheer will to endure the wrath of Fate and Irony "whom" quite literally threw the book of Karma at us in a last minute life that cost us every god forsaken asset within a marathon middle of constant beginnings and genuinely shit living arrangements thanks to an un-absolved criminal and credit record leaving us to exist out of the basement of an old lady with dementia without a fridge, stove, or internet, which meant wifi of fast food joints in a chore process to access self-publishing and editing services within in a never ending balancing act of relay writing…

That is, until we met Jonathan Cooperman, the self-made billionaire entrepreneur whom is also strong with The Energy of the same "freaky" and "twisted" nature previously seen, and whom gave us a position within one of a multitude of his transnational companies where, ironically, we, as a heavy metal fan and working man without a movie deal, find ourselves delivering specialty steel and "heavy" metal products to a long list of Jon's many clients all over Mob City, all the while spending every waking moment away from work to accomplish our mission of honoring a long awaited fan letter and hardcore resume revealing the real dirt about random labor jobs, all without the help of editors and professional publishing houses, until finally …we wrote the end of a hard fought story.

It was here, upon seeing our commitment to both the job and our writings that Jonathan Cooperman hired us to be his Professional Shadow not just in business, but also within his adventures worthy of their own book series chronicling the last minute life of a freewheel burning, styling and profiling, corporate CEO …and secret agent code named SLICE, whom is called upon to solve crimes when conventional means fail, at times calling upon us to aid his task as "the other option" charged with coming up with hard rock solutions in those dire and difficult moments which, now finds us at the conclusion and end of this interview, where, you, the reader and our potential "employer", can now choose if you would hire us as that Certified Crazy Person to be your unwavering friend, your chosen author, and most importantly, your Professional Shadow whom is capable of seeing The Energy we all carry both as a music fan and as the hardest worker in the room, where it is our sincerest hopes to include you within our foundation, our career and our purpose of Dreams-Reality-Heart.

Professional Shadow

## Acknowledgements

At this time we wish to thank every musical group or artist past and present that were not honored within these pages, but whose influence upon our lives and our journeys was the only thing keeping us going...

Therefore, to everyone, and **a tout le monde**...

Thank you.

## Special thanks to the following...

Trevor Macdonald, Harley May, Shawn Collinson, Haley Zimmer, Christie Coughtrie, Destany Buwalda, Jeff Gallant, Joey Gaudet, Randy Yakimowich, Louise (NSQ) Cantera, Broly Rotthauser, Chanse Gagne, Marie Oceane, Ezra & Farrah, Claude Jake, Violet Revolver, Vanessa Doyle, Jerome Pesant, Tammy Allan, Isabelle Leblanc, Jonathan Bourget, Brandy B Sweet, Eve Amore, Sayna, Maude Beaudoin, Destany Buwalda, Big Franky, Bass Bass, Poi Sin, Clare Ann Higgins, James Robichaud, Sophie Lagace and Jonathan Cooperman.

# FOR YOU

**AARON**

## FOR YOU

**Andrew, Natasha, Damyn**

# FOR YOU

# JAMES

# FOR YOU

**MOM**

## FOR YOU

## THE READER

Professional Shadow

# COMING SOON

## THE ADVENTURES OF

## JONATHAN COOPERMAN

### Code Name: SLICE

Professional Shadow

dreamsrealityheart@outlook.com

**Follow us on…**

TIK TOK

INSTAGRAM

THREADS

X

Made in the USA
Monee, IL
17 August 2025